THINKING CHRIST
CHRISTOLOGY AND CONTEMPORARY CRITICS

JANE BARTER MOULAISON

FORTRESS PRESS

MINNEAPOLIS

THINKING CHRIST
CHRISTOLOGY AND CONTEMPORARY CRITICS

Unless otherwise noted, scripture quotations are the author's own translation or from the New Revised Standard Version Bible, copyright © 1989 by the Division of Christian Education of the National Council of Churches of Christ in the USA, and are used with permission.

Chapter 6, "'To Judge the Quick and the Dead': Christ and the Redemption of Memory," originally appeared in a different form as "He Who Brings Light to Dark Places: Christ and the Redemption of Memory" in *The Church Made Strange for the Nations: Essays in Ecclesiology and Political Theology*, ed. Karl Koop and Paul Doerksen (Eugene, Ore.: Pickwick, 2011), 139–51.

Cover art (from left to right, top to bottom): *Jesus Christ* ©iStockphoto.com/Christian Kahler; *Worrying Jesus* ©iStockphoto.com/Marianna Raszkowska; *Christ And Stained Glass* ©iStockphoto.com/Stephen Moore; *Christian Suffering* ©iStockphoto.com/Ekspansio; *Jesus Profile* ©iStockphoto.com /Allan Brown
Cover Design: Joe Vaughan
Interior Design: Timothy W. Larson, Minneapolis, MN

Library of Congress Cataloging-in-Publication Data

Barter Moulaison, Jane, 1969–
 Thinking Christ : christology and contemporary critics / Jane Barter Moulaison.
    p. cm.
 Includes bibliographical references (p.   ) and indexes.
 ISBN 978–0–8006–9873–7 (alk. paper)
 1. Jesus Christ—History of doctrines—Early church, ca. 30–600. 2. Nicene Creed. 3. Jesus Christ—Person and offices. I. Title.
 BT198.B2685 2012
 232—dc23   2012001157

The paper used in this publication meets the minimum requirements of American National Standard for Information Sciences—Permanence of Paper for Printed Library Materials, ANSI Z329.48-1984.

Manufactured in the U.S.A.

À Luc Joseph et à Sophie Christine,
Avec amour pour tout ce que vous êtes,
et avec admiration pour tout ce que vous êtes
en train de devenir.

CONTENTS

CONTENTS

ACKNOWLEDGMENTS

A BOOK IS READ OR WRITTEN, IN OUR TIMES at least, in an irreducibly solitary manner. It is a solitude carved out in early hours and quiet spaces set apart for one set of hands, one set of eyes, one mind, and no more. But to say that the task is solitary is not to say that it is private, for the hands, the eyes, the mind are ineffectual or worse if they are not directed toward others in the quiet conversations that call insubstantial thoughts into being. For those who have molded my thinking and my praying and for those who have afforded the distraction and amusement to keep me from taking myself and my words too seriously, I give thanks, and I now name. I will leave it to them to sort out to which category they belong.

There are many friendships that have deepened due to a shared and obdurate devotion both to Jesus and to justice: I am grateful to the Rev. Canon Erin Phillips, the Rev. Canon Donna Joy, the Rev. Dr. Cathy Campbell, the Rev. Don Johnson, and Dr. Walter Deller (whose invitation to present lectures at the College of Emmanuel and St. Chad was the impetus for this book) for their friendship and for their exceptional theologies. Kristian Klippenstein, my research assistant, did just the right work at just the right time. I thank him for his reliability and his precision.

I thank The University of Winnipeg for its generous support. I am especially grateful to participate in such a universe alongside my husband, Dr. Glenn Moulaison. Glenn shares an academic vocation, but not (thank God) a compulsion to discuss it. Without his humor, friendship, and shared labor, not one word could be written, not one class taught, not one sermon preached—or, at least, there would be little inspiration for any of these!

Finally, I thank our children, Sophie and Luc. I thank them for being purely and unintentionally sure signs of God's beauty, truth, and goodness in this world. It is to them that this book is dedicated.

INTRODUCTION
"PAY THE DEBT"

Recently, I have begun work with a community of South Sudanese refugees in the city of Winnipeg. In learning about Dinka culture, I have also discovered something about my own. It is common for indigenous cultures to look to teachers of the past as guides to how we ought to comport ourselves today. The Dinka do not have the same attitude toward the past as the vast majority of contemporary North Americans: that is, they do not believe that contemporary knowledge is an achievement over what was known in the past.[1] It is generally held that the present generation forgets our ancestors' teachings to our own peril.

Upon learning this, I remembered something that I discovered some time ago about Western Medieval understandings of history. The term "Dark Ages," or *Tenebrae,* was assigned to his age by Petrarch (1304–1374), who represented a consensus belief among medieval scribes that a golden age of antiquity—with its brilliant execution of the *ars memorandi* ("the art of remembering")—was long gone, and thus he and his contemporaries, who wait in darkness, must attend to a reawakening of the mind and a restoration of the creativity and eloquence of the past.[2]

Read in relation to these other cultures, the contemporary West is strangely critical of its ancestors. It tends to see them as benighted, intolerant, and unprogressive. In spite of postmodernity's protests, the modern picture of inevitable and perpetual progress hangs ever in the air, clouding our view, and cutting us off from the past's wisdom and insight.

To argue for a hearing of the luminaries in Christianity's past is not the same as saying that Christianity's past was always especially illuminated. Contemporary critics are right to lament the colonizing history of Christendom as an utter distortion of the good news of Jesus Christ. To say that there are luminaries in the past from whom we ought to learn is also not to say that these past figures were impervious to sin, prejudice, or the many violences that characterized their times. Neither are we. My suspicion is that one of the ways that we inure ourselves to the violence of our time and our complicity within it is to look for answers outside of ourselves. Dead figures make easy scapegoats. But the violence of today cannot be easily attributable to the dubious and facile genealogies of violence that certain critics of the Christian past are quick to make. Augustine was and is not responsible for Hiroshima or Auschwitz or Batoche:[3] specific and real actors in modern world history were, and we continue to be.[4]

One of the best remedies to the past's ills is to understand our Christian past with greater nuance. This involves seeing the teachers of the past as caught in theological and moral struggles analogous to our own; as confronted, as we are, with a dramatically compelling gospel; and as seeking, as we do—and often failing, as we do—to live that gospel faithfully in our fallen time. To see the past clearly involves separating the wheat from the chaff of history, and becoming capable of recognizing those men and women of rare intelligence and wisdom as ancestors worthy of our respect and our remembering, and therefore also of our critical engagement. In his analysis of the task of remembering the past, philosopher Paul Ricoeur speaks of our relationship to tradition as a kind of debt that is owed:

> The idea of debt is inseparable from the notion of heritage. We are indebted to those who have gone before us for part of what we are. The duty of memory is not restricted to preserving the material trace, whether scriptural or other, of past events, but maintains the feeling of being obligated with respect to these others, of whom we shall later say, not that they are no more, but that they were. Pay the debt . . . but also inventory the heritage.[5]

What kind of obligation does the past demand of us? Clearly, it involves careful attentiveness to the words and contexts of past figures for the sake of representing them accurately. The student of the past who is also the inheritor of a heritage, however, is also required to offer a measure of receptivity to past figures because it is not the case that they *are* no more but, instead, that they *were*. That they *were* demands of us a measure of restraint before judging too harshly or too finally. Because they *were,* there is always a conversation left unfinished. There can be no closure on the past because they continue to assert a silent pressure upon the present that resists our efforts at closure or forgetting. This is so because it is not the case that they *are* no more. We pay a debt to them through our willingness to receive what they might offer.

TRANSCENDING THE LIMITS OF PRIVILEGE

A difficulty undoubtedly arises by virtue of the fact that all of the primary writers I deal with in this book are male: Irenaeus, Athanasius, Basil, and Augustine. Their influence upon Christian theology no doubt has something to do with accident of birth: for instance, Basil was an aristocrat, while Augustine was a highly educated North African. All were privy to an education that would not have been available to the vast majority of men and to virtually all women in antiquity. No doubt their writings are skewed by such privilege. The writings of all of them have been preserved, in part, because the powerful judges of history selected their writings to be preserved, while others—particularly those of heretics—were occluded.

However, their writings can, as I see it (admittedly by faith), transcend the limitations of their worldview, even of their privilege. To dismiss their writings because they were rich seems to me as irrational as dismissing the writings of those who are poor, of those who are female, of those who are non-Christian. What I have attempted to do in this book is not to follow their insights slavishly, but to allow their (in my view, remarkable) insights to engage and penetrate the questions at hand that are of contemporary concern. Seldom do I find in their writings teachings that are immediately applicable to the moral and political questions that I pose and that have inspired this book. This book is not an effort to show that Augustine was really a feminist, or Basil of Caesarea an environmentalist. Instead, I find them abidingly helpful (often in spite of their problematic teachings in specific situations) in the spirit, rather than the letter, of their writings. By spirit, I mean first principles, or the fundamental architecture of their arguments, which I believe can offer support and insights of enormous value to contemporary theologians.

THE IMPORTANCE OF INCARNATION

If we think of first principles as organizing theological affirmations that shape doctrine and practice,[6] we find among the Nicene and pre-Nicene teachers guidance that enables contemporary Christians to make greater sense of the faith that we confess and its relevance to the world. The relationship of these principles to Scripture is of profound concern for contemporary Christians who are often left the equally impoverished alternatives of historicism or literalism in reading the Bible. It is part of this book's contention that the Nicene teachers surveyed here read Scripture through a specific first principle that is christological in nature. That is, we can understand something of the meaning of Scripture because of the consummate and world-shaping knowledge that we have received in God's becoming incarnate in Jesus Christ. This fundamental principle—the incarnation of the word of God—will affect how Scripture is to be read, but not in a way that is inimical to Scripture. It is Scripture, after all, that discloses the event of the incarnation and governs the incarnation's meaning.

The main question animating this book is, What difference does the word becoming flesh make to our thinking and to our acting (although I am reluctant to separate these two too strenuously)? In the early church, we might say that Christology or, better, the revelation of God in Jesus Christ signaled a veritable revolution in ordinary patterns of thinking about the world. Although much ink has been spilled in noting how the figures whom I am engaging were indebted to pagan philosophy, for me what is far more interesting is how the pagan philosophy—by which they were admittedly profoundly influenced—was transfigured by their faith in the word becoming flesh decisively and finally in Jesus Christ.

Given the revolutionary nature of Christian thought upon prevailing philosophies within antiquity, is there an analogous "reading" that can be done by the contemporary church? Christians are influenced wittingly or not by many discourses other than the gospel. This is a good thing. God does not encounter us as a blank slate, and God, I believe, acts in and through non-Christian and nonreligious knowledges to offer knowledge of God. Contemporary understanding of the gospel has been shaped profoundly by critical discourses—for example, by pluralism, secularism, feminism, postcolonialism, and environmentalism. Might it be the case that these discourses can also be revolutionized or transfigured in such a way by the word becoming flesh that they are given not only a distinctive Christian shape or form, but also a greater depth and clarity?

By bringing the Christian tradition of the early church into conversation with these contemporary critical discourses, I am also intimating that the insights of the Nicene teachers cannot be easily left behind in a renewed theology. For whatever reason, most of those who have been advancing a critical theology have abandoned Nicene orthodoxy as "Constantinian" or conservative. By and large they have tended to treat the figures of the fourth and fifth centuries as foes rather than friends. But this period of emergent Christendom is not only more complex than it has often been characterized (for instance: Was Athanasius a friend or foe of the emperor? His track record of multiple banishments by imperial decree might nuance the picture that is often painted of him.), but it is often richer both in theological depth and in sociopolitical configuration. Who cannot be compelled by both the Eastern and Western church's turn to monasticism as a way of eschewing the newfound favor they had won? Can the ascetic turn within nascent Christendom be a resource or inspiration for those who lament the incessant consumerism of Western culture or the lack of seriousness of many of the spiritual practices of our time? Might the manner in which the Nicenes read Scripture *spiritually* and *ecclesially* open it up beyond a wooden literalism on one hand and an anemic historicism on the other?

THE GIFTS OF NICENE THEOLOGY

"The Fathers" and "patristics" are terms that I avoid in this book for rather straightforward reasons: that is, they perpetuate the concept that it was only "Fathers" and their thought that contributed to the life of the early church. Nevertheless, the period that I am engaging requires some justification and clarity. I use the term *Nicene teachers* not in the narrow sense of actual participants in the Councils of Nicaea or Constantinople,[7] but as referring to those early teachers who affirmed and defended the principle of Christ's full consubstantial unity with God the Father that was won at those councils. For the Nicene teachers, this christological principle was central to their thinking about all subsequent doctrines and practices.

I speak of these authors—Basil of Caesarea, Irenaeus of Lyons, Athanasius of Alexandria, and Augustine of Hippo—as teachers, for their chief task in their sermons, commentaries, pastoral letters, and more systematic treatises was to guide the faithful and to rule out what they took to be false teaching. For the most part, the ancient writers with whom I am engaged in this book belong to the period of early Christendom that was marked by the intellectual work required to offer specification to Christian thinking about the Triune God in the midst of controversy. The majority of the controversies of the Nicene period concerned the second person of the Trinity whom they confessed to be a historical man who was born, lived, was crucified, and was raised from the dead in a particular set of historical circumstances, and who was the eternal word "eternally begotten of the Father." The "development" of doctrine during this period was the result of the reappropriation of Scriptures in light of this affirmation. The intellectual task of clarifying these teachings in midst of theological controversies that sought either to reduce or exaggerate Jesus' identification with the Father was exacting and at the service of safeguarding the soteriological logic of the good news in situations that threatened to undermine such confession. Trinitarian rules of faith were normative in the third century in ruling out false teaching in various controversies, and became the normative grammar that enabled various theologians to carry this teaching forward in the midst of alternate accounts of the nature of salvation.

In all of this, these thinkers were teachers of the apostolic faith. They sought to give an intellectual account of the Christian faith in a world in which philosophy was prized. They sought fidelity with the teachers of the past, all the way back to the apostles, and they sought to "hand down" the good news at times to the catechumenate, to the unbeliever, and to members within their community so that they might grow in wisdom and in virtue. These two were closely related. The media of their teachings were various: they were highly exegetical, often direct commentaries on Scripture; many were sermons; some were polemic writings. Always, they were aimed at building up the faith.

The Nicene period was particularly rich in formulating such arguments, in part because the church moved from being a marginal sect to one that came to be at the center of political favor. Although that move was not a salutary one in many respects for the church, it did compel its theologians to give a rational account for the life that they lived in a manner that was accessible and intelligible within the intellectual world in which they inhabited and within a context in which large councils of bishops were convened at the emperor's behest. Although early Christendom (after the conversion of Constantine in 312 CE) does not represent the beginning of this apologetic work—certainly the pre-Nicenes were engaged in defending the gospel in light of the teachings of the philosophers—this period, with the advent of catholic conciliar processes for the debating and adjudication of doctrine, proved immensely fertile as this context provided the occasion for the teachers of the church to pay particularly close attention to doctrine. The Nicene period was by no means uniform and there are key differences in the theological emphases among those who support- ed what would become a Nicene consensus, which was worked out in Nicaea in 325 and later ratified and expanded in 381 in the Council of Constantinople. Nevertheless, Nicaea and Constantinople articulated a catholic creed that was trinitarian in scope, that signaled the importance not only of the unity of the Godhead, but also of the status of each of its "persons" as having salvific power that is effective and not merely derivative.

This book is primarily concerned with the christological confessions of faith of the Nicene period and their appropriation by several key theologians. While the creeds and creed-like sayings—the rules of faith or *regulae fidei*—ar- ticulated a common conviction in the saving capacity of the Son that can be traced to biblical witness,[8] what emerges in the fourth century is greater clarity given to christological confession fueled by various controversies that emerged in this period. Chief among the controversies was Arianism,[9] admittedly itself a problematic appellation that came to be used polemically against a wide range of opponents to orthodoxy who subordinated the Son to the Father. Accord- ing to "Arians," the Son was a mediator or an auxiliary to the Father because of his derivative status as Son, a status that the so-called Arians determined to be ontologically inferior. In spite of their being branded teachers of anathema, those who were identified as Arians would not strike us today as particularly heterodox. They, too, worshiped Jesus Christ as God, as had been the virtually universal practice since apostolic times.[10] What the Nicene defenders had to ar- ticulate against those opponents whom they identified as "Arian" is the manner in which the Father can be at once said to be the origin of the Godhead, while the Son is also his ontological equivalent—neither ontologically subordinate nor merely auxiliary. This confession, too, had to conform to the grammar of divine simplicity—a fundamental affirmation of the unity and aseity of the

Godhead, thus displaying how the Triune God can have distinct "persons" and also be united in activity and intention in the world.

This has enormous consequences how we may speak coherently about Christ. Christ is not a partial revelation of God. He is, rather, the "fullness of God" in whom God "was pleased to dwell" (Col. 1:19). Thus Christ is irreducibly God. He is not an instance or occasion of divine revelation, but is in himself unequivocally God dwelling "in bodily form." This central affirmation, of Jesus as the fullness of God revealed, is one that admittedly chafes against much of contemporary critical theology. To regard Jesus Christ as a partial revelation would appear at first glance to offer a more hospitable theology for those concerned to "make room" for other revelations of God within other religions and within the natural world. Seeing Christ as partial revelation also would seem to be more credible in a scientific, modern age, and therefore more hospitable to human knowledges outside of theology. Moreover, according to certain lines of feminist theological reasoning, the adoration of a male savior would appear to reinforce patriarchy.

I have attempted to avoid drawing terse parallels between the contemporary theologies that tend to diminish Christ's stature with ancient "Arianism." The historical gulf is just too wide to make such a comparison useful, and the legacy of Christian theology marginalizing heterodox thought too problematic. I have no special desire to impose a unity upon modern Christology or to invalidate alternate construals of Christ for their own sake. Rather, my reappropriation of Nicene Christology has as its aim chiefly the upholding of the saving efficacy of Christ for the sake of communicating Christ's salvific power over the fallen "powers and principalities" of this world, including, and perhaps especially, those political structures that hem us in. My argument is not that this realistic Christology is more "useful" or "expedient" than others in inaugurating a better political order. Rather, I would argue that a better political order has already been inaugurated in Christ, albeit only partially at this time. Yet an awareness of this emergent new order can inform a robustly political theology. Nicene orthodoxy does not make it so, or enable us to inaugurate such transformation in a more expeditious fashion; rather, it gives us the lenses to "see" such transfiguration as has already taken place, to see the riches that have already been given.

Nicene theology also articulates an account of the world in which the salvation that is won in Christ does not magically interfere with the activities of creation and God's creatures, but neither does it remain distant and distinct from these. Rather, the Triune God, as articulated and defended by the Nicene teachers, works through and within the world, while also transcending it, thus bringing *this world* to *its own* proper completion. Such action is delivered through God's renewing and regenerating power, which makes use of our action toward the God-given ends for which we were created and toward which the whole creation groans.

Christ's role within this divine drama is perfectly identified with that of the Father. We know and we experience God's liberating and creative love *through* Christ. But that experience of love is not merely a private intuition; it is instead an objective affirmation of this world, given at its very foundations, in the love that is poured out to the Son, who is sent to be the pioneer of true humanity and thus to be our redeemer. In becoming flesh, the Son unites what is divine to what is all too frail—our humanity—but in so doing, restores our humanity to its proper standing. Thus Christ takes up, or receives, our humanity, and indeed, as I argue in chapter 2, all mortal flesh into God's own unending and abundant life. In God's coming in Christ, God pronounces and confers the most profound blessing upon this life. There is nothing that needs to be done to add to this blessing: it merely requires our reception and our thanksgiving for it. In the gift of creation and the gift of Christ its perfection and perfecter, the order of the universe is revealed to be love, not violence; abundance, not sacrifice. Our role in response is simply to conform our peace making and our justice seeking to a prior peace, to a prior justice or order. While this peace and this order are not immediately apprehensible within this fallen world, the Nicene teachers are instructive in articulating the types of intellectual and spiritual disciplines that make wisdom possible. In each case, this vision is not understood as contingent simply upon human positing but, rather, upon a certain receptivity, a preparation of hearts and minds for God's adding to and infusing human wisdom.

CHRIST AS *EXEMPLUM* AND *SACRAMENTUM*

I have settled on three figures from the Nicene period (Augustine of Hippo, Basil of Caesarea, and Athanasius of Alexandria) and one pre-Nicene teacher (Irenaeus of Lyons) because I believe each of these can help us to overcome deficits in contemporary Christology for particularly urgent moral and political questions of our time. This book brings together *the* great figure of Western Christendom—Augustine of Hippo—with Eastern teachers of the church, Basil of Caesarea (one of the so-called Cappadocian Fathers) and Athanasius of Alexandria. It does so because I am convinced that the differences between East and West have been overdrawn by scholars of that period, and because recent readings of the Fathers have been extremely helpful in leaving old polemics between East and West behind. Most of the writers I engage are from the fourth and fifth centuries, with the exception of my brief treatment of Irenaeus of Lyons (c. 115–c. 202) in chapter 4. My treatment of his insights give way to a more in-depth engagement with Athanasius of Alexandria as a fourth-century figure who appropriates and develops them.

Each of the christological malaises with which this book wrestles has to do with a kind of immanentism, a tacit assumption within much of contemporary "critical" theology that human striving and knowledge are the chief sources of liberation, and that Christ serves primarily as an exemplar to guide our practices. What the doctrine of the incarnation in the Nicene period presses us to consider is how, in the union of humanity and God in Christ, every aspect of the *humanum* is already taken up and therefore is on its way to transformation. Thus there is no caducity in human affairs, no abject domain of human life or human affairs that cannot *de facto* be incorporated into God's redemptive purposes. Whereas critical theologies often begin in negation, a political theology that takes its cues from Nicene Christology must begin instead with an affirmation of this world. Thus there can be no primary motion of critical separation, even if it appears politically expedient to do so. This does not mean that there can be no judgment; there has to be judgment or justice in any theology that is concerned with political life. However, a theology guided by the incarnation of the word cannot be one that stops short of commending reconciliation as the theological end to which all parties must strive.

Put differently, the freedom that is won in Christ is not merely a negative liberty. By negative liberty, I mean merely that the type of freedom that much of contemporary political discourse envisions is primarily one of removing the constraining bonds of one's opponents or oppressors. Philosopher Charles Taylor defines negative liberty this way: "The basic intuition [of proponents of negative freedom] is that freedom is a matter of being able to do something or other, of not having obstacles in one's way, rather than being a capacity we have to realise."[11] In this passage, Taylor tellingly links a fuller notion of freedom with capacity, thus pointing to a notion of freedom that is very congenial to the one shared by the ancient teachers of the church.

Freedom, in this view, is the capacity to realize the self to be what it was created to be. Thus human freedom has as its background picture an ideal or prototype. We cannot answer the question of freedom without having a set of prior answers to questions such as, What is the goal of human life? or Toward what end does human life strive? The answers that are given in the Nicene period are ones that are entirely christological in shape. If Christ is the picture of perfect freedom, how does our knowing and our acting conform to him? This is clearly an exemplarist model of determining questions of freedom, based upon Christ as perfect human example. But Christ, according to the Nicene teachers, is not merely an *exemplum*; he is also *sacramentum*. That is, he imparts and endows our human quest for freedom with a desire that transcends its own fulfillment, because the home of human fulfillment is rest in God. Such desire is an awakening of our capacities not simply for self-realization but for a self-realization bound to the self-realization of the entire world. Christ gives us the pattern of human freedom which is service for others, but gives it not merely as a pattern to be followed, but as a gift in which we participate, and to which he, God incarnate, opens our hearts, minds, and embodied actions.

THE VIRTUE OF HUMILITY

A retrieval of these various insights from the past is predicated upon a destabilization of the kind of identity that modern criticism upholds: that is, viewing the self as a singular agent who determines for itself the course of action and the aims of political struggles. Nicene theology has the effect of problematizing the notion of autonomous agency, displaying how our knowledge of ourselves—like our knowledge of God—is partial and can be distorted and riddled with illusions. As moderns, the primary illusion we hold (at least in the North Atlantic) is one of mastery and control—of our world, of our language, of our encounter with God. Nicene theology is a surprising corrective to this, for it maintains that God is at work even when we are unaware, and that God continues to work in us and beyond us even when our confessions and praise of God have ceased.

Thus the chief theological virtue that is upheld among all the Nicene teachers that I engage is the virtue of humility. By this I do not mean a wallowing in guilt or self-contempt but, rather, the capacity to imagine a world in which activity abounds outside of the immanent and closed circle of human cause and effect. Instead, the world, the cosmos, and human selves within it are participants within a greater drama that has an intelligence and a purposefulness that transcends our own. To say that there is a transcendent intelligence and will is not to say that we are somehow mere puppets in a cosmic drama. It is not to say that such intelligence and will are arbitrarily imposed against us. Rather, they work with human intelligence and will, as well as those of other creatures, even when we rebel against them. They do so in bringing things to their proper completion, in ordering the universe toward ends that are pacific: in bringing light out of darkness, order out of chaos, life out of death. Such word or such wisdom is the animating energy of the world, that creates and sustains it. This word or wisdom is not only given at creation, it is spoken again in clarity and fullness in the life, death, and resurrection of Jesus Christ. Or, as the writer of Hebrews puts it, "in these last days he has spoken to us by a Son, whom he appointed heir of all things, through whom he also created the worlds" (Heb. 1:2). In him the proper destination of all things is made known, because he is their beginning and end. Christ, as the Nicene teachers have argued, is not derivative, but is the creative, generative word that is fully one with God the Father in intention and will. To posit such power in the incarnate God may lead to the confusion that Christ stands above us and over us in depriving us of a fully human nature—depriving us of our wills, demanding our obedience, and punishing our transgressions. Yet, this Christ does not stand against us as alien or antagonistic; he is "nearer to us than we are to ourselves," as Augustine put it. For Christ is also the internal word, the one in whom our own broken intelligences and wills receive their healing. In becoming human, Christ assumes for us all the messy stuff of our human nature and unites it with God, thus restoring in us our proper heritage as sons and daughters of the living God (2 Cor. 6:18).

The affirmation of God's immediacy within created life and its strivings is not to say that it is identical with it. Creation is still waiting with "eager longing for the revealing of the children of God" (Rom. 8:19). It remains captive to an alien rule, one that is contrary to us and to God, and one that is now in "bondage to decay" (Rom. 8:21). Yet life that has been created and affirmed by God admits no decay or violence. The life of God and the life that we were created for in God is a life of lasting peace. This affirmation will test other theologies which would argue that God is the author of violence or that the heavenly city is attained by calculated sacrifice. Therefore, although in relation to human life God may *make use* of the conditions of fallen time and of fallen nature—including its violences— toward God's peaceful and loving ends, God is not the author of these because God cannot act contrary to God's nature. Therefore, violence and sacrifice have no intrinsic place in the divine life or the economy of salvation. Violence is never an ingredient within divine salvation; it is always denied, always overcome in the infinite and abundant motion of love that God pours out into the world. Thus the divine economy is to be contrasted quite sharply with the economy within fallen creation that maintains peace through sacrifice and loss.

READING THE TEXT OF SCRIPTURE AND THE TEXT OF THE WORLD

One of the difficulties of being a Christian in modernity is that we have inherited a way of reading texts that tends to, on the one hand, seek to get at the "real meaning of the text," or, on the other, concede to multiple textual "performances" and thereby abandon any quest for more fitting or plausible performances. This leveling of scriptural meaning leaves the modern reader without much of a road map for interpretation. Of course, one could write volumes about patristic hermeneutics, and it would be foolhardy even to attempt to characterize such diverse practices by way of summary. Yet, one can establish within the Nicene period several common characteristics that serve to challenge critical hermeneutics.

The first distinction that one might assert between critical and Nicene hermeneutics is a distinction in the interpretative agent(s). Whereas both historical-critical and reader-response theories would focus upon the individual reader's interpretative processes in discovering the text's meaning, for the Nicene teachers the community—that is, the church—took precedent in textual deliberation. This community was demarcated by its practices, particularly its sacramental practices and its confessional *sensus fidelium*—the sense of the faithful that together formed the tradition "handed down from the apostles." The *regulae fidei* or the rules of faith were the creeds and creed-like confessions of faith that guided scriptural interpretation and liturgical practice. These rules were trinitarian in character in the Nicene period and were also centered upon upholding the identity of Jesus Christ as not derivative or subordinate, but as consubstantial with the Father. Thus the Nicene teachers read Scripture as a diversely interglossing canon that was centered on the saving kerygma of Jesus Christ. They therefore found within the Old Testament hidden signs of Christ's salvific work foreshadowed in its figures. Such a *figural* reading does not necessarily diminish the primary sense of the text, for the figures retain the solidity of identity and purpose, but it nevertheless allows the text to point proleptically to a revelation not yet fully known. Thus the text cannot be closed to the future, not because the reader might ascribe to it a variety of meanings, but because it can be used by God to become a "sign" that resists easy identification with this world alone. In other words, God speaks God's word through Scripture in a manner that is not historically closed, but open to a future unfolding of the revelation that it speaks. John David Dawson puts it well:

> Although one may refer to a figure "announcing" its fulfillment, it is ultimately God who does the announcing, for a person or an event is a *figura* precisely because it begins an extended divine utterance that embraces subsequent persons and events. "Figuralness" denotes the status of things as significant—not in themselves and not in their meanings—but insofar as they are, in all their concrete reality, the enacted intention of God to signify. If Jesus is the fulfillment of Joshua, it is because both Joshua and Jesus are moments within a single divine intention to signify. Discerning the intention as a literary congruence, the figural reader makes explicit the similarities by which otherwise separate events are related to one another as moments in a single, divine utterance.[12]

The Nicene teachers were exceptionally adept not only at reading Scripture as a living sign of God's self-disclosure, but guided by Scripture they learned to "read" the "text" of the world thus as well. In reading the world, as in reading Scripture, the Nicene teachers were able to discern traces also of God's beneficent will toward creation. However, they learned to *see* these traces, again through the pattern of the world that was revealed in Christ. If shadows of Christ stretched back into history, as they read the Hebrew Scriptures, they also leaned forward, disclosing the proper identity of the world that was redeemed in him. Thus the community of the faithful—the body of Christ—and its sacramental practices had a special role in revealing the ongoing divine intention in the world for it was here, particularly within Baptism and Eucharist, that it was foretasted. For each of these writers, the eucharistic sharing in Christ connotes a realistic participation in divine life that becomes, in a way, the measure of authentic living and the pattern of knowing God's presence. The doctrine of participation—a term that is far more prominent in the Eastern writers that I explore than in Augustine—connotes precisely this ontological sharing in God's eternity through the condescension of Christ and his ascension with us to eternal "knowledge."

This is not to say that participation is limited to the sacraments and those who receive them. Because God in Christ has blessed this world in his assumption of flesh, all flesh has the capacity to communicate his truth. The Eucharist is a particularly evocative sign of this redemption, because in it we see how the grape and the fields, the waters, sky, and the earth conspire to reveal to us Christ as the hidden center of all life. Like the lovely line from George Herbert's poem "Easter," "The cross taught all wood to resound his name," all creation is charged with immeasurable significance according to the Nicene teachers because Christ has come among us. The world is a sign because it derives from God. Because it is the work of God's creation, it utters the Creator in the very structure of its being. Thus correspondence to God is not contingent upon creation fitting a predetermined pattern or ideal, but is a revelation given gratuitously and surprisingly, and in a manner always exceeding our grasp. The beautiful (or the good or the true) is so because it cannot be exhausted, because it participates in an economy that springs from a ceaseless source. Thus the very particularity that is proper to the creature is not to be overcome in the contemplation of divine beauty, truth, and goodness, but is to be dwelled in, to be contemplated in its very material identity. David Bentley Hart puts it well: "Christian thought—whose infinite is triune, whose God becomes incarnate, and whose account of salvation promises not liberation from but glorification of, material creation—can never separate the formal particularity of beauty from the splendor it announces. . . ."[13] Thus the world's creatures can be seen as heralds to God, but their function as heralds pointing to something else should not obscure the fact that it is they who do the pointing and none other. They are not to be overcome or overlooked in order to reach splendor: these are the splendor themselves on their way to becoming.

Thus Christian representation can never overlook the sign or text as being merely auxiliary to its "true" or "deeper" meaning. The surface meaning is intrinsic to the story in Christian representation, because God has communicated through it. Thus God's revelation never supersedes the sign or herald, but completes them. This pattern of understanding participation as an essential affirmation of materiality is crucial to the interpretation of Scripture. This understanding of God's participation within the very *concretessima* of human life endows human life in its particularly with a profound significance. Because all people are potentially a "sign" opening toward God's glory there is no one who can be left behind for the sake of a common good.

WHAT IS THEOLOGICAL CRITIQUE?

What, then, is critique? What, in particular, is theological critique? Critical theory is not a term that is used with the regularity that it once was. Earlier forms of social criticism within theology acknowledged the critics' indebtedness to a tradition of inquiry that was intent upon challenging the assumptions of privilege in representing reality. Going back to the Frankfurt School of the 1920s, such critique signaled a veritable revolution in thought insofar as it understood that tools of the social sciences could be purposefully used to bring about emancipation from sinful orders. This work gave rise to a questioning of culture insofar as culture—and religion within it—often supported the oppression or the alienation of a vast majority of people. It did so by positing as normative the kinds of assumptions and values of the culture that only empowered a select few. In response to these critical insights, theologians began to question the church's own complicity with sinful power and sought to break the ideological hold of the church over our freedom. Thus, as Canadian theologian Gregory Baum likes to put it, "Thinking begins with negation":

> Knowledge begins with the critique of society and its ideologies. This is in keeping with the biblical perspective where God's Word is judgment before it is new life: God reveals the hidden human sins before forgiving them and renewing the human spirit. Critical theology subjects to an ideology critique not only society and its secular culture, but also and especially the Christian tradition, the source of its inspirition [sic].[14]

While I will leave to the side for a moment Baum's tantalizing conviction that God reveals Godself first in judgment (which, even more suggestively, he identifies with negation!), I will nevertheless aver that, in spite of the datedness of this perspective on theology, it remains the operative modality for a wide variety of theologies that seek social justice and environmental activism. There are three interwoven themes that Baum lifts up that, in spite of the lack of self-professed identification with "critical theology" of the writers I am engaging, remain common among them.

First, *knowledge begins as a self-knowledge*. That is, the contemporary theologians with whom I am engaged take their own situatedness within a particular society as an epistemological starting point. Thus "context" becomes that which the theologian identifies as the home from which she draws theological insight. This generally is a particular place of privilege, but also often of willing solidarity with those on the underside of history. There remains a confidence among such theologians (in this book this tendency may be seen in J. Denny Weaver, Rosemary Radford Ruether, Sallie McFague, and, to a degree, Miroslav Volf) that one can name, at the very least, who I am and where I stand. The assurance of one's position is thus grounded not externally—by reference to God or a metaphysical order—but internally: in the self and its insight. This, of course, will be a mark of distinction between the contemporary and ancient writers whom I engage, but not entirely so. The self is not bereft of significance to the ancient writers, but they hold much less confidence in its "knowability" and perhaps in its goodness. We shall see this more clearly particularly as we engage Augustine, the great skeptic of self-knowledge.

The second common feature shared by the critical theologians with whom I engage is *negation as a methodological starting point*. Negation, or the a priori conviction that the received thought of the dominant culture must be in some sense undermined, flows through the writings of many of the contemporary theologians addressed in this book. Interestingly enough, it is not the dominant modality of a number of the "postcritical," non-Christian writers whom I engage, including Hélène Cixous, Michael Hardt, Antonio Negri, and Saba Mahmood, for whom culture (biblical and otherwise) does not inspire an a priori negation but, rather, an engagement and a hearing. It involves receptivity prior to judgment. Judgment is still intrinsic to such postcritical writings, but it is done with an aim of preserving and upholding those features of a culture that resist the violences which the culture engenders as not incidental to the culture but ingredient within it.[15]

Third and finally, critical theologians share a common assumption that *biblical and theological writings are not immune to ideological distortion*. Indeed, because of their foundational status within Western culture, the biblical narrative and Christian theological tradition must be especially interrogated for it "generated, sustained, and communicated"[16] the values under which we are burdened and that require to be liberated from their oppressive distortions. Thus the task of the theologian is to look to the biblical and theological foundations of social malaise and thereby seek to remedy these through critical scrutiny of and, where possible, the advancement of a "usable" meaning that may be drawn from Scripture or other texts.

The critics that I engage in this book are far more haphazardly selected than the church fathers. In some cases, they represent Christian thinkers who engage the Nicene teachers more or less head-on (as, for example, Rosemary Radford Ruether's challenge to Logos Christology). More frequently, the critics whom I engage are those who do not take specific exception to the Nicene teachers, but are instead critical of more general tendencies within orthodox Christian confession (Wilfrid Cantwell Smith, J. Denny Weaver, Sallie McFague). At still other times, I engage Christian writers whose insights would not necessarily appear critical of the Nicene tradition, but whose treatment of a subject matter demands (in my view) clarification from the Nicenes (Miroslav Volf). Finally, I engage a number of non-Christian thinkers, either because they have had a profound influence upon contemporary Christian thought of a particular kind (Michael Hardt and Antonio Negri, Jacques Derrida), or because—by some gratuitous circumstance—their thought corroborates the position I am advancing through the Nicene figure with whom I am engaged (Hannah Arendt, Saba Mahmood, and Hélène Cixous). As I hope will become apparent in this book, I am engaged with most of these critical voices because I am sympathetic with their political ends. It is my hope that, whatever the theological differences that are named here at times, this does not undermine my debt of gratitude for their insights and wisdom.

This book is heavily indebted to secondary sources in the field of patristic studies. I am not a patristics scholar, and so I rely heavily on the careful work done by those within the field. I am therefore grateful for the revival of interest in the Nicene era, and for the willingness of scholars to do careful exegetical work in order to assist tenuous appropriations by theologians like myself. I am also indebted in this book to conversations that are much broader within theology in which a *ressourcement* of ancient material is a lively and growing source for constructive theology. The Radical Orthodox movement is a good example of this trend. However different the political directions that I may take at times from them, I am indebted to the careful attention that have given to thinking Christ in a culture that presumes anything but peace, anything but humility, anything but charity—both in our time and in Christian antiquity. What revolutionary effects did such Christian thought have in transfiguring the commonplaces and the wisdom of the Hellenistic world? And how did "the grain of the universe," a grain that is the hidden structure of peace in the midst of the vast dark forces of violence, explode in the hearts and minds of these figures? And, of course, behind this question is a tentative analogy with our own time. What difference does Christ make in our own world given over to violence and death?

How does he explode the parameters of our best thought today? How does he heal it? How is he reconciled to it? This book is dedicated to such an end.

THE DESIGN OF THIS BOOK

In each of the chapters, we will see how the desire of humans for liberation is one that is Christ shaped and Christ infused. In chapter 1, a chapter dealing with contemporary empires, we see the conflict that emerges within competing pictures of freedom, or competing notions of the good that might be realized. Augustine's two cities are driven by a love of self on the one hand, and a love of God on the other. The city fueled by self-love is trapped in an immanent plane in which the chief good to be realized is the good of self-preservation. In a world in which such aspirations are primary, citizens soon abjure their own capacities in order to enshrine a sovereign authority who will protect the city's citizens from external obstacles or threats. Augustine's alternate city, a city founded on peace, is one in which Jesus Christ is the sovereign, and his sovereignty is not based upon the violence of exclusion, but upon humility. Augustine of Hippo enables us to see the limitations of political theologies aimed merely at the preservation of the sacrificial order, rather than toward the heavenly city to which Christ calls his citizens. In this chapter, I bring Augustine into conversation with contemporary theorists of empire Michael Hardt and Antonio Negri, who share many of Augustine's misgivings about empire procuring a true and lasting peace. Unlike Augustine, however, Hardt and Negri are reticent on the nature of a good life toward which citizens might aim, and therefore their theory falls short of delivering the kinds of political goods they promise.

Chapter 2 takes up the theme of Christ as the one in whom the entire cosmos is made and thus alerts us to its beauty and depth perceived by humans as a real indication of God's blessing and power working within and through the natural world. In engaging Basil of Caesarea on creation, we find that creation is a sign to be read, which is a heavenly affirmation of this world. Thus creation care takes on a depth and significance as we learn to read its signs, but this reading requires our entire bodily engagement, including our disciplined refusal to dominate the Earth. Thus my engagement of Basil of Caesarea on the healing of the earth involves a form of renunciation or *askesis*, which, properly understood, is the condition not for human abnegation but for its joy. Again, in this chapter, we will explore a notion of liberty that is Christ shaped and Christ infused as the ascetic finds within her renunciation not deprivation but abundance.

Chapter 3 examines the creative capacity of Christ the Word through whom the world is created. It is also an analysis of the creative capacities within human beings themselves to represent God in language. It argues, with other feminist commentators, that the language that we have is often woefully inadequate to capture the ineffable otherness of God, who transcends all language. This chapter locates the origin of language within human desires, which are desires that are only partially articulated. Drawing on the philosophical work of Hélène Cixous, I argue in favor of an understanding of language as not neatly transparent or amenable to reconstruction, but as representative of desires not yet fully known, of gaps and lacunae that accompany its meaning and render language opaque. However, I also argue here that the caesurae in language are not destined to be language's final destiny, but, with Augustine, that language about God, like desire itself, has a "home" in which we might hope for true communication. Just so, this pledge of the redemption of our signs, which is itself implicit in the word being made flesh, is a pledge already partially enjoyed, even in the wounded words we use.

Chapter 4 turns our attention to the challenges that the existence of many religious languages present to Christian self-understanding. Particularly, what sense are we to make of the confession that Jesus is "true God from true God" in a world in which there appear to be many like claims to God's true identity? In this chapter, I examine the kinds of responses that this question has engendered in contemporary secularism, and argue that the concessions that this secularism often asks religious persons to make are too great. In this I engage Muslim scholar Saba Mahmood, whose analysis of the remaking of religious identity in the post–9/11 antireligious rhetoric of secular politics is a drive to conformity that seeks to undermine any alternate conceptions of identity. Mahmood's analysis of women in the pious Muslim revivals prods me to look to Christian sources on the nature of the self and how this picture challenges those secular accounts of what it is to be human. In this, I examine Athanasius of Alexandria on the difference that the incarnation makes to our conceptions of the self, and posit that such an account actually shows more promise than the secular accounts in allowing other religious pictures of the self to narrate their own anthropological claims. At the very least, Athanasius provides an account of the self on account of the incarnation that counters the acids of the contemporary picture of the deracinated self as an ideal.

If the picture of human flourishing that is lifted up in the incarnation is so salutary to an ethic of peace, what then are we to make of its seeming contradiction in the crucifixion? Do we, like many critics, abandon the cross as a primitive symbol of "divine child abuse"[17] or as a justification of violence and suffering more generally? In chapter 5, I engage J. Denny Weaver's now (in)famous critique of theologies of the atonement in conversation with Irenaeus of Lyons and Athanasius of Alexandria, finding much in keeping with "the non-violent atonement." However, I also find Weaver's and others' abandonment of the cross problematic and turn to the theme of recapitulation as an entrée for thinking about the cross in ways that both take biblical and later construals of the atonement seriously, while also denying (together with Weaver) that God can be the author of violence.

Chapter 6 is the concluding chapter of the book, and it is an exploration of memory and its redemption in Christ. It is a chapter that is future oriented, in spite of (or, better, because of) its dominant theme of memory. In this chapter I take up the work of Miroslav Volf on "remembering rightly in a violent world," and argue that Augustine's understanding of memory challenges Volf's concession that under certain circumstances the past may be more fruitfully forgotten than retained in memory. This chapter looks to the other-worldly nature of remembering as I explore the promise that our memories will be retained and transfigured in Christ, and that remembering is key to a just future.

To repeat Ricoeur's words, "The duty of memory is not restricted to preserving the material trace, whether scriptural or other of past events, but maintains the feeling of being obligated with respect to these others, of whom we shall later say, not that they are no more, but that they were. Pay the debt, . . . but also inventory the heritage."[18] In each of the chapters that follow, I attempt to pay a debt, to attend to a kind of pressure of obligation that the past exerts upon our current circumstances, precisely because the figures whom I engage in these pages *were*. There is a way of discharging the debt that is merely perfunctory, a settling of accounts. But there is another way of viewing a debt or obligation: that is, not as bound by compulsion, but by gratitude. It is a gratitude that seeks to recognize how they *were*, and how, because of them, we *are*.

1

"WE BELIEVE IN ONE LORD, JESUS CHRIST"

PROCLAIMING CHRIST'S LORDSHIP IN THE MIDST OF EMPIRE

The study of empire has become somewhat in vogue of late. In the area of New Testament, particularly Pauline studies, much fruitful work has been done in exposing the manner in which the apostle Paul conveys a Jesus who points us to a kingdom posited in radical opposition to Rome. Recent scholarship has drawn attention to the particular imperial context in which Paul encounters and proclaims Jesus, the Jewish Messiah, as one who offers political liberation from the oppressive political order that is Rome.[1] In this reading, Paul proclaims Jesus as one who has broken the hold of the powers and principalities and who will bring all worldly power under his dominion (Rom. 8:38-39; 1 Cor. 15:24; Col. 1:16; Eph. 1:20-21; 6:12). Such a rereading not only corrects the long and tragic tendency of Christians to de-Judaize Paul, but also offers an insight into the precisely political struggles of the apostle and his community within an often hostile imperial regime. This critique of the system of Roman political power is simultaneously—either implicitly or explicitly—a critique of the prevailing imperial ideologies of our time and, in this, theologians and biblical scholars keep company with a much broader assembly of critics of the new global order that structures contemporary life.

The New Testament writers were by no means singular in their chafing against Roman imperial power; this they share with the postapostolic witness of the early church. While it is often assumed that, after the "conversion" of Constantine, the church lost its critical edge against the empire and grew ever more captive to it, this picture also warrants challenge. Augustine (354–430), of course, is the great commentator on empire, as his magnum opus, the *City of God*, was written as an effort to refute those critics of Christianity who blamed Christians for the empire's demise. Augustine defended the Christian faith by writing a treatise on the nature of empires. For Augustine, there are two cities: the worldly imperial city (symbolized by Babylon), which is governed by love of self, and the City of God (Jerusalem), which is governed by love of God. The former is ephemeral; the latter, eternal. The former is given over to violence; the latter, to peace.

Yet his is no dualistic reading of history, as though the borders of these two cities were impermeable. In this life, until the coming of Christ, the cities are consigned to being intermingled. When Christ comes again, he will separate out the two cities, the righteous from the unrighteous. But until that time we live as sojourners within the earthly city, yet also as those who are called to follow Christ, and therefore are simultaneously those who properly are heavenly citizens.

Augustine of Hippo shares with contemporary critics of empire a fundamental misgiving about the capacity of empires to sustain the good and to preserve its citizens from violence and death. Yet, throughout this criticism, Augustine also sounds a cautionary note that is worth comparing with the contemporary analysts: the empire is not only "out there," but it is also within. Therefore, its eradication is not for him easily feasible. But this is to anticipate: before we examine Augustine's empire, it is helpful to take a brief detour through the cultural critics who have piqued our interest and shaped our analysis of imperial power in recent times.

POSTCOLONIALISM AND EMPIRE ANALYSES

The emergence of empire analysis is difficult to trace because it appears to have emerged simultaneously within a variety of fields. Certainly postcolonial analysis formed the first line of argument against Western colonialism and the devastating effects that this has wreaked on indigenous cultures. Here we may note the profound impact that literary theorist and cultural critic Edward Said has had upon academic discourse. Said's book *Orientalism,* published in 1978, signaled a profound challenge to the West in its representation of the Orient as the exotic other. Western scholarship and cultural production produces an idea of the Oriental, which it seeks to understand, manipulate, and ultimately annihilate in its otherness. In so doing, it justifies its conquering and domination of other peoples. As he examines the colonial literature, Said uncovers a constellation of forces—ideological, religious, and economic—that sought to bring the Oriental other under Western control:

> Imperialism is . . . a commitment . . . over and above profit, a commitment in constant circulation and recirculation which on the one hand allowed decent men and women from England or France, from

London or Paris, to accept the notion that distant territories and their native peoples should be subjugated and, on the other hand, replenished metropolitan energies so that these decent people could think of the empire as a protracted, almost metaphysical obligation to rule subordinate, inferior, or less advanced peoples.[2]

Said's analysis of the cultural production and reproduction of Western society found deep resonances among theologians in the two-thirds world who were wrestling with the ideological biases that inhered in a theology which was brought to them by the very people who subjugated them. The Bible and its tools for interpretation (that is, through biblical studies and theology) often became forces for their own domination. Hence, the reading of the Bible in a postcolonialist vein was and continues to be experienced as tremendously liberating for many men and women.[3]

While postcolonial readings opened up the Bible in profoundly life-giving ways, they tended to treat the colonial era as a period of expansion confined to the past. More recently, contemporary theorists have exposed the manner in which the habits of colonialism are far from a thing of the past; indeed, we belong to an era that is *hypercolonial*; the difficulty, however, is that the colonized space is more difficult to map in a world in which nation-states are no longer defined by clearly demarcated boundaries, and in a world in which the cultural values of the West are ubiquitously promulgated and reproduced through the market and technologies.

CONTEMPORARY RESPONSES TO EMPIRE

In 2001, just after the attacks on the World Trade Center and Pentagon, philosophers Antonio Negri and Michael Hardt released a most timely book entitled *Empire.* The purpose of the book is to trace the features of the new global order in which sovereignty rests not primarily with civil rulers or nation-states, but is characterized by invisible and more diffuse power regimes—chiefly, of course, the United States and the G8 countries, as well as multinational corporations that drive public directions and policies.[4] The power of multinational corporations and those countries that spawned them, particularly the United States, is, according to most analysts, a form of political power that is unprecedented, unregulated, and ubiquitous. The form of such power is evident in the extent of its reach, which Hardt and Negri describe thus:

> The machine [of empire] is self-validating, autopoietic, that is, systemic. It constructs social fabrics that evacuate or render ineffective

any contradiction; it creates situations in which, before coercively neu-
tralizing difference, seem to absorb it in an insignificant play of self-
generating and self-regulating equilibria. . . . The imperial machine
lives by producing a context of equilibria, and/or reducing complexities, pretending to put forward a project of universal citizenship, and
toward this end intensifying the effectiveness of its intervention over
every element of the communicative relationship, all the while dissolv-
ing history and identity in a completely postmodern fashion.[5]

While Hardt and Negri attribute clear danger to the proclivity of empire
to absorb territories, they also see within the movement toward globalization
certain promise. This promise is located in the capacity of individuals to refuse
the arbitrary ascription of identity in that which was imposed by the previous
regime of nation-states and opt instead for a global citizenship based upon
chosen solidarities and loyalties. In a globalized world, loyalties are no longer confined to nation-states, based upon arbitrary borders, and maintained
through coercive sovereign power, but are facilitated and cohered through new
technological developments that enable concerned individuals throughout the
world to connect and to engage in democratic forums for social change.

Hardt and Negri describe this process of a transition from the nation-state
to global empire as "a new world order" in which there has emerged a de-
centered and deterritorialized political structure that can also host networks of
solidarity across religious, political, and ethnic lines. Hardt and Negri's Marxist backgrounds enable them to see within this shift in power and in popular
politics several dialectical movements that undermine systems of sovereignty.
A new political configuration has arisen because of the struggles of the working class, of the anticolonial movement, and the "struggles against the socialist
management of capital—the struggles for freedom—in the countries of 'real so-
cialism.'"[6] Each of these movements resists the hegemony of sovereign control.

A second movement related to popular citizen uprising against national,
economic, and ideological hegemony is the reshaping of boundaries within
nation-states. Popular uprising has engendered increased suspicion and surveillance of citizens. At the same time, deterritorialization, thanks to the advent of electronic communications, has prompted heightened perceptions
of enemy threats that now lurk inside our borders, aspiring to invade and
overcome us from within. As Hardt and Negri write: "The enemy was not,
in other words, a stable sovereign subject, but an elusive and amorphous
network that could not be contained within boundaries—a contagious virus,
perhaps, rather than a bounded, autonomous entity."[7] The new norm for
conflict in such a world is not the territorial fighting between sovereign states,
nor is it any longer revolutionary uprisings against colonial power. The norm
for conflict now is the civil war, which is the result of the unraveling of the

old regime of colonial powers, which are now coming home to roost in the new global order.

In such a world, it becomes the task of citizens to discern anew the shape of political resistance and struggle. Several alternatives present themselves. One that Hardt and Negri advance is global citizenship and cooperation. Finding within the fluidity and mass communications of modern culture certain promise as well as peril, in *Multitude*, their sequel to *Empire*, Hardt and Negri urge leftist activists to use the networks and webs of communication and the free-market structure toward the amelioration of society. Through the deterritorialization of the world and through the emergence of new forms of production (informative and affective rather than material), the multitude may be able to control its own destiny without the interference of politicians or even the state. Thus the multitude—of a new form of democratic and economic engagement—can utilize the networks of mass communication, exchange, and mobilization toward humanitarian ends. For Hardt and Negri, multitude is a radical concept for it is the power to create social relationships in common without the mediation of external bureaucracies to regulate these.

The multitude is comprised of singularities, individual political agents, each with a unique political history and set of aspirations. These singularities are often excluded from political processes, but are now "plugged into" global politics and economics in an unprecedented way. They come together to form a "new race," a multitude of global citizens unconstrained by the borders of a nationalistic system that is dying away. One can be an activist in solidarity with other activists from behind a computer screen, ostensibly participating in democracy, or fueling innovation, or moving capital from anywhere in the world. This new collectivity, according to Hardt and Negri, is much like an orchestra without a conductor.[8] The multitude, so it is claimed, is the first fruits of a new kind of political belonging, for it is one that is governed not by sovereign power—that is, the sovereign governance by the majority or of royalty—but by the immanent autonomy of the multitude itself through a network of global self-governance. Now, suddenly, for the first time in history, radical democracy is truly possible.

This radical democracy is not to be created by a form of global solidarity in any organized sense. For Hardt and Negri, it is precisely the lack of centralized power that contributes to the potential for the multitude to be effective in challenging the new imperial order. This is to be done through local sites of resistance, where there is the free flow of information and communication; but that information and communication do not become hardened into a political program: "It is not true that there can be no multitude without being unified. We have to overturn the line of reasoning: the multitude is not and never will be a single social body. On the contrary, every body is a multitude of forces, subjects, and other multitudes."[9]

As I write this, the philosophical prognostications of Hardt and Negri would appear to be flowering into full force in the "Arab Spring" and beyond. Current protests worldwide for participatory democracy are spreading across North Africa and the Middle East, in countries such as Libya, Algeria, Tunisia, Egypt, and Yemen, as well as in the recent "Occupy Wall Street" movements that proliferate throughout North Atlantic cities. Throughout, the human struggle for freedom is fueled by global communications that reproduce similar protests within diverse public squares. Hardt and Negri contributed a perspective on these struggles in late February 2011, in the *Guardian*. According to them, what is novel and significant in these protest movements is their lack of centralized leadership. Here, we see their philosophical project attached squarely to specific protests:

> The organisation of the revolts resembles what we have seen for more than a decade in other parts of the world, from Seattle to Buenos Aires and Genoa and Cochabamba, Bolivia: a horizontal network that has no single, central leader. Traditional opposition bodies can participate in this network but cannot direct it. Outside observers have tried to designate a leader for the Egyptian revolts since their inception: maybe it's Mohamed ElBaradei, maybe Google's head of marketing, Wael Ghonim. They fear that the Muslim Brotherhood or some other body will take control of events. What they don't understand is that the multitude is able to organise itself without a centre—that the imposition of a leader or being co-opted by a traditional organisation would undermine its power. The prevalence in the revolts of social network tools, such as Facebook, YouTube, and Twitter, are symptoms, not causes, of this organisational structure. These are the modes of expression of an intelligent population capable of using the instruments at hand to organise autonomously.[10]

Hardt and Negri envisage the expansion of communications through social media as an outcome of an existing reality: one in which the mobile labor of communications has become the chief mode of production within our society. This kind of production empowers young and intelligent members of society who will not settle for anything less than full participation within public processes. For Hardt and Negri, however, there is no teleology to such political participation. Like a living organism that adapts and responds to various assaults upon the body, the multitude is responsive, in flux, but not externally determined. Instead, they call for a resistance to any form of power that might seek to overtake the production and the knowledge that the multitude generates for itself: "[The] multitude . . . resides on the imperial surfaces where there is no God the Father and no transcendence."[11]

Although the fullness of this form of citizenship is not realized yet, Hardt and Negri offer some broad brushstrokes of a portrait of global citizenship at the conclusion of *Empire*. Here we get a fuller sense of the telos of human political striving in their vision. According to Hardt and Negri, the new world order will produce the kinds of citizens who demand "the right to control [their] own movement."[12] According to them, the migration of citizens in the new global order can be turned into a normative and ideal form of citizenship. Nomadism, they argue, is "the struggle against the slavery of belonging to a nation, an identity, and a people, and thus the desertion from sovereignty and the limits it places on subjectivity. . . . Nomadism and miscegenation appear here as a figure of virtue, as the first ethical practices on the terrain of Empire."[13] We will return to Hardt and Negri's concept of nomadism as an ideal ethical subject shortly, but first it is helpful to visit Augustine's critique of empire by way of comparison.

AUGUSTINE'S AMBIGUOUS RELATIONSHIP WITH IMPERIAL POWER

Augustine had an ambiguous relationship to the imperial power that waned steadily during his life. He was born in the colonial outpost of Thagaste, North Africa (modern Souk-Ahrak), and some have claimed that his experience living on the outposts of colonial power shaped his theology in a decisively anti-imperial way. As Elizabeth Clark has pointed out, however, North Africa was hardly insurrectionist in its relation to Rome. Of all the Roman provinces, North Africa was most thoroughly Romanized. By appropriating African elites into the governing powers of North Africa and through a process of cultural assimilation, North Africa adopted steadily many Roman ideals. Those who were educated in North Africa received a classical education, and Augustine was a clear benefactor of such a practice. Clark analyzes Augustine's "hybrid" identity brilliantly:

> A recently discovered inscription from Roman Arabia reads: "The Romans always win." In the case of Augustine and others, the "winning" was not through the type of conquest that had demolished Carthage centuries earlier, but through engaging the hearts, minds, and aspirations of young intellectuals and those eager to assume positions of authority at home or abroad: "conquest by book" seems an appropriate description.[14]

Augustine had no stake in dismantling colonial power or advocating for the emergence of local identities. Although he did not lament the demise of the

Roman Empire, his vision involved the carrying forth of the booty of pagan knowledge for the sake of a universal church,[15] a church that admittedly took several of its administrative cues from the Roman Empire itself.

It therefore appears to be an odd choice to situate Augustine within a critique of imperial power. After all, in addition to his blithe acceptance of much of Roman education, Augustine hardly eschews the use of hegemonic force by ruling power over the dissident subject, as his invocation of imperial coercion against the Donatists and the Pelagians attests.[16] Certainly Augustine fell short often of his own insights that lauded the political virtue of humility. Nevertheless, the thrust of Augustine's work reminds us ever of the fallen nature of human reason and its capacity to discern justice. So, not through Augustine's own faulty example, but through his teachings on the nature of human justice and our capacity for self-deception as we strive toward that justice, do we find some clues as to how the imperial habits take up residence within our hearts and minds. Indeed, the sheer proof of their tacit work upon us is Augustine's own incapacity to "see" the problem of imposing a coercive silence upon his opponents in the name of the Prince of Peace. Yet Augustine's own insights should challenge any view that would accommodate itself so quickly to the use of coercion in ruling out heterodox teachings. Robert Dodaro sums it up well when considering the frank tenor of Augustine's self-scrutiny at the end of *De Trinitate* regarding his own misapprehension of the norm of Catholic faith:

> The reader of *De Trinitate* is rightly surprised at the personal tone with which he concludes this work, and with the frank admission, unique within Augustine's discussions of *regula fidei*, that the bishop's comprehension of the norm of Catholic faith is obscured by his own sin. . . . Augustine does not ascribe his lack of adequate comprehension of the *regula fidei* to a lack of study, to an inadequate application of dialectic to the scriptures or to the theological conclusions of his orthodox predecessors. Here, we need no further "development of dogma" in order to achieve a fuller understanding of the rule of faith. No, instead, Augustine confesses that his deepening understanding of the rule of faith depends upon the extent to which God refashions his self.[17]

AUGUSTINE'S POLITICAL THEOLOGY

In spite of Augustine's ambiguous relationship to imperial power, his *City of God* sounds many of the same warnings as do leftist theorists Hardt and Negri. Augustinian political action shares with Hardt and Negri a wariness of worldly empires and a recognition of their violent and unsustainable nature. As Augustine's book is occasioned by the shocking demise of the Roman Empire, he names an experience very close to that of contemporary North Americans: an incredulity over the fragility of an empire that seemed so impervious to destruction. It is fascinating to recognize that *Empire* and *Multitude* were written around the time of 9/11 and that Augustine was writing *City of God* just after the sacking of Rome by the Visigoths in 410. Both books were influenced by debate surrounding the "new world order"—Christendom in the case of the *City of God* and a globalized world in the case of *Empire*. It would perhaps be an overstatement to say that both were apologetical treatises for the new world order. However, it is the case that both Augustine and Hardt and Negri exposed the fragility and the violences of the old world order—Roman imperialism and state nationalism—and had little nostalgia for these, unlike many of their contemporaries.

Another parallel between the two works is their respective reticence in advocating a particular political strategy for a new world. Neither work is a political treatise in the sense of offering a programmatic way out of the political struggles that citizens face, Instead, they offer broad reflections on the nature and scope of the public sphere. Finally, both books advocate restraint in identifying too strongly with the prevailing political configuration. They understand strong attachment to political configurations as a potential precursor to violence, and thus they advocate a certain distancing and critical posture toward the dominant political agendas.

Augustine is wary of putting too much stock in earthly cities because empires are governed by the *libido dominandi*, the lust for rule, and as such are compelled by prideful self-assertion, which leads to violence in order to secure their own ends. In *City of God*, pride names the character of the *libido dominandi*, which is less an inherent weakness within the psyche or personality than it is an improperly ordered desire, one that aims primarily for personal glory rather than a higher good. Augustine does not altogether contemn the pursuit of glory, that vaunted classical ideal, recognizing that it can produce certain ends that are necessary for the proper ordering of society. Yet, glory, too, can become turned in on itself, as the citizen seeks recognition and praise rather than the truth. Thus the quest for glory is too easily prone to becoming corrupted, and the virtues that it seeks in the ordering of the self and society soon become vices in the seeking of praise rather than higher ends. Therefore, while glory can be useful in directing human will toward the recognition of others, such a quest soon becomes vain as it seeks ever its own ends. There is no peace within such a world, because peace can only be a temporary amnesty so long as the *libido dominandi* remains the primary modality of political life.

Augustine also goes against the grain of the political thought of his time in denying the *Patria* any divinely appointed significance. Indeed, whereas most ancient historians read glory and valor in Roman history as a sign of divine favor, Augustine finds instead in Roman history a long story of violence and exploitation contrary to divinely appointed ends.[18] Thus Augustine distinguishes the *City of God* from those treatises that would find the providential hand of God or of the gods working straightforwardly within human history. Michael Hanby puts it well:

> In denying Rome its noble history, Augustine implicitly denies a conception of progress that would grant a providential purpose to evil, a concept that would grant a providential purpose to evil, a conception that entails a perverse sacrificial economy.

> The voices of empire must transmute the war dead into victims and death into noble sacrifice in order to sustain this optimism. They must assuage their grief at the soldier's death, and enlist further victims for the cause, by making him heroic, by consoling themselves that his courage was expended for great cause or for a better future. Evil thus becomes a dialectical moment in the realization of empire, a moment that calls forth its victims' blood in exchange for "glory."[19]

In his critical rendering of Roman history, Augustine anticipates the insights of much of contemporary political theory, including those of Hardt and Negri. Like them, Augustine is wary of imperial configurations because of their propensity to collectivize and justify the *libido dominandi*, seeing in it a momentum that, once unleashed, becomes almost impossible to oppose. The unchecked drive of empire for self-sustenance and augmentation gives rise to several form of violence, not least of which is the violence to the truth that is intent on preserving illusions of the empire's rightness, even in the midst of the slaughter of human life.

Interestingly enough, however, neither of these works—*City of God* or *Empire*—represents a full-scale rejection of the political order in which the writers find themselves. Augustine finds within the Roman civic virtues that which is still worthy of recognition, even while that virtue—particularly its pursuit of glory—can far too easily be turned in on itself: "[Glory] . . . is nevertheless puffed up and has much vanity in it. Wherefore it is unworthy of the solidity and firmness of the virtues to represent them as serving this glory, so that Prudence shall provide nothing, Justice distribute nothing, Temperance moderate nothing, except to the end that men may be pleased and vain glory served."[20] Within Hardt and Negri's work, we have an even more positive assessment of the possibilities that inhere in a new global order. For them, as we have seen, the habits of internationalism can take a beneficent turn, and thereby use the technologies of mass communication for global good.

Yet the extent to which one appropriates the habits of the secular city is a fruitful point of contrast between Hardt and Negri and Augustine. For Augustine, the *libido dominandi* is likely to assert itself and corrupt individual citizens within the earthly city, for in securing its own good, citizens are trained to immanent and self-serving practices. Therefore immanence, or popular politics, is regarded with a good deal more suspicion by Augustine than by Hardt and Negri, who long for a politics without transcendence, a politics without sovereignty. Thus, according to Hardt and Negri, political possibilities are given only insofar as they are imagined by the multitude.[21] Such generative capacity is not, according to Augustine, a property of collective life in the earthly city. For Augustine, it is far more likely that citizens will replicate the original violence of empire than subvert it. Augustine reads the history of the founding of empires as a repetition of violence, whether that be the stories of Cain and Abel, Romulus and Remus, or the countless violences that have founded cities since.[22] Augustine is attuned to the manner in which city-states repeat violence generation after generation and holds little hope that the peace that governments might secure will be of a lasting or fulsome kind.

Hardt and Negri are far more optimistic than Augustine about the power of the political imagination to transcend the violent context in which it finds itself. To take one example from their theory of global citizenship, Hardt and Negri see statelessness as a possibility of an emancipated future for the multitude, as it affords individuals the capacity to elect social and political solidarities. Yet statelessness, to the vast majority of those who have experienced it, is a nightmarish scenario. And for the millions of refugees and internally displaced persons within the world today, nomadism is hardly an ideal form of citizenship. Further, statelessness, as we have seen amply in the millions of refugees displaced in the past twenty years in Kenyan refugee camps, does not connote freedom of movement, but quite its opposite.[23] One must ask difficult questions of Hardt and Negri such as, Is the African refugee experience accidental or intrinsic to a new world order? Is global citizenship the purview only of a select few, while the majority of the deterritorialized "citizens" of the world attain this status not by choice, but by the violent and cruel effects of political sovereignty in a new global order?

Political theorist Hannah Arendt, herself an Augustinian,[24] predicted some sixty years ago the dilemma in which we now find ourselves. Without a sense of place, without a tradition, it is unlikely that citizens can produce a genuine alternative to the violence of refugee society. Arendt, writing as a Jew after World War II, prophetically describes this condition as a new form of citizenship, but is hardly hopeful in her description:

> A man who wants to lose his self discovers, indeed, the possibilities of human existence, which are infinite, as infinite as is creation. But the

recovering of a new personality is as difficult—and as hopeless—as a new creation of the world. Whatever we do, whatever we pretend to be, we reveal nothing but our inane desire to be changed, not to be Jews.[25]

Thus the nomad, far from having an identity of her own choosing, has one that is scripted by the sovereign power that excludes her: to remain a "Jew" is to remain an outcast, to remain hunted. One has to become something else, but that something else is always determined and delimited by the sovereign authority of the state.

It is thus that Hardt and Negri's proposals appear naively optimistic about the political possibilities of the multitude, for, as Augustine knows full well, the desires of the empire will be reflected in the malformed desires of its citizens. We see this poignantly as we consider with Arendt the manner in which anti-Semitism shapes the Jewish refugee subject. The empire governs people based upon fear of being excluded or abjected from its protection, because sovereign imperial power is not simply an externality but, rather, is internal to an ever-expanding totality that knows no "outside."[26] Thus the stranger becomes a source of cohesion for the totality, as fear of meeting the same fate as the abjected members of society reinforces complicity with sovereign control. In this scenario, like the desperate Jewish refugees seeking to de-Judaize themselves, the subject internalizes the rules of the sovereign and imposes its sanctions within.[27]

The notion of a nomad as an ideal citizen thus is revealed to be a woefully wanting description. Because there is no common horizon among citizens, the multitude is as at least as likely to form deadly rivalries as it is to forge those allegiances where "cooperation and revolution remain together in love, simplicity, and innocence."[28]

While Augustine would agree with Hardt and Negri that overarching attachment to a city-state is perilous to the soul and the city because it is likely to be incited to violence in order to secure preservation and expansion, he would be disinclined to abandon earthly forms of preservation through the political order. Augustine would affirm that even the fallen political order offers a measure of goods that are themselves gifts from God and appointed to God's purposes in this world (Rom. 13:1-3). Indeed, Augustine takes up Scipio's (via Cicero) definition of a *commonwealth* as an ideal to be sought based on the commonweal of the people. According to Augustine, while this ideal pertains, Rome was never truly a commonwealth because it was never a people, according to the definition of people as "a multitude united by association by a common sense of right and a community of interest."[29]

Therefore, where there is no true justice there can be no 'association of men united by a common sense of right' and therefore no people. If, therefore, a commonwealth is the 'weal of the people', and if a people does not exist where there is no 'association by common sense of right', and there is no right where there is no justice, the irresistible conclusion is that where there is no justice there is no commonwealth. Moreover, justice is that virtue which assigns everyone his due. Then what kind of justice is it that takes a man away from the true God and subjects him to unclean demons?[30]

In arguing against the existence of a true commonwealth within Roman society, Augustine argues for a revision to the Ciceronian ideal. For Augustine there cannot be a commonwealth without justice, for justice attributes to all that is due to everyone, but because the people fail to give God what is due, it fails to be true justice and is inclined to become merely a throng. The multitude becomes a throng by being united by those things that are unworthy of it— unclean demons, yes—but Augustine is making more than a pious point here. For a commonwealth to have as its end merely its own self-serving is to deny citizens virtues that exceed mere instincts for self-preservation. This is both a form of idolatry and a guarantor of the corruption of the city. Augustine therefore argues that a true commonwealth is possible not only when it is united in the objects of its love but when it is united in the objects of its love *that are worth loving*. Thus Augustine brings together love and justice in his political theology as he implies here that the objects of the city's and its citizens' love will determine the virtues practiced within the city, and those virtues will become corrupted if they are not ones that have a telos beyond an immanent and self-serving frame.[31]

The connection of the republic to the goods it loves makes worship the basic form of human action. But worship can be performed to many gods, and in our culture, the devotion of hearts and minds seems to be regularly drawn to love of things. Desire for good is also a political tendency for individuals, and nations will strive to secure the good that they seek through a variety of means. Questions of the good, of the moral telos that animates political programs, need to be brought to greater articulation, for all political programs have an implicit overarching love that animates their actions, even while such a love or such loves remain hidden beneath the surface. Without bringing the objects of a city's love to articulation, it is possible that false loves, such as the love of annexing possessions, are really the decisive political motivators of a specific soul or city. Reflections upon the good, the "background picture" that shapes our political actions, are necessary in order to ensure that the good that we are pursuing are actually loves worth loving.

Philosopher Charles Taylor has pointed out the manifold ways in which contemporary politics is characterized by a reticence to articulate the background picture that shapes our moral and political action. Without an articulation of the good that orients our political actions, contemporary politics is given over to "negative freedom," that is, maximalizing the rights of individuals or community to resist heteronomous control of any kind. Therefore, the predominant note of contemporary politics is protest, challenging the status quo, undermining sovereignty, but it never really fleshes out what a life beyond oppression might look like. This modality of politics, of aiming at the securing of freedom from heteronomous constraint, characterizes Hardt and Negri's work. In both *Empire* and *Multitude*, there can be no loyalty of association that trumps the individual will. Thus the global citizen is governed primarily by her will; and it is a will that supposes it can elect political loyalties in something of the same manner in which it can elect a brand of automobile.

In this way, Hardt and Negri differ quite strongly from Augustine, for whom true political power, the power of the citizens of the City of God, is not yet a full possession of the inhabitants of the earthly city. Hardt and Negri wish not to posit a heavenly utopia, for such a utopia would merely replicate imperial sovereign power. In its stead, they believe that sovereignty of a new kind will emerge precisely by the disavowal of a transcendent sovereign power that is posed against people's wills. True sovereignty will be the sovereignty of the multitude—of singularities participating truly in democratic reform and in capital exchange.

It is the very absence of a transcendent object toward which desire might be directed that truncates the political possibilities of such a project. This lack of clarity has everything to do with a lack of vision, a lack of a transcendent object to our desire who might propel our future actions, but might also exceed them. Without such a vision, it is likely that the multitude will simply tacitly elect to reinstate the status quo. Further, when freedom is identified so squarely with individual choice, it is hard to imagine how durable and effective political solidarities might emerge, or how the market notion of choice as the capacity to elect the object(s) of my consumption from an infinite set of products can be overturned toward a more substantive kind of freedom.

What binds citizens together in the City of God is also the object of their love, and in the city, this love is eternal; it is God. That God be praised is the highest task of the citizen of the city, and for those who wish to approximate it, worship of, giving honor to, and lauding God (rather than *Patria*) are the chief activities. The City of God exceeds the grasping of political subjects. It is not a utopia inaugurated by concerted political will, but a heavenly and eternal gift that, in exceeding our grasping, also calls forth desires for justice and peace which are not easily appeased by the partial justice and the temporary amnesty that the world gives.

Just so, Augustine lauds humility as the primary civic virtue of citizens of the City of God. Augustine construes humility not as a form of self-abasement, but as a practical and other-worldly agency embodied in Jesus Christ. It is an agency that is displayed in Christ's receptivity to the Father, which is also a receptivity that seeks nothing less than God as the object of his desire. Humility for Augustine is also the practical political virtue that is necessary in order to enable justice to flourish. The citizen who is trained in the virtue of humility will be one who will not only assign what is due to God but also assign what is due to other humans, and this virtue will engender peace in the city. Such a capacity is not merely a political virtue that is cultivated but one that arises from right praise of a God who himself displays and makes possible humility in God's self-sacrifice.

Christ is both *exemplum* and *sacramentum* of humility. That is to say that his life, death, and resurrection are appropriated by the Christian as exemplary, a subject worthy of emulation. However, Christians affirm also that Christ's subjectivity is somehow active still long after his ascension, through his body, the church. Christ thus displays a personhood that exceeds the capacities of the multitude, because his life is not merely a singularity; it is instead a source of giftedness that does not cease being poured out for the sake of others. By the power of the Holy Spirit, Christ remains active in the world, even "to the end of the age" (Matt. 28:20). In other words, his life is not that of a singularity within a multitude, but his life is plenitude (or in the Greek, *pleroma*), for "in [him] the fullness of God was pleased to dwell" (Col. 1:19). The *pleroma* is, in turn, gifted to his body, which is not to be construed as an organic unity, each with one's own singular identity and entitlements, but as a community endowed with the capacity to serve one another through the "putting on of Christ."

Augustine derives the notion of plenitude from Paul, who made use of a concept that had great currency within Gnostic philosophies. Paul writes of the *pleroma* as a fullness or completion that describes the Son's relation to the Father and, in turn, the sanctification of the community or lover of God.[32] Augustine understands the fullness of the world in all its variety to be a manifestation of the divine gift. But such a gift has its own integrity; each of its agents has its own capacity for freedom and self-direction. Thus the *pleroma* is the fullness of God working within the fullness of singularities, bringing them to a proper completion, which is a profoundly intricate and interdependent system in time.

Plenitude, or *pleroma*, in the Christian story, unlike the Gnostic view of it, is not the transcendent, other-worldly sphere that the world of materiality conceals, nor is it a gift grasped and attained by a select few who have pressed on beyond this vale of tears. Instead, it is an at-once proximate, intimate, and erotic awakening in us of a desire that stirs up the self; while it also refuses assimilation or appropriation. As Augustine writes, "all creatures subsist from the plenitude of Divine goodness."[33] The fullness of God poured out upon us in God's coming among us in Jesus both awakens desire in the subject for the object, thus affirming a subjective and human love and vulnerability, while the object always remains ungraspable, always exceeds containment or possession. Which is to say that the object is also a subject. It is only in allowing the other subject to be subject that we are freed to love him or her. As Graham Ward puts it:

> Christian desire moves beyond the fulfillment of its own needs; Christian desire is always excessive, generous beyond what is asked. It is a desire not to consume the other, but to let the other be in the perfection they are called to grow into. It is a desire ultimately founded upon God as triune and, as triune, a community of love fore-given and given lavishly.[34]

As such, the proper posture of the lovers of God and citizens of the City of God is renunciation; it is exile, but it is exile that all the same loves and seeks to heal the earthly city. Therefore, although a perfect justice cannot be fully known in the earthly city, it can, through the prayers and *askesis* of the citizens of the City of God, be approximated, not in the sense of merely reflecting the heavenly city dimly but by finding within its common life traces of eternity to be shared among the citizens of the earthly city. We turn to Augustine to discover the possibility of such a power and such a community under Christ's Lordship. Such a community, united by the *exemplum* and the *sacramentum* of Christ, will cultivate virtues quite unlike the earthly city. Citizens will seek not the simple advancement of singularities within a multitude, but will turn themselves toward the other with a like generosity to that which was once poured out upon themselves. John Milbank describes it thus:

> [T]he only thing really like heavenly virtue is our constant attempt to compensate for, substitute for, even short-cut this total absence of virtue [i.e., in a human life dominated by conflict and violence], by not taking offense, assuming the guilt of others, doing what they should have done, beyond the bounds of any given "responsibility." Paradoxically, it is only in this exchange and sharing that any truly actual virtue exists.[35]

Milbank's description of Christian virtue is of a gift given in excess. Yet it is also a gift that subverts the sacrificial economy that funds earthly cities. Christ's sacrifice is different from the death of Abel or from the countless sacrifices that constitute violent histories because his sacrifice arises from the eternal and ceaseless love of the Triune God. The motion of gift within the Trinity is a making room for the other, a perichoretic love in which the three persons of the Godhead are constituted by their self-giving relationship. God's love for the world in creation is an analogous motion, of pure, unmerited love toward that which is not God. The motion is repeated once again upon a hill in Golgotha in which Christ's sacrifice is a recapitulation of that self-same eternal gift spoken into the world. The difference in tone and tenor of the gift has to do with the recalcitrance and violence of the world into which it was spoken. But this does not deplete the divine gift of the cross: it speaks into the violence of the world and renders it silent, a surd (i.e., something that is toneless), nonbeing, as God's eternal love is vindicated at Easter. Such is the economy of sacrifice into which we are called to participate in Christ. It is a life that does not keep stock of offense, but offers itself gratuitously to others in patience and humility. These are not just lessons learned, but they are virtues that are divinely endowed because the nature of that gift is a transcendence which has the power to act beyond and within our creaturely capacities and transform them. Augustine reveals Christ to be the perfect sacrifice upon whom the City of God is founded, not because it was upon his immolation that a city was built in war and enmity, but because his divine gift for the sake of worldly cities constituted another form of political sacrifice and political belonging that arises from plenitude. Christ's sacrifice founds the City of God as a city in which earthly sacrifices are not required, because the perfect gift of self-giving is one in which the one sacrificed is also the one whose life cannot be exhausted. For Augustine, humility is not primarily a moral position so much as it is a supernaturally endowed virtue that is given to humans as the benefit of Christ's suffering love. Christ, in uniting himself to humans, creates the possibility of this other-worldly virtue: "Against this arrogance of the demons, to which mankind was enslaved as a deserved punishment, is set the humility of God, revealed in Christ. But the power of humility is unknown to men whose souls are inflated with the impurity of inflated pride."[36]

Thus the city does not mete out justice as compromise; but justice, like love, is given abundantly from a source that has no end. God's plenitude in Christ always exceeds the gift received by the City of God, and thus the proper response to it is a certain confident dispossession, a knowledge that human life and human security are supported by an inexhaustible gift that transcends human efforts at securing justice and peace: "Christ's exemplary status therefore does not exhaust the plenitude it reveals. Rather the very structure of the exemplum reveals this plenitude to be inexhaustible, to be more than we can grasp. Thus our grasping must itself take the form of a letting go, a gift, which makes us partakers in the Son's response to the Father."[37]

The Nicene teachers spoke of the realistic capacity of God to transfigure this earthly vale of tears through the doctrine of participation. Participation connotes the eternal self-giving love of the Triune God as that which transforms and sanctifies human relationships. Participation in God's eternity in the world of fallen time is made possible by Christ's own identity as eternal and human, as he serves as the bridge that traverses us humans to the divine life. For Augustine, evidence of participation in God is the counterintuitive capacity of self-absorbed humans to care for others in a self-sacrificing manner. In order for persons to do this without resentment or violence, they must be recipients of divine grace: "That is why humility is highly prized in the City of God and especially enjoined on the City of God during the time of its pilgrimage in this world; and it receives particular emphasis in the character of Christ, the king of that City."[38] Political life, for the Christian, is thus not a resolute determination of outcomes so much as it is a willful renunciation of the self for the sake of others' flourishing. Although Augustine is reticent in using the language of participation, he does so here because he believes that participating in God's divinity through the incarnation is most likely to be manifest in humans' capacity to abjure the prideful *libido dominandi* and take on Christ's mantle of humility.

Unlike Hardt and Negri, Augustine sees as the model of citizenship within the earthly city not the nomad, but the pilgrim. The pilgrim is a sojourner on the earth because she belongs to a pilgrim church, a community *in via*, on its way to becoming whole, and doing so by participating in discrete practices that shape citizens in the heavenly virtue of humility. The pilgrim's final allegiance then is not, finally, to the earthly city, but to the heavenly one. Nevertheless, she must dwell in the earthly city, which offers real and tangible goods. The earthly city also contains those who have not been called to citizenship in the heavenly city, and who have reconciled themselves to its partial ends. In these times in between, the cities remain mixed and all citizens benefit from the earthly peace that is procured in this life: "Meanwhile, however, it is important for us also that this people should possess peace in this life, since so long as the two cities are intermingled we also make use of the peace of Babylon—although the people of God is by faith set free from Babylon, so that in the meantime they are only pilgrims in the midst of her."[39] Clearly, one cannot make Jerusalem from Babylon. The people of God do have to transcend Babylon, but such a transcendence does not eschew or negate the goods that a city-state can offer toward a peace. The pilgrim "makes use" of the goods that the earthly city has to offer even while she awaits a more perfect peace.[40] Indeed, as Augustine shows, it becomes the work of the citizens of the earthly city also to strive for such a peace, while also knowing that the peace that the world brings will be a compromised and ephemeral one. This engenders a critical view of all earthly programs,[41] as pilgrim citizens recognize that the earthly city has not yet attained that peace toward which it strives.

The self-critical capacity is stirred by an awareness that our political actions fall short of the peace that God wills, yet such self-criticism ought not to engender apathy or hopelessness; rather, self-criticism will issue properly in confession. Confession is a self-critical awareness of our need for God's grace; it is a referral of these shortcomings to God, who, it is prayed, will reorient our political aims toward God's end. Christian hope contains a proper lament, a confession that partakes of the humility that is hope's source and end. As Michael Hanby writes: "To those who would identify themselves as citizens of that other city, he extends a call to self-examination, to sort out the claims made upon our affections and our complicity in the distortion and disorder of the earthly city."[42]

CONCLUSION: CONFESSING CHRIST AS LORD IN THE MIDST OF EMPIRE

Without confession, cities are easily given over to the habits of the *libido dominandi*, justifying their power through coercion. Sovereign power therefore becomes a self-legitimating religion which seeks through ideological means to convince its citizens that there is no higher good than the good of the city. Throughout history, cultures and communities have always been founded upon sovereign power. Without a sovereign, there is no people. The body that is the people has always been tied in their allegiance, for better or for worse, to another body: that of its sovereign power, a rule that both transcends and embodies the equilibrium of the community—or seeks to do so. In our quest to rid ourselves from a rule that is foreign to our interests, we seek, as revolutionaries have always done, the slaying of the sovereign. But of course, history has shown amply that, as with Hydra, the cutting off of one head is likely to spawn another. The key is an allegiance based upon another kind of sovereign—one that does not sacrifice the one to the many, or absorb the singularity into the multitude, but who, as Lord, gives rise to a people through the preservation and care of "the least of these" through the heavenly virtue of humility. To confess Christ as Lord in the midst of empire is to belong to the church in which every knee shall bow before him, not because of his triumph and glory and majesty, but because he comes in the form of a slave, and through that very particular condescension, he reveals to us God's glory.

To confess Christ's Lordship in the midst of empire is to belong to a body that is not closed and self-contained, but open to welcoming the stranger who is also a sojourner. The stability that is offered the righteous in the City of God is sabbath rest. At the end of all our sojourning, there is a vision that animates political life in the time "in between": "He will be the goal of all our longings, and we shall see him for ever; we shall love him without satiety; we shall praise him without wearying. This will be the duty, the delight, the activity of all, shared by all who share in the life of eternity."[43]

This heavenly vision is a welcome one, in my view, for all those who are wounded, those who have been caught under the heavy weight of imperial oppression—including especially in the North American context aboriginal persons—and those within the two-thirds world who have heard the gospel only as the story of one nation's victory. After all, the one who calls us to praise him is precisely the one who has suffered under the blows of imperial violence, of a myth that states that we should be willing to sacrifice the poor for the good of the many. Any cultural representation of Christ's church that is too comfortable within the orders of the fallen world must always be reminded that God's love has been poured to all those who have been rendered broken by the world's political machinations. This community is not a closed body, but neither is it a ghostly or insubstantial one.

To confess Christ as Lord in the midst of empire is to abjure citizenship in a city that trains us merely to dominate over others through the imperious consumption of the fruits of cheap labor from the two-thirds world. Confession in this context involves repenting precisely in the imperial practices that we engage in today as well as in our historical past. And so, to proclaim Christ's Lordship in the midst of empire is to be humbled as Christ was humbled, taking the form of a slave, not so that we can wallow in an indulgent guilt over our privilege. Rather, in confessing our sin against the neighbor who is also our brother or sister, we are freed then to receive the grace of God, so that we are never destined to be an empire of violence and exploitation, but to be a pilgrim people whose boundaries are open, but not erased; to be heralds of God's gracious restoration that we await, even as we journey toward it.

2

"BEGOTTEN OF THE FATHER BEFORE ALL WORLDS"

JESUS CHRIST AND CREATION

FOR MANY CONTEMPORARY THEOLOGIANS, the connection between what we say about God and how we treat God's creation is clear. While some theologies have given rise to an antimaterialism, a belief that this world is to be escaped, contemporary ecotheologians have reminded us that it is precisely "among mortals" that God's "home" is (Rev. 21:3). To perpetuate the degradation of the environment and to contribute to its demise is an assault not only against other living beings who share this planet, but also against the God who created all things. Accordingly, theologian Wendell Berry calls environmental degradation "the most horrid blasphemy."[1] The exploitation of the Earth is a rebuke against God and God's creation for it arrogates to humans the power to destroy other living things that were pronounced "very good" by God (Gen. 1:31). In the past three decades, many theologians have rightly noted that, in order to be a church committed to justice, we cannot limit our theologies to the human realm. Creation, and the life forms inhabiting it, are also central to God's compassionate care. The task of theology, then, is to speak of creation with appropriate wonder and thanksgiving so that it is understood more fully as central to God's care and concern.

Unfortunately, theology has often perpetuated the exploitation of the natural world, as humans have sought to bring it under their control. The subordination of nature by humans has had devastating consequences to the degree that all nature now suffers under its effects. Christian theology has been blamed specifically for articulating a dualistic worldview that subordinates the natural world to humans, as though human beings were somehow above nature. This dualism would seem to be perpetuated in certain interpretations of the person and work of Christ. In particular, if a human being is seen as central to salvation, and if the salvation that he proclaims is primarily for other human beings, and if indeed, his life, death, and resurrection are viewed as a disruption of nature, then clearly Christology is at odds with a theological ethic that places creation care at its center.

This line of criticism has caused some ecotheologians to look to ways in which a nonanthropocentric Christology might be developed. An exemplar of this line of criticism is Sallie McFague, whose writings have been concerned with "rethinking theology," giving specific attention to care for the Earth as a theological imperative. Throughout her work, McFague asserts as a central tenet that it is the religious picture of the world that, at least in part, holds our actions captive. Faulty and outmoded language and models perpetuate our disordered relationship with creation. This includes Christians' faulty understanding of Jesus Christ, which has unwittingly contributed to our disregard or even hostility toward the natural realm.

ECOTHEOLOGY AND SACRAMENTAL CHRISTOLOGY

McFague tackles the question of Christology and its relation to Earth care most directly in her book, *Life Abundant: Rethinking Theology and Economy for a Planet in Peril.*[2] According to McFague, the "conventional" picture of Jesus that many North Americans share is one in which "a mythological savior . . . descends from heaven and, as the God-man, shows us how to live, forgives our sins, and wins eternal life for us."[3] While it might be unjust to characterize McFague's complaint with Christology as one that is concerned with classical expressions thereof, she is explicit throughout this book about the particular disorder of North American contemporary theology with respect to environmental ethics. Nevertheless, McFague also traces the origin of this worldview in the church's creeds and in Western art, literature, and music.[4] Here it is unclear if, by the West, she means the Western church, or if she means Western civilization in general, thus including perhaps the church universal, both West and East.

In any event, McFague spurns the cosmology to which Christians cling (of a hell below and a heaven above the Earth) as an "assault on the mind"[5] and as morally bankrupt in an age in which care for this world and this earth is of utmost importance. Therefore, she enjoins contemporary Christians to respond anew to Jesus' question to Peter: "Who do you say that I am?" In an age at the brink of ecological disaster, the responsible answer must place creation care at its center.

McFague thus delineates several typologies of Christ that have been of value to Christian ecotheologians, including prophetic, wisdom, sacramental, eschatological, process, and liberation Christologies. Although she acknowledges the slightly contrived nature of typologies, for they tend to separate that which is normally far more complex and interrelated, she finds within each of these Christologies promise for a renewed Christology, and therefore promise of a renewed relationship between Christians and the Earth.

McFague's theology never abandons the centrality of Christ. Although she sees certain Christologies as having deleterious consequences for Earth care, Christology itself is not to be rejected; instead it is to be rehabilitated. Of particular interest for this project, which is concerned with rehabilitating Nicene Christology, is McFague's interpretation of sacramental Christology. Although a rather confining type (for sacramental Christology surely also encompasses the prophetic and the eschatological, among other types), it is a helpful entrée into conversations with the Nicene teachers because it offers a point of connection between theology and practices, and between Christology and ecology.

Sacramental Christology is, according to McFague, a theology that speaks to the immanence of God throughout the world as related to the incarnation of God in Jesus. Such a theology overcomes the "traditional emphasis"[6] of Christian theology upon transcendence, and instead is invested in an understanding of Emmanuel, God with us, in the bread and the wine, in the fields and the vines, and so forth. McFague sees rich potential in such a theology, for sacramental theology views God as incarnate not merely in the man, Jesus Christ, but throughout nature as well. While clearly such a theology has potential to offer an alternate construal of our relationship to the Earth and bodies, it has not always done so. In spite of the abiding emphasis upon the body or bodies within traditional Christianity, McFague notes that sacramental theology has not always served the body or the natural world well, and she judges, somewhat problematically, that "until recently, great concern for starving, tortured, or raped human bodies" was absent from Christian consciousness and practice.[7]

In her own constructive ecotheology, McFague explores the model of sacrament as a viable (although not exhaustive) Christology.[8] Incarnation concerns itself with the here and now and, like sacramental theology, understands God to be "embodied in creation" as well as in the hope for a new creation. In order to be fully liberating from an ecological perspective, however, we need to understand all nature as the sacrament of God and not confine sacramental revelation to one man. This is not to say that Christ is insignificant. Jesus is paradigmatic of what is evident elsewhere as well. Christ, therefore, is not a unique revelation, but shares with the natural world the capacity to "reflect the divine glory"[9] and provides for humans an evocative model of God's love for the world.

But it is not only Jesus' flesh that is the incarnate word; it is also the flesh of "atoms and newts, black holes and elephants, giant redwoods, and dinosaurs."[10] It is difficult to deduce from McFague's Christology how Jesus is paradigmatic of creation, or whether he simply stands among creatures. Indeed, McFague goes to considerable length to display how Jesus is not, in fact, unique but, rather, shares with the entirety of creation the capacity to reflect God. While Jesus is "the model for Christians,"[11] it is not clear that his life, death, and resurrection serve to reveal God except in a partial and heuristic sense.[12] In other words, God is not understood to be ontologically related to Jesus in any special way, and indeed Jesus' creative capacities are the same as those of other members of creation. Jesus the man does not create, restore, or sanctify creation; he is contained entirely within it.

McFague makes the Bultmannian move to separate the Jesus of history from the Christ of faith. Christ, not Jesus, is divine insofar as he is principle or force that exists *beyond* his humanity. Christ is the Logos or Sophia that works within the natural world. Thus Christ as Logos or Wisdom connotes an energy or power working in and through the natural world, including, but not limited to, the world of humans. The Logos is embodied in Jesus of Nazareth in a special way for humans, and specifically for Christians, in order that they might come to know what Godly life looks like. However, Jesus, as parable for God, is not unique and there is no special ontological coordination between his life and that of God that might be distinguished from those of other creatures. McFague has no difficulty placing Jesus on the creaturely side of the ontological divide. Christ, Holy Wisdom, however, is identified more closely with God's own creative and effective will. The effect of this splitting is a curious truncation of the environmental possibilities of the doctrine of the hypostatic union, the very doctrine that affirms that God and creation are truly united in Christ, for this union preserves the possibility of God's working in and through the natural world in an effective and realistic manner. This possibility collapses when the disunity of the person of Jesus Christ is emphasized.

Clearly, there will be a good deal that will distinguish McFague's position from that of Nicene orthodoxy. My point in engaging her as representative of contemporary ecotheology is not to expose her heterodoxy. She would probably side more with an "Arian" position than a Nicene one on the nature of Jesus Christ. My question is not whether she particularly meets the standards of Nicene orthodoxy. Rather, I ask, Is it necessary to abandon normative Christian claims about the hypostatic identity of Jesus Christ in order to respond morally to a planet in peril? My second question that is inspired by McFague's theology is this: Is hers an adequate account of the natural world and its sacramental relation to God?

In responding to these questions I will begin by considering the latter question before moving to the former, and will do so by engaging an alternate construal of the natural world and humans' role within it to see if it might engender the kind of moral practices that McFague rightly and prophetically commends. Because of the depth of his insight on both Christology and creation, I will engage the writings of Basil of Caesarea (329–379), particularly his *Homilies on the Hexaemeron*, in my own consideration of a constructive ecological theology that is attentive precisely to the serious concerns that animate McFague's writings. The *Hexaemeron* was a text that Basil wrote toward the end of his life (c. 378), consisting of nine exegetical homilies that focus on the six days of creation and that are centered chiefly upon the creation of nonhuman life.[13] In spite of this focus upon nonhuman life, human beings are central to his analysis, for we receive from his account of creation insight into the nature of humanity. It is therefore faulty to read this work as a proto-ecological source. His sermons—remember they are sermons—are intended to illuminate the human condition as members within a created order governed and reconciled by God. Nevertheless, they offer us clues as to how the gulf between human and divine is overcome in Christ and what possibilities might therefore emerge for Christians concerned to address the environmental crisis of our time.

BASIL ON THE DIVERSITY AND DESIGN OF NATURE

The *Hexaemeron* is often read as an overly literal account of the nature of creation because Basil draws amply from the natural sciences as they were then understood, including botany, astronomy, and meteorology. Though he draws moral and pastoral conclusions from these sciences, he is, or so it is argued, reluctant to engage in a spiritual or allegorical reading of Scripture in its account of the creation of the world.[14] I am disinclined to read Basil as a literalist opponent of an allegorical reading in this or in his other works, because, as I shall argue later, I believe that it is a particular type of allegorizing that he rejects. Be that as it may, it is easy to pass over the depth of insight that this work contains because of the seemingly primitive science that it contains. However, Basil's work is not best read as a scientific manual, but as what it is: homilies, intended for a public hearing within the church for the sake of growth in faith. They draw upon the natural world to illustrate God's intrinsic care and work within it, and, by analogy, of God's care and work upon and within human life.

The natural world—or "creation," as we may call it theologically—is difficult in a technological age to name. In a world in which bioengineering is changing the very DNA of plants and animals, it is increasingly difficult to discover a nature that is "uncorrupted" by human manipulation. Both McFague[15] and Basil acknowledge the complexity of nature by exposing the manner in which the natural world is adaptive, alive, and relational. This shared insight is of no small significance in a world in which nature has tended to be regarded as inert matter available primarily for human consumption and use. Whatever the natural world is for these thinkers, it is alive and charged with energy. Creation is not designed merely for the use or appropriation of human beings; it is instead intricate and intrinsically good. It is adaptive life in its living, healing, reproducing, and dying. Basil, like McFague, celebrates the wonderful prodigality and diversity of nature, and sees in this the evidence of God's abundant gift scattered throughout creation. In his reflections upon plant life, Basil writes:

> What variety in the disposition of their several parts. And yet, how difficult it is to grasp the distinctive property of each of them, and to grasp the difference which separates them from other species. Some strike deep roots, others do not; some shoot straight up and have only one stem, others appear to love the earth and from their roots upwards, divine into several shoots. . . . What variety there is in bark! Some plants have smooth bark, some have only one layer, others several. What a marvellous thing![16]

Thus nature has its own intrinsic rhythms. As Basil moves from his exposition of the creation vegetative to animal life, he remarks how animals have a native intelligence, which procures for them what is necessary for survival. That intelligence is not quite the rationality of humans; nevertheless, it is not to be disparaged. Animals have God-given capacities for self-preservation that enable them to disguise or protect themselves in the face of prey. Thus even in their sheer and adaptive physicality, we see something of the goodness of the Creator toward creation, for God endows animals with the creaturely capacity to know and to will the good of self-preservation. Basil marvels at this ordering, which is not just evident in the bodily "design" of animals, but also is known intuitively as the animal self-appropriates the laws that govern them. When reflecting on the innate migration of fish, he extols: "Who puts them in marching array? Where is the prince's order? Has an edict affixed in the public place indicated to them their day of departure? Who serves them as a guide? See how the divine order embraces all and extends to their smallest object. A fish does not resist God's law, and we men cannot endure His precepts of salvation!"[17] Here Basil intimates that the Logos, conceived here as the divine ordering of God within the created universe, is reflected even in the government of a school of fish. The natural world is therefore not animated not only by the will to survive, but also—in certain instances—by commerce and mutuality. It is in these relationships that we see, straightforwardly, the goodness of the Creator:

> What a variety, I have said, in the action and lives of flying creatures! Some of these unreasoning creatures even have a government, if the features of government is to make the activity of all the individuals centre in one common end. This may be observed in bees. They have

a common dwelling place; they fly in the air together, they work at the same work together; and what is still more extraordinary is that they give themselves to these labours under the guidance of a king and superintendent, and that they do not allow themselves to fly to the meadows without seeing if the king is flying at their head. As to this king, it is not election that gives him this authority; ignorance on the part of the people often puts the worst man in power; it is not fate; the blind decisions of fate often give authority to the most unworthy. It is not heredity that places him on the throne; it is only too common to see the children of kings, corrupted by luxury and flattery, living in ignorance of all virtue. It is nature which makes him the king of the bees, for nature gives him superior size, beauty and sweetness of character.[18]

Nonhuman creatures participate in relationships not merely of mutual benefit, but of friendship and love, as is most amply displayed in the relationship between parent and child. Basil sees within the natural order a universal *sympatheia*[19] that secretly unites all of the diversity of nature. This *sympatheia* is the defining characteristic of life prior to the fall of humanity. Here we have a natural affinity between God and the natural world, to such an extent that nature reflects the very commandments that God gives: "Children love your parents, and you parents, 'provoke not your children to wrath' (Eph. Vi. 4). Does not nature say the same? Paul teaches us nothing new; he only tightens the links of nature."[20] Thus Basil would affirm that there is affinity between the relationships of nature to the divine activity within the world. Nonhuman animals are able to participate in and enjoy the bonds of affection that are the divine gift written in animal society. Creation participates in the beneficent and loving will of the Creator toward creation. The rhythms and patterns of creation are not antagonistic to God's intention for them but conform to them in a harmonious *sympatheia*.

Human beings share in the affinity, the *sympatheia*, that other creatures enjoy. They are distinguished from other animals because they possess the image of God, which for Basil was identified with the rational will or logos. Animals lack two interrelated capacities that, according to Basil, constitute their identity in *imago Dei*: rationality and language. These gifts do not necessarily secure human beings greater privilege, but they do charge them with greater responsibility. It is a responsibility that is soon neglected, the result of which is the loss of likeness to God, and thus are now prone even in their powers of language and of reason to sin and decay. Although Basil does not treat the fall in this treatise, we can find in his subsequent writings evidence and teachings to warn against human pride and to spur us toward creation care.

THE *IMAGO DEI* AND LIKENESS TO GOD

In their theologies of creation, it was common for the Nicene teachers to seize upon the distinction of Genesis 1:26a in which it is written that God creates human beings in God's image and likeness: "Let us make humankind in our image, according to our likeness . . ." Basil's own use of this distinction is one that separates the naturally endowed gift of reason as representative of God's image, and the capacity of humans to reflect that image through virtue as their likeness to God. Likeness is a human willful occurrence, whereas image is a divinely appointed gift. Likeness is response to that prior gift so that persons may conform themselves to it. Such a conformity is not so much a willful and stubborn persistence as much as it is a *surrendering* to the truth of our natures. Basil likens such "work" to that of artisans:

> 'Let us make the human being according to our image and according to our likeness' [Gen. 1:26]. By our creation we have the first and by our free choice we build the second. . . . Yet now he has made us with the power to become like God. And in giving us the power to become like God, he let us be artisans of the likeness to God, so that the reward for our work would be ours.[21]

A great deal of criticism is likely to emerge when rationality is considered to be that which separates humans from animals, and that which endows humans with the capacity to be God-like. However, this passage is instructive in its displaying the role of the will, of human freedom for securing our divinely appointed status in Basil's thought. Rationality is not a cold calculating from on high; rather, according to Basil, it is a freedom that is only manifest in electing the good, in "putting on Christ":

> If you become a hater of evil, free of rancor, not remembering yesterday's enmity; if you become brother-loving and compassionate, you are like God. If you forgive your enemy from your heart, you are like God. If as God is toward you, the sinner, you become the same toward the brother who has wronged you, by your good will from your heart toward your neighbour, you are like God. As you have that which is according to the image through your being rational, you come to be according to the likeness by undertaking kindness. Take on yourself 'a heart of compassion and kindness,' that you may put on Christ.[22]

Thus the purpose of the logos or the rational will within humans is to conform ourselves to the perfect Logos, to Christ. The characteristics of Christ are here enumerated not as power or capacity to control, but precisely their opposite: it is a divine receptivity, a willingness to forgive, good will toward those who have offended, kindness and compassion toward others. Clearly this rationality may also be extended to the nonhuman world.

Basil of Caesarea understands human rationality as that capacity which most perfectly reflects God's image. It is on account of the gift of rationality that humans are also given responsibility for ruling the Earth. Basil extols the power of reason to cause even the mightiest animals to succumb to humans, and clearly embraces an anthropocentrism that the contemporary environmentalist would wish to critique. Nevertheless, his understanding of the exercise of our rational capacities is hardly the exercising of dominion over it. In recalling the virtues that are given to man and woman created in *imago Dei*, he chooses women as models of virtue in representing God: "The woman also possesses creation according to the image of God, as indeed does the man. . . . Through compassion (the body) is vigorous, in patient endurance and earnest in vigils. When has man been able to imitate the vigor of women in fastings, the love of toil in prayers, the abundance in tears, the readiness for good works?"[23] Clearly, Basil was a man of his times with respect to his understanding of humans' superiority in reason and the propriety of their dominion; however, dominion and rationality are understood in ways that are tempered by faith in Christ. Thus the prototype that he assigns to being created in *imago Dei* is a praying and compassionate woman. Clearly there are worse options for understanding Christian stewardship of the Earth.

The most consistent trope that Basil uses to represent human rational activity is not rational manipulation or control but, instead, *theoria* or contemplation. Contemplation for Basil is primarily a receptivity of thought to the divine working within the universe. Thus it is able to see in the diversity and diffusion of creation a unity of intention or purpose. The goal of contemplation is not manipulation, but attention to the created world as a sign of God's purposive activity. Basil cites Paul as a proof text for his argument for knowledge of God from creation: "Ever since the creation of the world his eternal power and divine nature, invisible though they are, have been understood and seen through the things he has made" (Rom. 1:20). This capacity is available to human beings not on account of a divine property existing within the psyche, but because the Logos has healed the logoi of men and women in condescending himself and accommodating himself to human knowledge. The Spirit completes this work in giving humans a pure heart to see the benefits of salvation and a will to work in accordance with this vision.[24]

CREATION AS SIGN AND SACRAMENT

In creating the word and pronouncing it good, God declares God's blessing upon that which is not God. Creation is both derivative, limited in time and in space, and also free. Thus God does not dwell *in* nature, but neither is God remotely detached from it. God's transcendence is such that God is freed to take up residence within the natural world without denying its integrity. Thus God is to be found in nature not by looking through it to something ineffable and other than nature, but to see God reflected in nature itself, to be willing to risk finding God in nature's stark finitude, in the word entering into history, into nature, into fallen time, and yet see the purposes of the natural world that God intends.

Thus the created order, according to Basil, is to be loved in all its complexity and particularity. Yet the natural world is not God; between God and creation there exists a profound ontological interval. God in God's essence transcends the composite and mortal character of the created world,[25] in God's simplicity and in God's eternity. Nevertheless, God elects to speak the world into being, thus creating from God's very lips that which is other than God—that which is finite, composite, and temporal. God speaks this world into being through God's eternal word, the Son, who is, for the sake of all creation, its "firstborn." That the Triune God enters into a world of time through the word speaks something about the nature of God. It speaks to a love and care for creation that flows from the very heart of the divine life toward the world. Thus, on the one hand, there exists for Basil a distinction between the divine life in itself and the divine life in relation to the world. The inner-triune life (or immanent Trinity) cannot be known in its essence, and therefore can only be spoken about by way of negation (God is uncreated, undifferentiated, apathetic), which highlights the analogical impasse between God and creation. On the other hand, we can know something of the nature of God in relation to the world (the economic Trinity), as God pours out God's divine life and blessing for its sake.

For Basil, there remains an ineffable and impenetrable mystery of God which is not reducible to the divine energies that God displays throughout the world in calling forth natural life. This *ousia* or essence of God is beyond all understanding, and constitutes the limit of our capacities to penetrate the divine life. Because God's essence is hidden from human understanding, we cannot straightforwardly identify creation with God, although we can identify creation with God's active love within the world. Therefore, unlike many modern commentators, Basil is reluctant to locate divine agency within the *processes* of nature. God's essence is not known in this world, because this world is still encumbered by sin and death. The natural world is not impassible. As interconnected life cannot help but be affected by the presence of other parts of the organism, particularly of the parts that have wielded such unencumbered and often violent power—human beings. Thus creation is encumbered by violences, including and especially the violences of human beings. God is not the author of these violences; these are instead manifestations of a creation that is not yet complete, not yet divinized.

In distinguishing God's essence and God's energies, Basil of Caesarea is also making a distinction between the types of language that can be used for God. In the instance of God's essence, there can be no ascription to God except by way of negation. Our signs can only point here to what God is *not*. God is impassible, immortal, unmoveable, beyond signification. In her theory of language, McFague also wishes to underline the unknowable character of God. It is for this reason that she finds in metaphor a safeguard against idolatry—of making God too small by identifying God too tersely with human properties. And yet, the distinction between these respective negative theologies is important. The *kataphasis* or negative theology of Basil does not signal that nothing can truly be known about God and that therefore there are myriad ascriptions that can be given to God. Rather, he is saying that because we cannot know God in God's essence we are compelled *not* to say certain things about God. We cannot say that God is finite, composite, or passible. We must say that God is eternal, simple, and impassible, even while those categories exceed our grasp of them or we cannot know them except by indirect analogy.

In the category of divine energies, there is a great deal that can be said about God as God relates to the world through the word. Through the word, God accommodates Godself to our creaturely capacities, God speaks the idiom of creatures so that they might understand. This divine idiom is creation itself created through the word. Creation is itself a trustworthy sign of God's love for the universe, not because it is a *symbol* representing God's love, but the very communication of that love. All creation participates in God not through its willful cooperation in reflecting God, but because it is God's eternal yes spoken in time and in the beautiful utterance that is creation. It is a sacramental theology because created matter is made holy not by becoming something or representing something that it once was not, but because it is the very language of God's blessing.

In this way, creation is the irreducible sign of God's blessing. One need not overcome the distance between God and the world through the mediation of human metaphors or symbols; rather, creation is the very language of God's love for the world. In this way, Basil gives a more robust account of the relationship between God and nature. For him, the relationship is one of immediacy of a kind that is lost in many contemporary writings on symbol, analogy, or metaphor. Consider for a moment McFague's description of the relationship between the creation and God: "If God can be present . . . in what one sees then potentially anything and everything in the world can be a symbol of the divine. One does not preach to the birds, but a bird can be a metaphor to express God's intimate presence in the world."[26] Rather surprisingly, McFague is presenting here a far more anthropocentric account of God's relationship to the world than is Basil. For McFague, birds *can be* metaphors of God's intimate presence through human mediation. For Basil, birds simply *are* signs of God's intimate presence. It is unclear from this description of the natural world as symbolic or metaphorical how these symbols or metaphors are more suggestive or appropriate than others, or whether they might be fruitfully or expeditiously substituted for other symbols as taste and/or circumstances warrant. In other words the lack of intrinsic affinity between creator and creation makes the correlation of these two arbitrarily dependent upon human symbolization, and therefore attaches far too much weight to human mediation in the giving of signs.[27]

As David Bentley Hart argues, a symbolic taxonomy is blinded to the sheer gratuity of the gift itself and tries to capture or explain it. "Beauty," rather, lies in "the immediacy of a certain splendor, radiance, mystery or allure." Efforts to capture its symbolic import, or to ascribe to this immediacy a theory of divine relationship to the natural world, is to lose sight of the immediate or the surfaces of things: "In the moment of the beautiful, one need attend only to the glory that it openly proclaims, and resist the temptation to seek out some gnosis secretly imparted."[28]

To find a hidden depth of meaning or an edifying morality within the world of nature is also to miss its point. The "terrible beauty" of the natural world ought not to be domesticated by ascribing to it a hidden organic morality. There can be no preemptive closure on the meaning ascribed to nature. To do so would be to treat the natural world instrumentally, as less than fully alive. Such a tendency is particularly evident in those ecological theologies that accommodate themselves to the violences of nature by identifying providence too straightforwardly with evolutionary processes. Because God exists beyond nature, and because nature is created with its own freedom, we do not have to look for hidden theodicies within the book of nature. To do so is to pay too high a price by attaching a divine morality to the often terrible processes within the natural world, a world that can be ravaged by earthquakes, floods, tsunamis, and other "natural" disasters.[29]

Much debate has been engendered over Basil of Caesarea's so-called rejection of allegory that seems to grow in intensity in the *Hexaemeron*. It is helpful for our purposes to examine Basil's line of reasoning in some detail, for it gives us a clearer sense of the profound importance that he gives to creation. As Basil writes:

> I know the laws of allegory, though less by myself than from the works of others. There are those who truly, who do not admit the common sense of the Scriptures, for whom water is not water, but some other nature, who see in a plant, in a fish what their fancy wishes, who change the nature of reptiles and of wild beasts to suit their allegories, like the interpreters of dreams who explain visions in sleep to make them serve their own ends. For me grass is grass; plant, fish, wild beast, domestic animal, I take them all in the literal sense.[30]

Although Basil of Caesarea does not reject allegorical reading *tout court*, he does reject those readings that render overly complex the literal sense of Scripture, as though the exegetical difficulties of the Genesis text overrule a discovery of God's creative will within nature as described in that text. Therefore, Basil finds within the natural world hidden traces and signs of God's handiwork and marvels at them in their unique manifestations. The capacity for such wonder is one of the gifts that is given uniquely to the human condition. It is the propensity to see within the diversity and temporal material of the natural world a proleptic opening toward simplicity and eternity. In short, human beings are endowed with the capacity to interpret natural signs that point to God: through their rational souls they are able to discover a hidden depth of things, not by abandoning natural appearances, but by dwelling within them. As Jaroslav Pelikan puts it: "The sovereign and overruling power of God was not comprehended in words, not even divine words, but it was witnessed to by the works of God. . . ."[31] Thus the world proclaims the glory and the grandeur of God, not by being something that it isn't, but by being what it is which, as Rowan Williams writes, "includes, paradigmatically, creation being itself in unfinishedness, time-taking, pain and death."[32]

The capacity to recognize creation's participation in divine life comes not through a human faculty per se, but is itself a divinely endowed gift of the Holy Spirit, as the eschatological consummation of ordinary life is illumined for the rational mind to partake and participate in. It is upon this basis that the Holy Spirit is declared divine for Basil: for it takes ordinary matter in the liturgy and transforms these into instruments for our salvation. The Spirit renders complete what is merely pointed to in ordinary time; it sanctifies matter and displays its proper end. Thus Basil's rejection of allegory is not a rejection of seeing within the "text" of the world signs of God; rather, it is a seeing the signs of Scripture in the Genesis account as pointing to something other than the world. The world is worthy of human contemplation and praise and ought not to be overcome or subdued in scriptural interpretation. Allegory is not needed to overcome the world, or to supplant it with another taxonomy. The taxonomy of nature is sufficient and perspicacious in manifesting to rational beings the benevolent care and the abundant beauty that God bestows freely upon the world. Robert Stillman sums it up well: "As the handiwork of God, the world does not need a figurative reading in order to reveal spiritual meanings."[33] The *Hexaemeron* is therefore a celebration of an artisan maker who creates both word and world and a celebration of the "art" which is the masterful creation that God gives. More than this, contemplation of nature enables us to participate in something of God's own beauty and goodness in praise. As Basil enjoins his hearers: "May He who filled all with the works of his creation and has left everywhere visible memorials of His wonders, fill your hearts with all spiritual joys in Jesus Christ, our Lord, to whom belong glory and power, world without end. Amen."[34]

For McFague, the natural world is a sacramental manifestation of God. Christian sacraments are instances—given to the church in the story of Christ— of God's miraculous coming into the world within ordinary things like bread and wine. These meals serve as a reminder of the goodness of creation and the equality of the women and men who participate in the ordinary gifts—the fish and the bread—of Jesus' ministry. McFague reminds us of the early communions of fish and bread particularly, because they represent more fully an ordinary meal in which God satiates ordinary hunger with the fruits of creation. These ordinary meals are miraculous! Too often North Americans confuse abundance with excess. Jesus' own meals remind us to take from the Earth only what the body needs, allowing it to replenish itself. As McFague writes: "An insatiable appetite is the mark of global market capitalism; it is also a definition of sin within the model of the world as God's body."[35]

Thus the world, as the body of God, constitutes an organic whole in which humans are but one small species. Human consumption must limit itself so as to preserve the whole. Self-sacrifice or asceticism are thus pragmatically lifted up as means to partake in the Earth's limited resources more equitably. McFague's asceticism is therefore temperate self-restraint. In this she shares with the early church a discipline that is all but forgotten in contemporary expressions of Christian life. Yet for McFague, asceticism is chiefly a *moral* discipline to which we are enjoined by the teaching given in the religious metaphor. While the moral level is indeed an important strand in Nicene theology, temperance gives way to abundance in a manner that I believe is helpful in the reappropriation of the meaning of ascetical practices for the contemporary church. This has everything to do with the judgment that Christ is not a symbol or a metaphor of God, but a reality who truly communicates himself within the created world through his divine radiance and beauty. Thus reflection on the immediacy of creation and its goodness also gives rise to thought concerning the unity of intent of the Father and the Son. It is not in a willful exercise of creation that the world is made in its variegated splendor, but in the immediate overflowing of God's creative love through the Son. Jesus Christ offers a foretaste of this superabundant joy in his earthly ministry as he offers through the miracles a transfiguration of fallen nature into their proper splendor. He does this through the ordinary things of the world, not to impart a lesson, but to restore created matter to their proper natures. In so doing, Jesus is not overcoming the natural world, but working precisely within it and through it. David Bentley Hart's reflection upon miracles as the fulfillment of nature is significant to our purposes here:

The incarnation is the Father's supreme rhetorical gesture, in which all he says in creation is given perfect emphasis. This is particularly evident in the Gospel accounts of Christ's miracles: the healing of infirmities, the raising of the dead, the feeding of the hungry, even the transforming of water into wine. These are not acts that manipulate or negate the order of nature in order to achieve an outstanding effect; in them the goodness of creation is reaffirmed, its peace is restored: they repeat God's gift of creation by imparting joy in the good things of the world—food and wine, fellowship and rejoicing, life and vision and health—to those in whom such joy is lacking. Christ's miracles—as do all the aspects of his life and ministry—constitute his *semeiosis* (John's Gospel, in fact, calls them *semeia*) that restores the original *semeiosis* of the world, the language of divine glory, and all that reorients all the signs of creation toward the everlasting sign of God who walks among them.[36]

Basil distinguishes between the essence (*ousia*) of God and God's energies (*energia*), arguing that while the former remains veiled, the latter is available to us through the reflective practice of *epinoia. Epinoia* is a form of embodied knowledge, one that derives principles and ascribes common traits to the things of their world through sense perception raised to contemplation. While we can know God in God's relationship to the world, we cannot apprehend God in God's essences, which remain yet obscured to human beings, and which defy clear analogical relation. Thus Basil remains apophatic on the nature of God with respect to God's essences. However, this is not to say that knowledge of God is impossible. Indeed, we know God insofar as we know how God acts within this world. As we have seen, this knowledge is available to us through nature, but it is crystallized for human beings in the knowledge that becomes incarnate in the Logos, Jesus Christ: "Just as perfect knowledge is manifested in the true human being, Christ, it is shown as lacking in Adam, precisely because of his inattentiveness to the fullness of what God had given. It is a movement of the eye from 'light to shadow' or of the mind which strays from God and the abundant life bestowed."[37]

These energies are known through the attentive knowledge that is *epinoia*, and they form a trustworthy account of God's revelation to us through God's creative activities within the world. However, we do not bypass the energies of God in relation to the world in order to press on to discover God's essence. The essence remains hidden, while the activities are revealed. From a hidden font of blessing derives an abundance of divine energy or motion toward the world that originates, according to Basil, in the Father, and appears to us through the Son, and is completed in us and in the world beyond us by the Holy Spirit.[38] We can know God's activities in the world because they are not of another order from the properties of creation. The created world teeming with life is a real reflection of the Creator because it cooperates with its initial calling forth given at creation. This symmetry between God's activities in the world and the creative creation offers a source of knowledge and of faith. Basil believes that through *epinoia* we can enhance our knowledge incrementally of both creation and Creator. As he writes: "A single plant, a blade of grass is sufficient to occupy all your intelligence in the contemplation of the skill which produced it."[39] Such knowledge requires moral and spiritual preparation in addition to intellectual rigor. For Basil, a clearing out of sinful distractions is necessary to gain a proper perspective.

CONCLUSION: ASCETICISM, INCARNATION, AND THE FLOURISHING OF CREATION

Although the gifts of human beings created in God's image and likeness are heavenly gifts, the restoration of God's likeness also requires the cooperative activities of human beings through durable practices aimed at spiritual growth. Christ provides the model of full and perfected humanity in his own earthly life of receptivity toward God. Christ also fulfills our knowing by being united to human nature. Thus knowing, for the Cappadocians, was not simply a discipline of the mind but involved a spiritual awareness, whereby the proper ordering of knowledge was made possible through wisdom. It is here where the christological dimension of knowledge becomes the most prominent. Because it is God's will that the light of wisdom should penetrate the world in the coming of Jesus, it is also God's will that we should conform our own rational wills (our logoi) to perceive and to receive that coming. While this is true of knowledge in general for Basil, it is of particular interest here in our pursuit of an environmental ethic that might be drawn from his Christology. In this, the conforming of our wills to Jesus Christ takes the shape of ascetic renunciation, a renunciation that, among other things, has the effect of harmonious living within the cosmos.

Ascetic discipline is not limited by any means to Christians of antiquity. The term *asceticism* has its origins in rigorous military training. To practice self-restraint was a widely shared ideal, reflected in the Homeric models of virtue (*arete*), and developed into a systematic philosophy by the Stoics. Greek education inculcated such virtues as temperance and prudence in its practices. The Neo-Platonists, whom Basil studied, regarded asceticism as a means to the purification not only of the body, but also of the soul. All these would share in some way the organic metaphor of the body described above: in order to have a balanced body, we must exercise self-restraint.

Basil founded a monastic community based upon these principles. He created rules that instructed men and women on the disciplines of common life and through cenobitic monasticism commended for Christians a life in which the presence of constant community is itself an ascetic practice. Basil saw the role of the monastery as not merely a self-contained unit, but as one that welcomed the poor, the infirm, and the traveler. His vision for the monastery was that it ought to be a reflection of the divine life which was poured out so generously within creation. Thus it is not the task of humans to hoard possessions, but to share them, as the possessions do not properly "belong" to humans at all:

> Recall, my friend, who has given these things to you. Remember who you are, what you are asked to manage, the one from whom you receive it, and the reason you have been privileged before so many others. You are, in fact, the steward of a good God, the household managed for your fellow servants. Do not think that all of this has been prepared simply for your belly. Make plans about what you hold in your hands as if it belonged to others; you may enjoy it for yourself for a little while, but then it will melt and vanish, and you will be asked to give an exact accounting for all of this.[40]

While for Basil there is a clear moral injunction to ascetic disciplines within the Bible, "in imitation of Him who for our sakes becomes poor,"[41] such renunciation is not merely a disciplined act of self-sacrifice, but it is instead an ordering of one's life in such a way that God's abundance is more fully apprehended and experienced.[42] In his appeal to a solitary monk to take on the training of a new Christian, Basil compares the struggle of the new Christian to that of a wrestler, overthrowing an opponent, "the prince of darkness of this world."[43] Thus, for Basil, asceticism involves a reorientation of one's life so that those things which are distractions from the love of God are overthrown. This practice is a self-purification that is ancillary to a greater pleasure, but *askesis* is also constitutive of that very pleasure as monks and other disciples receive a foretaste of the world to come, a world in which we would be redeemed from the overwhelming demands and limits of our bodies.

In his *Homily on Deuteronomy*, Basil points out that the disciplines required for monastic living among other persons are also transferable to our relations with the natural world, a world in which receptivity to the truth that creation reveals also engenders a respect and a love for fellow creatures:

> "Take heed to thyself." Every living creature possesses within himself, by the gift of God, the Ordainer of all things, certain resources for self-protection. Investigate nature with attention, and you will find that the majority of brutes have an instinctive aversion from what is injurious; while, on the other hand, by a kind of natural attraction, they are impelled to the enjoyment of what is beneficial to them. Wherefore also

God our Teacher has given us this grand injunction, in order that what brutes possess by nature may accrue to us by the aid of reason, and that what is performed unwittingly may be done by us through careful attention and constant exercise of our reasoning faculty. We are to be diligent guardians of the resources given to us by God, ever shunning sin, as brutes shun poisons, and ever hunting after righteousness, as they seek for the herbage that is good for food.[44]

Monastic *askesis*, then, is not a self-denial, but is instead the attuning of oneself with a reason that is naturally conferred. Thus asceticism, self-denial, is not merely self-sacrifice for the righting of an imbalanced system; it is instead a spiritual vision in which human beings are sustained by the spiritual gifts of God. This is facilitated by ascetical practices in which the demands of our body are met, but are not the primary object for fulfillment: "Let us . . . turn to the example of the three thousand [in the early Christian community of Acts 2]; let us imitate the first band of Christians, when all things were held in common—when life and soul and harmony and the table all were shared, when fraternity was undivided, and unfeigned love formed many bodies into one."[45] The discipline of ascetic self-renunciation not only has the pragmatic benefits of living more responsibly within a fragile ecosystem (although this is crucial),[46] it also offers something of the sensuous joy of a life given over to "unfeigned love." Basil marks therefore something of the spiritual and of progress in renunciatory practices. Clearly they are of practical benefit, but they also lead to higher ends as they bring clarity to the purpose and direction of human life that is receptive to God. For Basil the monks may even attain proleptic vision, which enables them to anticipate a life freed from violence against fellow creatures, and encourages monks to become vegetarians, living as though the world were already perfectly restored.[47]

Perhaps the fundamental distinction between ancient and contemporary theologies on creation has to do with differences in the condition for such changes to take place. For McFague, responsibility toward the Earth is a moral given in an ecological age, and her special task as a theologian is to awaken Christian hearers to previously hidden resources within the tradition and beyond it that might challenge us to respond to the environmental crisis more boldly and more faithfully. Thus she "tests" various models and metaphors for their efficacy in encouraging right relation to a wounded planet. In this way, religious language becomes instrumental to the primary goal, which is to form ecologically conscious Christians.

Implicit in this argument is that Christian doctrine has to do the "work" necessary to correlate its confession to the needs of the planet through symbol making. This is because human beings are understood to be makers of signs.

Signs are not somehow given by God, or somehow expressive of an already existing affinity to the divine. Therefore, signs can be treated instrumentally, and we can posit a better sign than others by virtue of the strength of our ecological convictions.

Against this, Basil would have a more realistic account of signs—both the nonverbal signs that permeate the natural world, and the signs that are our language about God and God's creation. Although he would agree with McFague that all our language about God falls short with respect to the Triune God's essences, he would aver that, nevertheless, God speaks to the world in the clarity of God's self-communication with it. "The world is charged with the grandeur of God" in the perspicacity of a budding flower, a tree stretching toward the sun, or a colt nuzzling its mother. Because these signs are perspicacious and trustworthy, we can also say that our representations of them display a fidelity to the living relationship between God and the world. Our relationship to God may be described variously, given the sheer variety and effusiveness in which God bestows God's energies upon the world. Therefore, in terms of the economy, Basil would concur with McFague and other contemporary theologians that it is appropriate to "bring many names" to God. This is so because God encounters us in a great variety of ways, ways that exceed singular ascriptions to God:

> Then again, on account of the divers manners wherein grace is given to us, which because of the richness of His goodness, according to his manifold wisdom, he bestows on them that need, Scripture designates Him by innumerable other titles, calling Him Shepherd, King, Physician, Bridegroom, Way, Door, Fountain, Bread, Axe, and Rock. And these titles do not set forth His nature, but, as I have remarked, the variety of the effectual working which, out of His tender-heartedness to His own creation, according to the peculiar necessity of each, He bestows upon them that need. Them that have fled for refuge to His ruling care, and through patient endurance have mended their wayward ways, He calls "sheep," and confesses Himself to be, to them that hear His voice and refuse to give heed to strange teaching, a "shepherd." For "my sheep," He says, "hear my voice. . . ."[48]

For Basil, there can be a plurality of names for God's energies as they penetrate the world. The basis of this confident pluralism resides with the christological affirmation that the world was made by God through God's word. The world itself is the "language" or idiom, expressed in a plurality of ways, through human signs. This indirect speech about God is derived from a direct encounter with the divine energies as the word of God penetrates the world. It is on this basis that Basil argues for the literal sense of Genesis—in this case, the world of creation does not need to be overcome or compensated for in order for it to be a window to the divine. This is not to say that he is arguing for a scientific reading of Genesis as though the world were demonstrably created in six days; instead, he finds within the "language" of creation a trustworthy sign of God's abundant care for the world. Thus language that represents the *energia* of God in the world requires a certain fittingness to the word spoken in creation, but because of the intimacy of the word coming into the world in many forms, and in intimate affirmation of creatures, it is appropriate that the language reflecting it conforms in some way to the apprehension of that word by the creature who is addressed and saved by it.

Ecotheologians such as Sallie McFague have served theology enormously by turning its attention away from a sole focus on the affairs of humans, and have helped us consider the manner in which all created life deserves our compassionate care. McFague's project is to enlist theological language to rehabilitate Christian ethics and to reform it from its anthropocentricism. In this chapter, I have attempted to argue that such a moral project is, although commendable, in a way redundant. Because creation is the idiom through which the word of God speaks, it need not be augmented or supplemented by a symbolic system that seeks to give it special attention. Creation itself is the sign; all human signs are merely an echo of God's self-communicating yes to the world.

In spite of the myriad ways in which God's grace is given, we cannot, according to Basil, depart from the biblical idiom entirely in our linguistic representations, because this is the place where knowledge of the word becoming flesh is given. God's activity in the world is paradigmatically given in Jesus Christ, as Christ enters into creation in order that it be restored. Thus God's energeia is revealed in a distilled form in the affirmation of the world given in the incarnation. Without this knowledge, we could not apprehend the effects of God's word dispersed throughout creation. Therefore the plain sense of the word is referred to another order of meaning when interpreted christologically. As God enters into creation through the word, God redeems it all, human and nonhuman alike, so that each particularity within creation may be an instance of the utterance of God. The task of the Christian who seeks wisdom is to allow the intrinsic affinity or *sympatheia* to speak to the nature of its Creator. Through *epinoia* or meditative contemplation upon things, one might ascend from the signs of the world given with great and rich prodigality in creation, to prevail upon an understanding of the God who spoke it into being through the word.

What this means for Christians concerned with the environment is that creation itself is the surest sign of the goodness of God and therefore cannot be disparaged. Wendell Berry is right to understand the diminution of the natural world as a kind of blasphemy because it speaks against the word of God poured forth in creation. Jesus Christ is the word in whom all creation is made and is the perfecter also of it. In Christ, in the word made flesh, we come to see and to understand the meaning of the words God has spoken in creation. Such words reflect Christ insofar as they are receptive to God's creative will. The perfection of the wills of creatures after the fall involves a certain correspondence with the *sympatheia* or the affinity given in creation. In coming among us as humans Christ restores our capacity to demonstrate such *sympatheia* with other creatures. Basil commends a life in which the *sympatheia* among creatures becomes more transparent. In this rule, we live in ascetic renunciation not because we wish to set right the balances of nature, but because we have learned that a sacrificial economy is alien to the world as God created it. Read in this light, the ascetical disciplines are not merely a moral injunction, but a proleptic glimpse of a restored creation where all creatures flourish.

3
"BY WHOM ALL THINGS WERE MADE"
USE AND ENJOYMENT OF THEOLOGICAL LANGUAGE

IN 1983, ROSEMARY RADFORD RUETHER wrote what was to become one of the most influential books of feminist theology, *Sexism and God-Talk*. This book was pivotal for a number of reasons. For one, Ruether made the connection far more explicitly than had other theologians between theological language or representation and the mystification of patriarchal structures within church and society. The power of representing the world, according to Ruether, was also the power to claim as legitimate one's own authority. Thus Ruether identifies the one-sidedness of the androcentric biblical tradition as not only historically inaccurate in its solipsism, but also dangerous because it perpetuates injustice through its privileging of male experience and representation of the divine. As Ruether writes: "God did not just speak once upon a time to a privileged group of males in one part of the world, making us ever after dependent on the codification of their experience."[1] Ruether's entire theological project involves correcting the distorted sense of the Christian churches that male experience from a certain time and place is the only normative expression of religious experience within the Christian tradition. Ruether seeks to redress this imbalance by making the church mindful of those without a voice within the Christian tradition.

The task of feminist theology, as Ruether sees it, is therefore twofold: it is to challenge the hegemonic claims of patriarchal texts, "the codification of privileged male experience," and to articulate women's experience of the divine. Both tasks—the deconstructive and the reconstructive—of feminist theology are to be guided by the same principle. Theology is to be judged according to its capacity to become a "usable tradition" for women and other marginalized groups. According to Ruether, this "critical principle" serves as a norm to determine a religious message or work's authenticity in relation to the divine: "Whatever denies, diminishes, or distorts the full humanity of women is, therefore, appraised as not redemptive."[2] She also articulates a correlate critical principle positively: "What does promote the full humanity of women is of the

Holy: it does reflect true relation to the divine, it is the true nature of things, the authentic message of redemption and the mission of redeemed community."[3]

The sheer fact that representation of divine encounter has been done by men within the Christian tradition requires theologians' critical attention and correction. There are admittedly scant resources within the Christian tradition that represent the divine life from women's experience, thus the canonical patriarchal texts need to be supplemented and women ought to create a "new canon"[4] drawn from a variety of sources, sources that give voice to women's experience. Like many of her colleagues and contemporaries within feminist theology, Ruether traces a narrative of fall from the early grace of the egalitarian and eschatological worldview of the New Testament era. She judges that the church increasingly betrayed its original revolutionary narrative by conforming to the culture and its patriarchal biases in which they found themselves. The nadir within this narrative of fall was the conversion of Constantine in 312 CE, and the subsequent diminution of a messianic Christology and the concomitant ascendancy of "kingship ideology."[5]

In such a worldview, according to Ruether, Christ, the Logos of God, is the author of the existing social and economic world, who is understood within Christendom to underwrite the increasingly hierarchical structures of church and society alike. Thus Christology secured the desires of a new hierarchical ordering. Christology lost its critical capacities, its ability to represent the longings, aspirations, and desires of those who were excluded from the privileged place of authority within Christendom. According to Ruether: "Christ as Logos or Nous (mind) of God discloses the divine mind and provides the plan and government of the established social cosmos. All is integrated into one vast hierarchy of being."[6] Representation of Christ the Logos as the order giver of the world had vast and deleterious consequences for women, for it enshrined Jesus' maleness as constitutive of this authority, thus allocating to women a subservient role within religion and society, while also allowing women and other oppressed groups within antiquity to be brought under increasing surveillance and control:

> Women, slaves, and barbarians (as well as religious minorities, Jews, Pagans, and heretics) are the *a-logoi*, the "mindless" ones, who are to be governed and defined by the representatives of divine Logos. Christ had become the Pantocrator (All-Ruler) of a new world order. Christology becomes the apex of a system of control over all those who in one way or another are "other" than this new Christian order.[7]

The sheer usefulness of this model of Christ—as Logos, order giver, Pantocrator, and King—within the new that was Christendom had the effect of closing christological conversations from alternative construals of Christ's saving power. Thus language creates a social reality for women that has a self-generating effect because it is reinforced within the political and social structures. As Christ became increasingly powerful and kingly, so, too, do the men who operate within the socioeconomic and religious order of Christendom.

The "mindless ones" are also those who are excluded from such representation. The rational ordering of the world is given by God and safeguarded by men through the power of naming. Women are occluded not only from holding positions of authority, but also from naming their world and their understanding of God. Ruether's now-classic book sought to remedy precisely this, and it became profoundly influential for subsequent generations of feminist theology in articulating a theory of Christian language as a tool for enshrining of patriarchal privilege and desire.

The picture of language that Ruether presents is one that I believe is highly influenced by Marxist conceptions of ideology and mystification.[8] Language for Ruether functions as an ideological tool that perpetuates gender disparity. According to Marxist literary critic Terry Eagleton, there are several interrelated ways in which a dominant power will reinforce itself through cultural production and representation:

> A dominant power may legitimate itself by *promoting* beliefs and values congenial to it; *naturalizing* and *universalizing* such beliefs so as to render them self-evident and apparently inevitable; *denigrating* ideas which might challenge it; *excluding* rival forms of thought, perhaps by some unspoken but systematic logic; and *obscuring* social reality in ways convenient to itself. Such "mystification," as it is commonly known, frequently takes the form of masking or suppressing social conflicts, from which arises the conception of ideology as an imaginary resolution of real contradictions. In any actual ideological formation, all six of these strategies are likely to interact in complex ways.[9]

Thus religious representation, according to Ruether, works rather straightforwardly to normalize and reproduce existing social relations. It does not name a reality that is God (for God is beyond description); instead, through its patriarchal images, it fills in the spaces where, properly, there should be reticence or multiple metaphors, and offers instead projections of masculinist ideals and desires that function to perpetuate the status quo within patriarchal society. The representative function of theological language is primarily, then, a mirror of a patriarchal and oppressive church/society. Religious language serves to obscure the dissident subject; it imposes a preemptive unity upon experience and therefore language, while it also perpetuates dominant language through the sheer ubiquity of normative signs.

Because of the multiple deleterious effects of ideologically deployed religious language, Ruether calls for creative redress by women theologians and other marginalized groups. Thus she challenges theologians to interrogate the religious language being deployed for its usable capacity in creating a more equitable understanding of God, and therefore a more equitable understanding of society. This pragmatic approach to language and the past is evident in Ruether's and others' quest for a "usable past," as well as in her "critical principle" in which language is judged by the social behaviors that it produces.

RELIGIOUS LONGING AND LINGUISTIC REPRESENTATION

The problem of linguistic representation is, of course, a problem that has vexed philosophers and theologians long before feminist theory. Within continental feminist theory, particularly in France, feminist philosophers have offered a more complex account of the role of language, and indeed, one might argue that this has been their chief philosophical concern. Feminist theorists such as Hélène Cixous, Julia Kristeva, and Luce Irigaray, often problematically grouped together as "the French feminists," have, like Ruether, understood linguistic representation of women to be central to understanding their oppression and to imagining its alternative. Yet these thinkers, who have been influenced by psychoanalytical theory, see within linguistic representation a surplus of meaning that resists being brought under rational control. Language thus is not closed, but it remains a contested site that may seal the oppression of women, but it might also open up new possibilities for imagining the world and living in it with joy.

Although not a theologian, Hélène Cixous has developed throughout her career a theory of creative expression that is deeply indebted to Jewish and Christian theology. Although hers might be considered an *atheology*, because she locates the divine power within—rather than beyond—the subject and because she subverts traditional theological language in writing about this power, she nevertheless is instructive to theologians, particularly to feminist theologians in their nuancing feminist theory of representation beyond ideology critique.[10]

This is not to say that Cixous neglects the ideological function of language; on the contrary, she sees it as more insidious than most pragmatic critics of language would wager. Cixous regards the entire system of representation within the West as distorted by male, rational privilege, as "phallocentric"—that is, a symbolic universe that derives from the phallic drive for mastery of the world. Phallocentrism is paradigmatically encoded in the Genesis story as it is the male God's action, through the word, that creates life. Similarly, Adam, created in *imago Dei*, alone is given the power to name, and hence dominate the world. So far, this critique has resonances with Ruether's thought and that of other North American feminists. The occlusion of women from the power of naming has deleterious consequences. And yet, for Cixous, while women are alienated from language, such alienation does not constitute merely a silencing, but also a possibility. For women, it is from the gaps, the fissures, that creativity emerges and not only creates possibilities for women's self-expression, but also for a veritable revolution in language and literature. Cixous refers to this playful subversion from the margins of language as *jouissance*—a word that has connotations both with enjoyment and with orgasm. She sees *jouissance* as the special provenance of women because women's bodies are characterized by multiple and diverse sites of erotic desire. Women's writing emerges, according to Cixous, from the body and the multiple desires that the feminine body issues. Women writers have the capacity to revolutionize language because of the otherness of their bodily desires that have not yet been attended to in literature and art. Women's writing (*l'écriture feminine*) represents a departure from phallocentric mastery and control and concerns itself with desires hitherto unarticulated in literature—where the boundaries of subject and object are permeable, such as in women's experience of pregnancy and mothering, or sexual encounter itself:

> Almost everything is yet to be written by women about femininity: about their sexuality, that is, its infinite and mobile complexity; about their eroticization, sudden turn-ons of a certain miniscule-immense area of their bodies; not about destiny, but about the adventure of such a drive, about trips, crossings, trudges, abrupt and gradual awakenings, discoveries of a zone at once timorous and soon to be forthright [11]

Thus women's desires form the basis of a writing that is yet to be discovered, yet to be revealed. According to Cixous, this is not destiny, not a predictable essentialism that traps women in yet another confining paradigm; rather, desire is wide open, its telos nowhere in sight. It is exploratory, adventurous, open, and unending. It is from the particular site of bodily experience and its opening of desire that, according to Cixous, myriad adventures and possibilities are made possible.

Cixous's development of an *atheology* of language culminates in her 1998 book *Stigmata*.[12] *Stigmata* represents an effort to deconstruct the mythology of a God-given word or language that ought to be normative or that pretends to speak to the entirety of the human condition. By reflecting upon stigmata as image, we can delve deeper into the gratuitous *atheology* that Cixous imagines. Clearly, stigmata are a sign of death; they immediately call to mind Christ's torture upon the cross. Yet, as she plays with the notion of the Christ's wounds, Cixous likens them to the mark inflicted upon the page in writing. "Stigma stings, pierces, makes holes, separates with pinched marks and in the same movement distinguishes—re-marks—inscribes, writes."[13]

In writing, there remains a *trace* of life, and as such, life is not condemned to eternal suffering, but is instead re-membered, transfigured, revealed:

> Every language artist is an artist of the struggle against the condemnation to death. Sentences and their words always lead elsewhere than the place we were expecting them. Neither the reader nor above all the author knows, foresees, commands, calculates, anticipates, prepares for the event of revelation. This *incalculable* is the text's promise and taste of triumph.[14]

Thus writing and representation, even within a patriarchal society, one in which wounds are indeed a trace of suffering, are capable also of releasing the writer from this suffering. In Cixous's view, this potentiality has less to do with the creative genius of the writer herself than it does with a kind of epiphany that comes in writing. Women have been indeed marginalized from the opportunity to write and express themselves; nevertheless, they are not cut off from the capacity to reveal and to be revealed through the *jouissance* of writing. Indeed, their standing as strangers within an alien linguistic world actually enhances their creative capacities. Women's writing within a patriarchal world "celebrates the wound and repeats the lesion."[15]

While women's writing speaks to their resistance and survival, it is also reflective of the precarious place in which women often find themselves: on the border between life and death. Women, as bearers of children, have special insight into life and death, a knowledge that is hidden or repressed in phallocentric discourses that covet and fear this power. Cixous enjoins women to celebrate this opening, this gap; for it is a gap that gives life: writing is a "trace reserved for the passage of death."[16] Yet it is not only mothers or women in general who have access to an alternative language. All those who have been abjected from the mainstream of society may possess the capacity to subvert normative language. Recounting a story from her childhood in Algeria in 1940, Cixous, a Jew, tells of being tormented verbally by Nazi children in a playground. Singling her out, she becomes a representative victim whom the children taunt in a mimetic and cruel game. When she seeks to use words to overcome the violent distance between them, the children react brutally: "Liar!" they taunt. The word falls upon her brow like a gash. "All Jews are liars!" Cixous describes this incident as a parable for her birth as a writer. She is cast out of the garden of blond-haired "hard angels," just as she is cast out by language, by a "superior force" that transcends the interactions of the children. And yet, she finds within this banishment not simply the verdict of exclusion, but also that release which "engendered all [her] literature."[17]

While the utterance of the word *liar* signals for Cixous violence, she also has come to see it as also a form of liberation. Later she will become grateful for her exclusion from this garden because it enables her to hear and to understand the cruel untruth of dominant utterances. Her exclusion also enables her to create for herself and with other strangers an alternative language of lies. Writing is an act of defiance against the wound and the false symbolic world that perpetrates it: "Writing is the place from which boundless desire is unleashed. 'Writing is God. But it is not your God.'"[18] The God who is revealed through writing is not the God of the law, nor the God of order, power, and hierarchy that Ruether exposes in her critique of Logos theology. This God is a God of the composite, a God of the rejected and the "wordless ones":

> I have never written without *Dieu*. Once I was reproached for it. *Dieu* they said is not a feminist. Because they believed in a preexisting God. But God is of my making. But God, I say, is the phantom of writing, it is her pretext and her promise. God is the name of all that has not yet been said. Without the word *Dieu* to shelter the infinite multiplicity of all that could be said the world would be reduced to its shell, and I to my skin. *Dieu* stands for the names that have never yet been invented.[19]

While this God looks quite unlike the transcendent Logos that Ruether rejects, Cixous is not claiming that "the God of her own making" is merely subjective, merely an inner word. Indeed, this God who "is her pretext and her promise" is the source for names that have never been invented. Hence, while writing is a clearly personal form of discovery, it is a discovery of that which exists partially outside of the individual imagination.

Cixous is never direct about the source of this epiphany. *Dieu* is clearly not the *Dieu* of the theologians. *Dieu* resides in unconscious and unarticulated desires of the self. *Dieu* is the source of awakening and birth to desires that remain repressed or unarticulated within a patriarchal culture. So while writing proceeds from woundedness, from gaps, this writing is at the very same time inherently creative. It is a creation *ex nihilo*: "My voice repels death; my death; your death; my voice is my other. I write and you are not dead. The other is safe if I write . . . [Writing] is what never ends."[20]

Thus Cixous points to a kind of transcendence from finitude within writing itself. The author, in her desire to stave off death, also preserves that portion of identity which would otherwise be absorbed by the forces of death that hem her in. She self-creates, but what she creates is a self that expands beyond the stifling world into which she was born. She creates and recreates herself through the language of her illicit desires, not as the inevitable feminine subject that the patriarchal world begets but, rather, as a self who is freed to be other—to express *différance*. Graham Ward puts it well:

What Cixous' (and Lyotard's) project affirms is an ineluctable concern with transcendence generic to the human condition. The concern manifests itself because the compulsion to transcendence is the nature of desire itself. Desire requires the other, outside or inside. For Cixous, writing embodies (materially) this desire and therefore the journey towards the unutterable other. In writings and reading we experience this transcendence which is fundamentally a deconstruction of subjectivity; in writing and reading we live the economy of différance.[21]

Cixous's crossing over is not merely the liberation of the subject from restraint, it is also crossing toward the other who also is constitutive of one's identity. Hers is hardly a solitary project, for writing upon the page is at every stage provoked by the desires of others that also constitute the human subject and human language. In crossing over beyond the language of dominant desires (i.e., the phallocentric drives of the dominant discursive subjects), she does not leave that world behind, because she cannot. Instead, she navigates the phallocentric world and the desires that have begotten it into her own journey, and yet she is, somehow, able to find another world that exerts an erotic pressure upon her. This is a world not of differentiation, but of erotic proximity; it is a world where legitimate desire includes the desire for union.

As we have seen with Cixous, the desire of human subjects, particularly subjects on the margins of human society, are not easily brought under phallocentric language's rational control. Instead, the desire of the subjugated belongs to a subterranean world—a world of dreams and creative power. Unleashed, this desire exerts a power that is God-like; it is a power to speak, and therefore to create the truth. It does this not by abandoning language, not even phallocentric language, but through the *jouissance* of writing it works within it, until that language is internally subverted; until the world, to quote a famous feminist phrase, is "split open."[22]

While I do not wish to make too much a point of challenging Ruether's view of religious language in light of Cixous's insights, I wish to signal but a few points of contrast that will be of benefit in considering the manner in which the world is "split open" by the word in this alternate feminist construal of linguistic representation.

First, religious language is not exclusively or necessarily ideological. It certainly can function thus, but it can also function in a way that addresses the female subject anew, not through her identification with the patterns of patriarchy therein, but precisely through her alternate position within it. In being excluded from traditional patterns of representation, women are not doomed to absence from linguistic and cultural representation, but do indeed occupy an alternate relationship to those dominant patterns. This alternative vista, reading from the "underside of history," has been acknowledged by feminist theologians from North America, including Ruether. However, her seeking a usable past may not adequately describe the intricacy and subtlety of the manner in which we not only use language, but are also *used* by it. Cixous's feminist theory shows how language constitutes subjectivity in ways that exceed use or function.

Cixous also captures with greater depth the power that language holds upon our unconscious. Because biblical language belongs to a "dream world," it is not easily eradicated from our consciousness, even if we will it so. The symbolic depths of religious language work upon us even when we are unaware, not only because of the Bible proper, but also because of its repetition throughout literature and art. Further, Cixous would argue that the language of the Bible speaks more thoroughly in the language of unconscious desire than it does in rational concepts. Therefore the human reader or writer does not work as an arbiter of the biblical or literary text; rather, the text is the arbiter of us, even, or perhaps especially, when we are unconscious of it. It gives to us language, and even when that language is seemingly foreign or hostile to us, it cannot be easily dismissed and certainly not abandoned.

It is helpful here if we add an illustration. In a beautiful "reading" of Rembrandt van Rijn's painting *Bathsheba at Her Bath*, Cixous engages upon an extended meditation—a reading of a "text"—that is, Rembrandt's painting, based upon a text, the "subject," Bathsheba, understood through the biblical text of 2 Samuel 11, who is, in turn, reading a text—a letter—presumably, the illicit summons from her would-be lover, David. Cixous's reading, like Rembrandt's painting, draws our attention to the absences. Cixous points us to the missing but essential features of the text, without which the painting—and her interpretation of it—lose their power:

> Rembrandt paints the secret: the trace of what escapes us: he always paints what escapes us: what has just happened, what is going to happen, and which traverses us suddenly, pierces us, turns us upside down, escapes—beyond the painting, beyond thought, and leaves us there panting, suspended, grazed, he paints the body that remains, maybe the skin, maybe the cadaver. The painting is the place of passage.[23]

Cixous's interpretation of this painting displays the incredible complexity of theological interpretation and of religious symbolism. It would be easy to dismiss this narrative for its patriarchy. After all, we are given very few explicit clues about Bathsheba's will in the biblical narrative; she is treated merely as an object by David. How did Bathsheba experience the whole affair? What choice did she have in responding to David's call? And yet, for Cixous, and indeed for Rembrandt, it is precisely within this silence that the drama of the narrative exists. And it exists, not through positing another, better, narrative, but by meditating upon the "trace."

This trace risks escaping our notice if our efforts are simply to render the past "usable." On the surface, the immortalization of woman as adulteress would not seem good news; but the text points to so much more than the usable; it speaks of a desire only partially articulated in the biblical narrative, and when contemplated by the artist's hand, becomes unleashed. The power of the story does not cease in the artistic rendering. Cixous, the writer, in reflecting upon Rembrandt's rendering, creates yet another performance of the text that gives it meaning, not by circumventing the patriarchal world that it reflects, but by dwelling in it subversively, by listening to the pained and exuberant deliberations of desire of this woman suspended in time just as she is summoned by the king. Cixous captures this moment in the original in a way that the English does not do justice to her intricate play on words: "*David est l'hors. Le hors. L'ordinnateur.*"[24] In this creative play, Cixous recreates Bathsheba as a subject of desire, and transforms what is admittedly a patriarchal text into a rendering of it that both dwells within the surface of the patriarchal world, but disarms it and sets it free. It is not a usable feminist text in Cixous's hands per se, but it is a profound and a vivid one, because it emanates from the complexity of desire. It is a portrait that cannot be cast aside, because it commands not only our political attention, but also our dreams.

USING THE THINGS OF THE WORLD

Such a celebration of the creative desires of the artist or interpreter is not, as such, a theme that has a cognate among the Nicene teachers. Cixous hands over far more authority to the writer than would ordinarily be affirmed in premodern, let alone Nicene, theories of exegesis. Indeed, the creation of the feminine subject in her encounter with art and in her assertion of her own artistic power or power to name is one that is, in the final analysis for Cixous, a kind of self-mastery. True, this involves transcendence, but the transcendence evoked is of psycho-linguistic in nature. The author writes *herself* into being, and brings from the darkness or nothingness of the unwritten self a desiring subject capable of self-rendering through her writing or art.

Yet the ideas Cixous introduces into feminist theory of language echo a much older question: What is the relationship between *res* and *signum*—the thing that is signified and the sign? Is the *res*, in religious language, God, ever to be known directly, or do we approach God better indirectly, through the very gaps of our known and inherited history? And so, while the Christian student of Cixous may part company with her on the question of the origin and the source of language, she assists us profoundly in seeing language in more than merely a functionalist manner. Furthermore, Cixous points us to the igniting of desire and the creation of identity by an external word/Word. Like ancient authors, she believes that the transcendent word does not just work outside of the interpreter, but within her, within her desires, which are themselves traces of a summons to love.

Like Cixous, Augustine develops an understanding of language as one in which God/*Dieu* communicates signs within this world that are available—in part—to the attuned "reader" of signs, in spite of the fallenness of our language. Like her, the mastery of signs does not involve so much overcoming the world of fallen speech, but a transfiguration, we might even say a subversion, of it. Like Cixous, Augustine is aware that the restless desire which we experience is one that is the very source of our transcendence, and that it is the gap between this desire and our representation of it that presents a problem. Like Cixous, Augustine believes that our desires are mediated in this world through signs that carry with them the capacity either to alienate us or set us free.

Augustine's difficulty with discovering the proper use of language is well documented in his *Confessions*. Recounting his experience as a young man, he finds much to excite the intellect in the words of the gifted orators and is seduced by their words, but comes to recognize that their words invariably fall short of substance because their knowledge does not cohere with wisdom or virtue. Augustine experiences a fundamental alienation in language as the signs point merely to other signs rather than to their true source.[25] As Peter Brown reminds, for Augustine, the fall is a "a fall from direct knowledge into indirect knowledge through signs. The 'inner fountain' of awareness had dried up: Adam and Eve had found that they could only communicate with one another by the clumsy artifice of language and gestures."[26]

One of the chief effects of the fall, according to Augustine, is not only humans' groping in darkness in naming divine things, but in naming properly the ordinary stuff of life. Even the self, in this fallen world of human signs, is a mystery, and uneasily penetrated by the signs that we use to designate it. The other, and even the self, although seemingly self-evident, is, in fact, unknowable in any direct sense. Whereas in Paradise Adam and Eve had direct access to one another's souls, after the fall, signs become necessary for communication. "Things are learnt by means of signs,"[27] writes Augustine, but signs can confound more than they illuminate.

In his *On Christian Doctrine*, Augustine creates something of a theory of the interpretation of signs. Augustine distinguishes between two types of things: things to be enjoyed (*frui*) and things to be used (*uti*). Augustine warns us against improperly distinguishing between types of things, and indeed urges that only God, and not the things of this world, can be properly enjoyed. Even human beings are to be used rather than enjoyed. This blunt segregation has caused a fair amount of criticism of Augustine.[28]

It makes a great difference when we understand the meaning of the term *use* in Augustine's hands, for he is not suggesting that we ought merely to use persons as objects of our fulfillment. Augustine's idiosyncratic employment of the concept of *uti* is, I believe, drawn from Paul, for whom "making use" of the things of this world was central to the unfolding of messianic time. Because the Messiah was near, Paul would urge his readers not to put too much stock in the things of this world and to "make use of your present condition."[29] Things of this world are not useful merely in the sense of being instrumental to us; instead, they are to be used rather than enjoyed because the world is, in fact, passing away and therefore cannot give the kind of stability that we desire from them; only God can give this. Because we are in a pilgrim state, the world is, in fact, a shadow of the world to come (Col. 2:17). Yet this shadow is not wholly dark or inchoate; the shadow of the world is also the very means by which wisdom may be received and desire properly ordered. The things that we use in this world are, therefore, according to Augustine, not proper to our desire, for our desire is to be eternal, because that desire is ignited in us by a Beloved who is eternal.

Thus Augustine's distinction is not a dualistic abjuring of the world; rather, he sees the distinction as primarily an eschatological one. In this time between the times, we are compelled to discipline our desires for the things of this world, in use rather than in enjoyment. To use a thing in this sense is not to treat it disparagingly, but lightly; to not cling to it as an object of fulfillment, but to allow it to be free from the compulsion of our desires. The things of the world are to be used rather than enjoyed for their own sake because they are not yet redeemed, not yet made complete, and therefore their significance is only partially available to us. At the end time, we will know things and people for what they truly are, for they will then fully participate (or become signs) within the divine life, and thereby will be given their proper and full meaning in reference to God who "will be all in all." Thus we use the things of the world in the sense that they are proleptic, anticipatory of their final destiny, which is yet hidden from the world.

We therefore are not entreated by Augustine to use people as objects of our fulfillment; rather, *uti*, in his specific sense, means not imposing a preemptive meaning upon their signification. The neighbor is yet mysteriously open to new possibilities that transcend any closure of meaning that I might impose upon her. Because my neighbor's life is yet "hidden with Christ in God" (Col. 3:3), I cannot presume to treat him simply as an object of my desires, as one to be simply enjoyed; I must attend his becoming.

To illustrate this, Augustine frequently uses the imagery of homecoming, drawing on the parable of the prodigal son to illustrate how the destination of the prodigal son's sojourn is only lately and gratuitously discovered in the

Father's welcoming. Therefore, the return journey of the prodigal son (and of us all), however beautiful, is anticipatory, not fully disclosive, of the beauty of that final destination: "We have wandered far from God; and if we wish to return to our Father's home, this world must be used, not enjoyed, that so the invisible things of God may be clearly seen, being understood by the things that are made,—that is, that by means of what is material and temporary we may hold upon that which is spiritual and eternal."[30] This is not to disparage the journey of the human sojourner; rather, it is to point out that there is no final closure or finality of the self or of her purpose apart from God. There is still unfinished business in redemption and were we to hasten to enjoy others as though the work of their redemption were finished, we might easily arrest theirs (and our) spiritual progress. There is always more to be discovered in the other; always more possibility of her gratuitous self-disclosure. Thus as the things of this world are passing away, their transfigured reality becomes more evident. Rowan Williams puts it this way:

> Real desire is about recognizing that I have no resting place: my home is what I must look for, eagerly, attentively as I grow and journey. And—the Christian will add—my journey only 'ends' when it reaches God—and even then it does not come to a comfortable full stop because God is himself a region of unending new discovery and reappraisal and fresh vision.[31]

CRITIQUING AND ORDERING DESIRE

Although Ruether is certainly no fan of Augustine, much less of Paul,[32] there is much here that runs parallel to feminist criticism of both sign and patriarchy within a fallen world. Central to Ruether's analysis is that the world and the representation of it are not fully redeemed; indeed, they are "groaning" in anticipation for the redemption of our bodies (Romans 8); specifically, for Ruether, this redemption is from patriarchy.

Because the world is not yet fully redeemed, it cannot be fully enjoyed. Ruether's critical lens is not unlike Augustine's conviction that we are often bewitched by the things of the world, and we presume that our sense of them *is* their ultimate meaning. Patriarchy functions in this bewitching manner for Ruether, and she and other feminist interpreters share with Augustine a conviction that signs can often be alien, even hostile, to us. Like him, feminist theologians would emphasize the merely conventional relation of linguistic signs to the reality to which they point. These conventions emerge from a fallen world, in which sign making is disordered and representative of the fallen relations we inherit.

Like Ruether, Augustine is aware of the ideological nature of God language, particularly insofar as God-talk reinforces particular and misbegotten desires of human beings, according to the pleasures that they seek: "And since men are moved by different kinds of pleasures, partly by those which pertain to bodily senses, partly by those which pertain to the intellect and soul, those of them who are in bondage to sense think that either the heavens, or what appears to be most brilliant in the heavens or the universe itself, is God of gods . . ."[33] Language about God is not immune from prideful misdirection of speech based upon illicit desires. According to Augustine, misbegotten desires will give rise to faulty concepts of God. We cannot perceive God unless our desires are rightly ordered. Otherwise we are likely to turn our fondest wishes into God or gods. Here we have a critique of desire that is not unlike that of Ruether. Because patriarchy is above all a misbegotten desire for the control and mastery of the world, it is likely to give rise to concepts of God that support this desire. Augustine is, like Ruether, wary of certain desires and of the ideologies they engender. In this way, Augustine is quite unlike Cixous, for whom the opening of many desires is legitimate and worthy of exploration. This is not to say that the range of desires in Cixous is infinite. They are given direction by what she understands to be bodily experience. Therefore, gender comes to play a huge part for Cixous in the operation of desire. Women's desire is essentially different from that of men based upon physiology. Women's writings emerge from their opening to the world, from the gaps, from the fluidity of their wombs, and from the diverse and diffuse sensory receptors in their bodies. For this reading of the body, Cixous has received considerable critique from other feminist writers, who see her work as a stultifying form of essentialism that reproduces predictable gender stereotypes.[34] Does Augustine show us a way beyond the impasse of essentialism and constructivism in language?

For Augustine, desire is a trace of a peace and a unity once enjoyed and a longing for return or homecoming. As Augustine famously writes in the beginning of his *Confessions*, "You stir man to take pleasure in praising you, because you have us for yourself, and our heart is restless until it rests in you."[35] For Augustine, desire for God is not fully perceived by the senses; desire's fulfillment—rest in God—cannot be attained by the things of this world that crowd out right desire. God is always at a distant land, far off from the human sojourner's immediate environs; and yet that distant land is also "our native land."[36] But that native land is not approached through the abandonment of ourselves, but through a return to the self, through the "cultivation of pure desires and virtuous habits."[37]

Words matter for Augustine, because the misuse of words has the potential to misdirect our desires. Conversely, words have the capacity to direct our desires properly. Augustine grows suspicious of the effects of rhetorical excess in the poetry he loved as a youth, a poetry that fueled his concupiscent desires. Although much castigated for his antagonism toward sexuality and the body, perhaps it is more correct to say that what Augustine challenged was an ideology of sexuality that, through the improper deployment of signs, rendered sexuality too important, contaminated friendship and charity, incited "jealously, suspicion, fear, anger and contention,"[38] and thus colonized the soul's space for other kinds of relations, especially relationship with God.

This is at once a recognition of the ubiquity of signs: we do not encounter the world without their mediation, and an acknowledgment of the force that signs can exert. This acknowledgment of the poverty of signs causes Augustine to turn to the biblical account of the fall for signs from origin and home. In creation, there is no rupture between intent and utterance, between *signum* and *res*. The works of creation, created by the utterance of God, are pronounced good. This native affinity of signs and things, of use and fruition, is present in creation, lost during the fall, and will be restored in the coming of Christ.

In *On Christian Doctrine*, Augustine points out how God is unlike the signs of this world. God is not merely a sign among other signs, but is the home and origin of signs. Thus God is outside of the realm of signification, because there is no human concept that adequately captures who God is. Yet God condescends, as we have seen in Basil, to give us a sign so that we might not be linguistically or noetically bereft. The peculiar way in which God communicates in signs is through the one sign that is reflective of the Father, Jesus Christ. In coming among us, Christ imparts the capacity to read the signs of this world, at least in a provisional manner, properly. This capacity involves not just a mental insight, but also requires the virtues needed to see the things of this world in terms of their proper destination on their way to being fulfilled. The capacity to "read" the signs of this world as objects of God's transforming speech is called wisdom, and is itself not just a natural endowment, but one granted by God to those who prevail to know God and to know the things of this world properly through the ordering of desire or, as Augustine puts it, through the "cultivation of pure desire and virtuous habits."[39] The cultivation of proper desire involves a renunciation of sorts from attempting to enjoy too immediately the things of this world. This is not out of contempt for the things of the world; on the contrary, it is a willing setting of them free to become what they, too, were destined to be without being threatened by our consumptive enjoyment of them, and without the arresting, therefore, of their development, which is now only partially complete.

SCRIPTURE AND SIGNS

At the very heart of early Christian understandings of creation, and implicit in the doctrine of creation *ex nihilo*, we see God doing what only God can do, being fully generative in speaking without prior determination and circumscription[40] of others' speech. God is not molding stubborn form into God's own purposes; rather, through God's word, God calls life into being from nonexistence out of a desire that the other be set free. Unlike Augustine's speech, God's is not predetermined by the habits and the vices of the society that God inherits. Only God's speech is free because it is the beginning and the cause of speaking. God speaks the Son eternally without loss or diminution in an overflowing speaking of abundant and eternal love. God speaks *through* the Son without loss or distortion.[41] This is to say that Christ is not an afterthought in the order of things, but he is ingredient within the very nature of what it is to be God. As Lewis Ayres puts it: "The existence and consubstantiality of the Word demonstrates that, unlike any human speaker, the Father has the power to reveal himself perfectly."[42] In other words, the action and the intention are united and come to fruition in the divine utterance only. In God alone there is no cleavage between sign and signified. God need not make *use* of anything for God's potency to come to fruition. Instead, in creating through the word, God is creating through that which is already united to the Father.

Although called into being by the word, the world, after the fall, is not receptive to the Logos, and that same word that is spoken eternally often falls upon rocky, shallow, or weed-infested soil within the fallen order. Those who hear do not often apprehend (Mark 4:12). And thus the word, once spoken, far too easily becomes silenced or interrupted among our creaturely clamorings. Augustine locates his intellect's and will's wanderings as, at least in part, in the false use of words, the alienation of signs in the linguistic world that surrounds him and that he inherits as a result of the fall. Such linguistic confusion, such misapprehension of the proper *use* of words, cannot be resolved through willful efforts at obtaining clarity, but instead require conversion—a conversion that, in Augustine's case, is made possible in the speech, not of the orators or philosophers, but in the sing-song voice of a small child that precipitates his conversion experience: "As I was saying this and weeping in the bitter agony of my heart, suddenly I heard a voice from the nearby house chanting as if it might be a boy or a girl (I do not know which), saying and repeating over and over again 'Pick up and read, pick up and read.'"[43] Signs are reoriented through the voice of a little child in the Garden of Milan who invites Augustine to language's redemption through the written (and holy) text. It will lead Augustine to embrace humility of this rhetoric—the biblical idiom. It is the Bible's humanity—its very vulnerablity—that makes it a fitting sign pointing to God.

This word, this injunction toward the biblical text, is the beginning of wisdom. From this other-worldly voice and Augustine's heeding it, issues the reorientation of desire from language and actions that have been hostile to him to those that are now life giving: "What is described is a transformation of our affections . . . it is Christ who removes the thorny hedge, the malice of our past sins, making possible our return to him. Thus, in a real sense, it is Christ who makes himself useful to us. He is the way and the means to blessedness precisely because of what he does for us."[44] According to Augustine, the language of wisdom involves the contemplation of eternal things, but the ascent to wisdom is precisely and necessarily through the use of things rather than their immediate enjoyment, in such a way that the thing is never left behind as a mere instrument for my use but, rather, becomes an essential part of homecoming.

Scripture is paradigmatic of the kind of approach we ought to take to signs and their meaning. In Scripture, God uses ordinary language in order to convey the extraordinary. The ascent of the soul is made possible by its entrée, which is the humility of the biblical form. Just as Christ, the word of God, came in the form of a slave, the Scriptures are mediated to us in demotic, ordinary speech. The task of interpreting and understanding Scripture would be a "great and arduous undertaking"[45] were it not for the fact that God encounters us in the reading of the text and incrementally leads us to greater understanding. Like the miracles of the loaves and fishes, Augustine urges, there is an abundant gift to be had in the breaking open of Scripture, and it is a gift that exceeds that of the minister of these gifts.[46] It is also a gift that, once received, ignites a desire for greater understanding. Thus reading Scripture is a kind of play, an opening, an exploration:

> The Christian life, itself, as we have seen, is in constant danger of premature closure, the supposition that the end of desire has been reached and the ambiguities of history and language are put behind us; and thus the difficulty of Scripture is itself a kind of parable of our condition. We cannot properly enjoy what we swiftly and definitively possess: such possession results in inaction and ultimately contempt for the object.[47]

Knowledge of Scripture is an analogue to knowledge of another kind of "text" or "sign": the human being that is before us. She cannot become preemptively the object of my desire as though her existence were primarily to fulfill my needs. There is always another opening, another layer of meaning yet to be attended to, another surprising depth or secret that her otherness conceals. The meaning of the "text" is deferred to an eschatological horizon where our desire for knowing the other—whether that be the neighbor or the scriptural text—

will be fulfilled. We remain, however, on a way station to that destination, and any attempt at the closure of meaning will mean both a thwarting of the text's true meaning and an arresting of our development.

CONCLUSION: GENDER AS PROVISIONAL SIGN

Cixous has likewise taught us something of the deferred meaning of the "text" that she encounters—the angry taunt, the stigmatic scar, the concealed letter in Bathsheba's hands—all speak of the capacity of texts to defy narrow circumscription. In this way, she would agree with Augustine that wisdom requires an attendant waiting upon a word that is not immediately under our possession or control. Yet, for Augustine, unlike Cixous, *frui* or *enjoyment* risks a preemptive closure, whereby the text becomes merely what the text means to me. We have seen in Cixous that enjoyment or *jouissance* is not a teleological surplus enjoyment nor is it the ending of signification through brisk orgasmic arrival. It is, instead, diffuse and circuitous, an endless play of deferred desires, always promising arrival, but returning again to the unconsummated text. In this way, Cixous differs from Augustine, even while both are wary of the foreclosure of the meaning of the text. In Cixous's case, the letter is always hidden from sight; desire is always partially concealed in Bathsheba's and therefore by the artist's creative hand. While Augustine would agree that desire is properly without bounds, this is so not because it is diffuse, but because it is eternal. It arises from a source that extends beyond the immanent letter, the immanent body, or the immanent desire itself. It arises from a source that awakens in the reader a boundless desire, to be sure, but also one that promises consummation, or the fulfillment of desire; it promises boundless and unambiguous joy.

Thus the economy of *jouissance* in a Christian aesthetics of creativity is not merely cyclical and self-referential; it contains the promise of progress, of knowledge. So while there is enjoyment (in Cixous's sense), there is also an acknowledgment of the partial nature of our creative offerings, and a hope (as well as a promise) that that rendering will be made complete:

> . . . where the smoke of offering does not vanish into an abyss, but ascends to a plenitude which has already received it, and therefore ascends with unquenchable hope of future benefit, there it will be seen that every production, just to the degree that it is produced only to be lost, expended and offered, nonetheless exhibits in its specific lineaments the benefit of participation, of further received gift.[48]

Liturgy is understood in this schema not to be play but, rather, work in a sense, as is commonly observed. It is work not in the technological sense of mastery and control, but in the sense of a cumulative appropriation and performance of heavenly signs for the sake of the upbuilding of a people. To cite Milbank again, liturgy is "The work of the people. Therefore it is not the occasional riot of festival and the steadiness of everyday tranquil craft. But festival as craft and craft as festival."[49]

While Augustine speaks of the infinite nature of desire, it is a desire that is not diffuse or inchoate. This is so because the object of our desires has spoken and has called us to "seek, knock, and find him." And although that object cannot be fully obtained in this world, he does infuse our desires, and through his word and the practices of the community sets it on a specific course and destination. This course involves traveling lightly through the fleeting desires of the world, not because they are not beautiful, but because they need to be set free from the dangers of our hastening to appropriate them. Language serves the end of setting right our desires so that we do not confuse the desires of this world with the desire by which we were created. In this time in between the times, all our "performances" have not yet been given their proper final specification, and as they await this, we might follow Augustine in questioning whether we cling tightly to the representative form to which the world currently subscribes. Augustine's deliberation upon signs might prompt us to wonder whether *l'écriture féminine* forecloses the possibilities of desire and of creative receptivity that women's bodies engender. Is there not yet an eschatological horizon in which they might be, not abandoned, but mysteriously transformed into signs of a further glory?

Seen this way, gender is also a provisional sign, a word on its way to its ultimate signification. While Cixous has served feminist theology profoundly in opening the word beyond a narrowly prescribed form of representation, her project risks making too much of the sign of the body from which, according to her, all desires flow. Perhaps it is better to consider with Augustine that manner in which gender itself is a provisional marker, a code requiring divine revelation in order to enable us to read it correctly. Perhaps then women and men will be liberated to interpret and direct their desires beyond the confines of biology, and toward a place where even this datum is "passing away." In this way, we may find that it can be used in such a way that the faulty stories we tell— drawing from the Bible and elsewhere—about the meaning of the gender signs are broken open in God's telling.

4

"VERY GOD OF VERY GOD"

PROCLAIMING CHRIST'S DIVINITY IN A PLURALIST AGE

THIS CHAPTER IS A REFLECTION on one of the most difficult and demanding theological exercises for our time, and that is the confession of Christ as God in a pluralistic world. And although I cannot hope to be exhaustive in this presentation, what I do hope to offer are some arguments in favor of not relinquishing claims to Christ's unique identity—as the second person of the Trinity, as the one who is consubstantial with God the Father, as the one who is God incarnate—as an immediate amnesty amidst the seeming agonistes of religious faith within the public sphere.

My argument rests upon critiquing not pluralism per se—that is, a belief in the meaning and value of world religions other than Christianity—but by inquiring into some of the assumptions that are implicit within pluralist discourse within a secular age. In doing so, I will argue first that pluralism, as it is commonly understood and advocated, contains within it several tacit assumptions about the nature of religious life that are actually deleterious to positive religious faith—for Christians and non-Christians alike. Second, I wish to argue that to abandon Christian claims to accommodate the demands of living in a multi-faith society is to forgo the very sources required to engage the religious other with a deep measure of hospitality. Such a capacity, for the Christian, has everything to do with the account of what it means to be human that is implicit in the incarnation. Therefore, this chapter on religious pluralism will consider the manner in which the self is understood within certain secular accounts aimed at promoting religious tolerance, and counterpose this account with classical Christian accounts of the *humanum* originating from the doctrine of the incarnation. Finally, the chapter will conclude with some reflections of what it means to say that the word was made incarnate, and what it means for humans to be created by that word. Toward this effort, I shall draw on the resources of Athanasius of Alexandria, whose theology of the word, in my view, offers us an account of the self who is both unmade and made in that encounter with the incarnate word which opens up rich possibilities for interfaith dialogue.

UNITY AND PARTICULARITY IN THE MEANING OF RELIGION

The generation of scholars of religion employed shortly after World War II in North America tended to come from Christian backgrounds, but scholarship and the temperament of the time prompted them to challenge common assumptions about the priority of the Christian faith by seeking to articulate a general theory of religion. The classical modern argument for pluralism has been articulated by such thinkers as Wilfred Cantwell Smith and John Hick Jr. and speaks to a fundamental unity that exists *behind* religious and cultural difference. Fundamental to each religious truth is a quest for a good that is known only in a limited way by each of the various religions. As John Hick writes:

> There are, first, important ideas within the different traditions which on the surface present incompatible alternatives but which can be seen on *deeper analysis* to be different expressions of the same more fundamental idea: thus the Christian concept of salvation and the Hindu and Buddhist concepts of liberation are expressions of the more basic notion of the realization of a limitlessly better possibility for human existence.[1]

Like Hick, Wilfred Cantwell Smith challenges the presumption of Christian normativity. He does this by resisting the notion that religion is first and foremost a belief system, and argues instead that *religion* itself is a highly Westernized concept which forces a premature limitation upon those broad areas of life that are more basic to the human experience. Faith, according to Smith, is a far more supple set of suppositions than those that are commonly ascribed to the special sphere of thought or belief that is called "religion." As he writes, "For this writer 'religion' is no system of observances or beliefs, nor an historical tradition, institutionalized or susceptible of outside observation. Rather it is a vivid and personal confrontation with the splendour and the love of God."[2]

This irreducibly personal confrontation between human subjects and their God is better described by the term *faith*, which for Smith is "a personal quality of human life and history." Such faith has a "living quality" and is the "throbbing actuality of a myriad of someones."[3] As such, it is to be distinguished from the "traditions" that encrust it. Whereas faith is personal, relational, and organic, tradition is a "human construct offered to order what is given."[4] Over time and across distance, local traditions give rise to what Smith terms a *cumulative tradition* that arises from various religious experiences within particular cultural contexts. The cumulative tradition also differs from religion for, as a concept, it concerns itself with the difference and particularity that exist as a result of the myriad of human decisions, commitments, errors, and triumphs that constitute it as a culture. As such, a cumulative tradition can become an empirically observable phenomenon. Because traditions are so varied, any insistence upon their unity by way of appeal to the abstraction called religion is bound to impose a kind of arbitrariness that obscures the commitment of actual men and women. This Smith calls *reification*.[5] Reification is the process by which the living faith of men and women becomes a thing, in this case a set of disembodied ideas and, finally, an institution.

Thus, as Smith traces it, there emerges within Enlightenment thought a departure from the faith of "literally individual persons"[6] toward an abstraction called religion. The task of the historian is to trace these diverse expressions[7] of religious faith, empirically and scientifically, but this task, important though it is, does not get to the heart of the matter, which is to understand that there exists a "similar variety" which is obscured by the changes and chances of religious traditions, within religions themselves, and even within the temperaments or moods of individual men and women.[8]

Religious experience is prior, according to Smith, to religious practices. He thus evokes Marx's notion of religion as reification, a making of a thing in which religion comes to be understood as an "objective systematic entity."[9] Thus, as Marx draws the strong link between religion and capitalism—both are forms of alienation through the abstract focus upon things as possessing a power that constitutes an end in themselves (fetishization)—Smith sees a process of object fetishization occurring in the preoccupation of religions (and those who study them) with external practices. And yet, Smith's appropriation of Marx's concept is curiously reticent on the manner in which the reified thing not only becomes an object of misbegotten meaning, but also a bearer of symbolic significance, a guarantor of the symbolic world's perpetuation and cohesion.[10]

For Marx, this fetishization within religion is bound to have a pernicious result: religion becomes the "opiate of the people" and indeed, the metaphor of opium trades on the notion of the self's willing appropriation and later addiction to the drug. The dependence upon the drug is guaranteed by the dissolution of self-awareness as the drug effectively gains control over the subject from without. Yet this tacit appropriation of subjects by—for better or for worse—the material givenness of the social order that they inhabit is never fully attended to in Smith. There always remains for Smith an ideal self who communicates with God (or better, the Transcendent), unencumbered by material reality or bodily habits and practices. Such practices are a mere digression from (and often a deformation of) the true faith, which is relational and unmediated.[11]

Although Smith is renowned for being one of the great early scholars of Islam, his writings suggest a curious ambivalence about its practices. According to him, Islam is "more reified than any other of the world's great living faiths."[12] To remedy this, Smith is quick to separate out the kernel of religious faith from the husks of reified practices, laws, and traditions. Yet adherents to Islam, he concedes, are unwilling to make this salutary distinction. Islam, he contends, remains the only religion to view itself self-consciously as a religion, that is, as a system with distinct and separate laws and practices that would govern the totality of human life. Smith finds in Muhammed the first self-conscious founder of a religious community, a community that resists being named by others, but is defined deliberately by its adherents. Thus we have within Islam the closest approximation to the concept of religion as a formal entity consisting of rituals and laws. According to Smith, the Arabic word for religion is *din* and, unlike its non-Muslim cognates, whose ideas of faith concern themselves with the relational and self-involving, *din* carries with it both inner and outer—subjective piety and systematic (reified) religion.[13]

A helpful critique of Smith's analysis of the "special case of Islam"[14] comes from Muslim scholar and cultural anthropologist Talal Asad. Asad takes issue with Smith on many grounds, beginning with Smith's interpretation of the history of Muslim-Hindu encounter, claiming that his analysis of the situation depends upon a faulty connection between monotheism and intolerance, and conversely, of polytheism and tolerance. Further, Smith is himself unaware about the particularity of his own perspective—his own theology—and how he as a liberal Protestant favors secular concepts of the privatization of religion, especially the preference for inner piety over overt religious bodily expression. For Asad, faith is inexorably and unproblematically bound to the inhabitation of the world in time and space—in a people and its language: "Faith is inseparable from the particularities of the temporal world and the traditions that inhabit it. If one is to understand one's own faith—as opposed to having it—or to understand the faith of another, one needs to deploy the relevant concept whose criteria of application must be public—in a language that inhabits this world."[15]

This excursus into the meaning of religion as debated by Asad and Smith is highly instructive for our purposes. Smith's pluralism is won by the abandonment of seemingly "external" differences—the practices and the doctrines to which religious adherents conform. In its stead, he locates faith within an inner living relationship between God (the divine, or the Ultimate) and the individual. While such an understanding of religion would appear to accommodate a greater plurality, Asad would disagree, claiming that appeals to a hidden unity beneath religious difference is actually a theology of a particular kind, and one that has little relevance to traditional Muslim adherents (among others).

The notion that there exists a fundamental religious unity is of course incredibly appealing. And yet, what is sacrificed in his efforts to identify that unity is the very particularity itself, in favor of what is considered to be a more neutral existential or moral meaning. Therefore, claims to historicity and veracity—claims that are clearly central to Muslim, Jewish, and Christian accounts of faith—are annulled for the sake of a deeper analysis. One wonders if such a deep analysis is only the domain of the scholar of religion.

TOLERANCE AS A SECULAR VALUE

In a penetrating study of the contradictions that inhere within pluralist discourse about religion, Saba Mahmood, a former student of Asad, observes the heightening of anti-Muslim sentiment in the aftermath of 9/11. She argues that the rise in public discourse on religious pluralism coincided ironically with the increased regulation of Muslims' activities in America and abroad. For example, in the wake of September 11, President George W. Bush made immediate overtures to the "Muslim community," declaring Islam itself to be as a "religious of peace and tolerance" in its inner essence. On November 19, 2001, one month after the invasion of Afghanistan,[16] and less than one week after the fall of Kabul, Bush hosted an *Iftar*, the evening dinner that marks the break of fasting during Ramadan, at which he spoke these words, which I quote at some length:

> America is made better by millions of Muslim citizens. America has close and important relations with many Islamic nations. So it is fitting for America to honor your friendship and the traditions of a great faith by hosting this Iftaar at the White House. I want to thank our Secretary of State for being here, as well as members of my administration. I want to thank the ambassadors for taking time in this holy month to come to join us in this feast.
>
> This evening, we gather in a spirit of peace and cooperation. I appreciate your support of our objectives in the campaign against terrorism. Tonight that campaign continues in Afghanistan, so that the people of Afghanistan will soon know peace. The terrorists have no home in any faith. Evil has no holy days. This evening we also gather in the spirit of generosity and charity. As this feast breaks the Ramadan fast, America is also sharing our table with the people of Afghanistan.
>
> We are proud to play a leading role in humanitarian relief efforts, with air drops and truck convoys of food and medicine. America's children are donating their dollars to the Afghan children. And my administration is committed to help reconstruct that country, and to support a stable government that represents all of the people of Afghanistan. We are working for more opportunity and a better life for the people of Afghanistan, and all the people of the Islamic world. America respects people of all faiths, and America seeks peace with people of all faiths. I thank you for your friendship, and I wish you a blessed Ramadan.[17]

Now, one could spend several lectures happily deconstructing this speech, perhaps beginning with the odd swiftness that moves from commending Islam for its peacefulness to justifying recent attacks on Afghanistan. Or, one might point out the history of U.S. involvement in Afghanistan, including its supplying of armaments to extremists as a way of countering Soviet rule there.[18] In any case, what is interesting for our purposes is the kind of religious pluralism that Bush presents. Deep down, we all really believe in the same thing—tolerance, peace, and cooperation.

There is this odd bewitchment that takes place with words such as *tolerance* and *pluralism*. They pretend to speak to an underlying unity, which is more significant than outward action. It is okay to bomb a Muslim nation so long as our intentions are pure—this is tolerance. Why am I tolerant? Because deep down I really like Muslims. Perhaps what Muslims would wish of Americans and Canadians is not that they would love them *deep down*, but would love them instead on the surface. As Mahmood will argue, the ideology of of state pluralism tolerates religion insofar as it amounts to private sentiment. But religion, or at least any religion worth its salt, is not this—it is a public commitment, it is a community, and it involves a set of practices that seeks to shape persons in decisive ways. While Smith, Hick, and pluralists are not responsible for the double standards of the recent pluralist discourse of the War on Terror, their distinction between a core essence of religious faith and its external practices clearly accommodates such confusion, and has engendered an interrogation of Muslims since 9/11 with which we are still contending.

The *Iftar* is not simply a religious ritual that points to a common meaning that we all fundamentally share, nor is it simply an arbitrary sign that we can all enjoy as it suits us—it is instead a claim to truth, and it is a claim that alters its practitioners. It is a claim that helps to orient and shape what Muslims mean when they speak of God—that it is God who provides nourishment and sustenance, and who therefore requires our submission, even of bodily appetites. How different a version of human flourishing this is from that of contemporary secular culture—although not altogether foreign to the ascetical practices of the Christian faith.

In any case, what I find interesting is how advocates of tolerance seem compelled to separate the form of religious expression (the *Iftar*) from its content (its perceived underlying meaning). It is this move—the allergy against identifiable markers of faith—that is seen regularly in various eruptions of Western distress over Muslim religious practices. In 2001, American feminist playwright Eve Ensler added a new monologue to her famous *The Vagina Monologues* titled "Under the Burqa." This monologue debuted at a star-studded, one-thousand-dollar-a-ticket gala and featured Oprah Winfrey as its narrator, who intoned:

"Imagine a huge cloth/hung over your body/like you were a shameful statue." The performance ended with the appearance of a burqa-clad woman whom Oprah Winfrey liberated through the dramatic lifting of the woman's veil, thus releasing her to the light.[19] In keeping with the success of this performance, Ensler chose the slogan the following year for her annual V-Day campaign, "Afghanistan is Everywhere." As she told reporters, "[I]n every place I go women are being raped and battered and burned and destroyed. We all wear a burqa, but it is a different burqa in every country."[20]

Somehow, in the aftermath of 9/11, even Bush's progressive opponents can deem a Muslim nation a symbol of evil. Further, the burqa and the veil have increasingly aroused an impression of a lurking threat from which women in particular and the West in general must be liberated, as various disciplinary measures taken against it amply display.[21] Pluralism as state policy, far from appreciating religions difference, is a stringent regulator of what kind of religious practice will be tolerated. Thus Muslim women have become the archetype of female victimhood and Western women the paradigm of their emancipated potential, as Mahmood notes:

> We need a way to think about the lives of Muslim women outside this simple opposition. This is especially so in those moments of crisis, such as today, when we tend to forget that the particular set of desires, needs, hopes, and pleasures that liberals and progressives embrace do not *necessarily* exhaust the possibilities of human flourishing. We need to recognize that, whatever effect it has had on the women who wear it, the veil has also had a radical impact on our own field of vision, on our capacity to recognize Muslim societies for something other than misogyny and patriarchal violence. Our ability to respond, morally and politically, in a responsible way to these forms of violence will depend on extending these powers of sight.[22]

The veil actually serves as that which obscures *our*, that is, the West's, vision for it both presents and conceals a subject who is not easily identifiable in contemporary liberal politics. Contemporary liberalism tends to be predicated upon the belief that there is no higher good than being free to express oneself as one so wills, and therefore any type of restriction or conformity placed upon or adopted by a subject is seen as a form of tyranny. And yet, Afghani women have told us repeatedly that, in comparison to the poverty and violence in their country, the burqa is a relatively minor issue. Further, many more Muslim women have conceived of the *hijab*, the veil, in ways far broader than as a sign of oppression.

Mahmood challenges the presumptions that so captivate progressives such as Winfrey and Ensler. That is, she undermines the assumption that untrammeled choice or freedom (the freedom to wear what one so chooses) is among the highest of goods. And thus she also challenges the fundamental commonplace of pluralism—that we are all either really aiming at the same thing, or that the differences that we exhibit do not make a pervasive claim upon us. As Mahmood helpfully points out, there are versions of human flourishing that are different from those of the Western individual. The virtues and disciplines that are embodied in Muslim piety both reflect and shape subjects who have different aims from those generally held by the West. Liberal democracies, far from tolerating religious difference, thus set firm limits on the kinds of difference to be tolerated. This regulation has an almost panoptical effect upon religious subjectivities for even theologians, like many scholars of religious studies, reproduce the canons of secularism and interrogate theological doctrines and practices according to these norms. Thus theology and the churches take for granted that religious faith is predominately a private affair; that its claims to truth cannot be argued peacefully and therefore need to be policed; and that it makes little difference to religious adherents in their public identities which form of religious belonging they take on. Religious subjects thus adopt an anemic pluralism because, under the conditions of secularism, there are increasingly fewer places available within society to develop or defend a particular moral vision. As Mahmood writes: "The political solution that secularism proffers, I am suggesting, lies not so much in tolerating difference and diversity but in remaking certain kinds of religious subjectivities."[23] How are religious adherents remade by the demands of secularism? Who are these reformed religious subjectivities?

First, secularism is not a space but a time—it is a time that is opposed to sacred time. And thus it orders time according to a logic of punctuality and efficiency. It is therefore wary of practices that require the inefficient use of time, like the *Salah,* the Muslim prayer to be practiced five times a day, or of Jews' keeping of sabbath; it is wary of patient practices like caring for those who require our time, as most great religions commend us to do. Secularism is a flattening of time. It is one damned thing after another in the long march of history and it abides no account of time that would permit us renarrate time as that which is seized by God and demands our attention. In its stead, it offers an endless array of distractions and simulated experiences designed to jolt us out of our boredom. Thus the religious subject becomes the seeker chasing after forms of entertainment, which the savvy churches at least are all too willing to offer up.

Second, in Christian theology at least, secularism convinces its adherents, even its theologians, that the particular features of their faiths are parochial and without any significance beyond the self or one's community. Religion is a private affair; it is truly privation—it denies any claim of knowledge of the good, the true, and the beautiful, and thus it becomes ever more insubstantial and insignificant until it fades away to nothingness.

Third, and finally, because it can abide no strong conception of the good, the true, and the beautiful, secularism creates the kinds of religious subjects who understand themselves as electing their own religious belonging, unpressured by the passé allegiances of culture and community. The religious consumer is thus freed to choose among the marketplace of religions, all of which reproduce a fetid and boring array of exotic difference, thereby reproducing the market's pluralism of goods for consumption. Secularism creates citizens who have no greater allegiance, and at times no other allegiance, than to the state. Such an allegiance to the state is no longer an allegiance to the good of citizenship, but to the good of perpetual and morally vacuous consumption. For example, in the wake of the worst economic meltdown since the Great Depression, citizens are told to buy our way out of it! Never mind the evaporating resources of the earth, never mind climate change; we simply exercise our citizenship by spending more!

It is at such a pluralism—one that is shaped by political and imperial imperative of the current political order—that I wish to take aim. This is because I believe that the differences between religious evaluations of how to mark time or on the nature of the good, the true, and the beautiful can be radically different one from another, although perhaps not so different among the religions than between religious faith and secularism. Further, because theological judgments from various faiths seek to shape their subjects in powerful ways, one cannot assume that doctrinal commitments about the nature of God (or of the gods' absence) will issue in a generic sensibility about the goal and purpose of humanity. The discrete way in which Christian subjectivity is formed has everything to do with its strong claim that Jesus Christ is God incarnate. That is, that God divested Godself of eternal glory in the taking on of human form, the form of a slave (Phil. 2:5-11), and in so doing made manifest the true destiny and glory of humanity. What is most significant about confessing Christ as God incarnate is not simply what it says about God, but also what it says about humans. As Athanasius of Alexandria said, "God became human so that humans could become god."[24] What the incarnation of God means is the heralding of the most profound kind of blessing upon human life. This is a life not to be squandered—not just Christian life, of course, but all human life. Secularism unmakes the Christian claim of the mystery of human life as God's good joy and turns it into a narrative of self-mastery through the exercise of private will. Proclaiming Christ as God incarnate will inevitably clash with such a narration of the human subject, not only because it makes God too insignificant, but because it makes humans so.

ATHANASIUS AND WHAT IT MEANS TO BE HUMAN

There are many Nicene writings that take up the theme of human dignity being assured by the incarnation. Indeed, the dominant soteriological motif within the patristic era concerns the elevation of humankind through divine descent and return. Thus God makes a way in Christ for human participation in the life of the Godhead through Christ's union of humanity and divinity. I have settled primarily on the writings of Athanasius (particularly *On the Incarnation of the Word* and *Contra Gentes* ["Against the Heathen"]) because human dignity is not, in the first instance, tied to human assent or righteousness or even to knowledge of Christ, but foremost to an ontological blessing that is conferred upon humanity in the kenosis of the Son. From here, I wish to consider how that blessing is at once a correction to human waywardness and its sanctification, and how this action is received in the specific community, not first through human positing, but through its pathos, its *askesis*, its renunciation.[25] These reflections will lead me to further writings in Athanasius that will, I believe, point to something of the paradox of Christian evangelization in the early church, and how that paradox is, in fact, instructive to Christian life today.

Athanasius of Alexandria would seem, at first glance, an unlikely ally for a chapter dedicated to theological questions arising from the plurality of religions. He is somewhat notoriously remembered as the staunch defender of Nicene Christian orthodoxy against the Arians and as the author of *Contra Gentes*, a treatise dedicated to denouncing the proponents of "false religion." This is hardly a treatise of religious pluralism! However, it is helpful here to remember the question that is before us: the question is not, first, How are the religions related one to another? (a question that preoccupies modern religionists such as Smith); instead, the question is primarily, What does revelation in this tradition have to say about the nature and destiny of the human creatures? This is a question to ask not only of the Christian narrative, but also of the secular one, which will, willy-nilly, be influential in individuals' self-understanding in this society. The answer given by each theology, including the secular paradigm, is neither universal nor neutral.

Like Mahmood, I would argue that secularism is, in fact, a kind of theological discourse which has very specific religious features, aimed to shape its adherents in specific ways. Like her, I would judge that secular pluralism, far from being neutral on the question of what it means to be human, actually takes upon itself as task the remaking of human subjectivity, particularly religious subjectivity. In particular, it chafes against any notion that subjectivity is somehow formed or disciplined in discrete ways by adherence to common practices and disciplines. What we receive from an ancient writer such as Athanasius is an alternate narration of what it is to be human. His account is not singular, but is still partially accessible through Christian practice and doctrine, particularly in the liturgy, and hence is a living (albeit somewhat forgotten) tradition. A call for a rehabilitation of Christian thinking on the *humanum* from the Nicene era is not meant to suggest that Christian theology since is bereft of such reflection, but it is to posit (although unfortunately all too briefly) that without an ontological grammar supporting anthropological claims—a grammar that was defended and advanced in the fourth century by thinkers such as Athanasius—the universal significance of Christ's saving work remains underdeveloped. In its stead, we receive from modern theologies of religion a universalism that is devoid of christological grounding and, because of this, an absence of a vision of the good that might orient our present action.[26]

DIVINE IMMANENCE AND TRANSCENDENCE

Athanasius (c. 300–373) was bishop of Alexandria for an impressive forty-five years, almost sixteen of which he spent in exile, a fate he experienced five times. Although a polemicist, and hardly irenic toward his Arian opponents, he later made peace with the so-called semi-Arians. *On the Incarnation* is actually the second part of a two-part treatise—*Contra Gentes* and *De Incarnatione* (hereafter *CG-DI*). Although a subject of much scholarly dispute, the precise dating of *CG-DI* is incidental to our purposes. It makes sense to understand this work as catechetical in nature, offering an apologetical treatise on the nature of salvation in Jesus Christ that is not thoroughly overburdened by immediate controversy with the Arians. Although several scholars have argued that Athanasius's lack of direct reference to the Arians signals an early dating,[27] the dating becomes a secondary issue when one focuses upon the coherence of his thought throughout his theological and ecclesial career. Here, the work of patristics scholar, Khaled Anatolios, is most helpful in overcoming earlier false dichotomies between the early Athanasius and the later, or between his writings on creation and soteriology. Athanasius's doctrine of creation is part and parcel of his soteriology, as we shall soon see. In any event, suffice it to say that Athanasius wrote *CG-DI* as an apologetic work, aimed at both Christian and pagan readers. The treatise is very important for our purposes because its focus is the nature and role of the incarnation of the word in relation to creation. Thus we find in these treatises a veritable treasure trove of scriptural and philosophical reflection on the ontological significance of Jesus' coming for the elevation of humanity.

There is much within the modern temperament that chafes against Athanasius's language, to the degree that many scholars are inclined to dismiss his writing as irredeemably inflammatory and narrow-minded. As Timothy Barnes describes him:

> If the violence of Athanasius leaves fewer traces in the surviving sources than similar behavior by later bishops of Alexandria like Theophilus, Cyril, and Dioscorus, the reason is not that he exercised power in a different way, but that he exercised it more efficiently and that he was successful in presenting himself to posterity as an innocent in power, as an honest, sincere, and straightforward 'man of God.'[28]

The purpose of drawing on Athanasius is not to make a case that he was "an innocent in power." Barnes is surely correct in pointing to the inextricably close relationship between imperial and ecclesial power in nascent Christendom. Nevertheless, there remains within Athanasius's writing a challenge to the temptation to coercive power that writers such as Barnes expose, even if Athanasius as a political figure failed to live up to that challenge.

With Athanasius we see a drive to defend the ontological status of the Son for reasons that are other than mere power politicking. Athanasius is intent upon defending the divinity of the Son as an ontological principle quite simply because he believes that, in him, the world was changed. The world has changed in a manner that is not merely symbolic on account of Christ's coming, but it has changed in the most fundamental manner: it has been recreated and repristinated according to its original form and shape. And this recreation or repristination of the original order involves especially rehabilitation of humans because God has come down and assumed our nature. Thus, the so-called Arian misapprehension of the nature of Christ is no small error, but it threatens to undercut the very logic of salvation. By failing to recognize the ontological status of the Son as the eternal and incarnate word, Athanasius's "Arian" opponents threatened to violate the semiotic system by which the Scriptures reveal divine being.[29] Or, to put it in positive theological terms, the ontological status of the Son was the necessary grammar for a coherent doctrine of salvation.

According to Athanasius, the origin of life from nothingness gives rise to its fundamental instability: created matter from nothingness threatens to return to nothingness. Although human beings are created from nothingness, they are also created by God, and as such receive from God God's own goodness. God as source cannot be a source of anything but good.[30] Furthermore, God creates human beings in God's own image, thus endowing them with a "portion even of the power of his own Word."[31]

Even further to this, God anticipates the waywardness of God's creatures and thus establishes a law and a land/garden whereby their flourishing might be guaranteed.[32] While in many respects this explanation of the fall is one that is in keeping with the teachings of the Fathers and Scripture, and represents a fairly predictable catechetical narrative, what is remarkable in *On the Incarnation* is Athanasius's persistence in drawing together the doctrines of creation and of incarnation. By the word the world is created. Being made in the image of God means participation in God's eternal word. Jesus comes not so that we can be divine like him; as though becoming partakers in the divine life were alien to our natures, that divinity is already assured in us in the very act of creation whereby human beings share in the word by being made in God's own image. Jesus comes instead to interrupt human degeneration and descent into nothingness and therefore to restore something that was indigenous to humans at creation. Thus the incarnation is the remedy for the willful turning away from God among the first humans, not merely by canceling out the original transgression in the garden, but it heals the effects of the multiplication of death and corruption that have been unleashed since Adam. The human story of fall is one in which the image of God upon humans was becoming effaced by human neglect of its proper purpose. In God's sending the word, God reiterates the first act of creation, so that the word, who dwells eternally and everywhere with God, might condescend to specifically human reasoning, human suffering, and human sin in innumerable distortions. As Athanasius puts it:

> For now He [God] has come to our realm, and taken up his abode in one body among His peers, henceforth the whole conspiracy of the enemy against mankind is checked, and the corruption of death which before was prevailing against them is done away. For the race of men had gone to ruin, had not the Lord and Saviour of all, the Son of God, come among us to meet the end of death.[33]

Here, in this foundational remark on the incarnation, Athanasius intimates salvation's objective scope. Christ's work effects a return to an original order that was lost due to human recalcitrance. His work is a rehabilitation of an image that is all but effaced. The restoration is sheerly gratuitous and is not contingent upon the personal assent of the believer; it is contingent only upon God's gift that shines forth in the very foundations of the world. The effect of Christ's repristination of humanity is experienced throughout the created universe. It is not withheld to any but is poured out to all.

This is not to say that human beings are inert recipients of divine restoration. In spite of its fallen condition, the fundamental orientation of humans is one of *desire* for God, which, being created in the image of God, propels the creature toward God. Humanity is ordained, by the radical logic of its constitution, to rise up above itself and maintain its being by virtue of its "conversation" (*sunomilia*) with God, whence its being is derived and sustained. This framework is consistently central to Athanasius's theological vision throughout his career. The world is by no means bereft of the Logos, which inhabits the entire creation and endows it with its resplendent beauty, even after the fall.

In becoming human, the word acts consistently with divine purposes from the very beginning, but those purposes are in him clarified, rendered intelligible in the coming of the word in human flesh, for the sake of assisting human beings to grow in knowledge of him. Such knowledge is not new; it is consistent with God's wisdom working throughout the world. As Athanasius writes:

> Consistently, therefore, the Word of God took a body and has made use of a human instrument, in order to quicken the body also, and as He is known in Creation by his works, so to work in man as well, and to shew Himself everywhere, leaving nothing void of his own divinity, and of the knowledge of Him. For I presume, and I repeat what I said before, that the Saviour did this in order that, as He fills all things on all sides by His presence, so also He might fill all things with the knowledge of Him, as the divine Scripture also says, 'The whole earth was filled with the knowledge of the Lord.'[34]

The Logos does not eschew taking on frail and human flesh. There is a consistency in Christ's condescension to frail humanity with the gift given by God in the beginning. It is God's very nature that God fills in freedom and love the universe with divine life and light. The coming of Christ is a repetition of this motion for our sakes. It is the pouring out of the fullness of divine life into humankind upon an unregenerate humanity. Thus creatures are filled with knowledge (with the Logos) through Christ in the same way as creation is filled with God's glory.

In his impressive study of the consistency of Athanasius's thought, Khaled Anatolios[35] identifies a consistent schema that is worked out as the relation between transcendence and immanence. For Athanasius, a uniquely Christian understanding of these two terms is central to understanding the logic of salvation. While it is clearly significant that Jesus Christ is the eternally begotten word poured forth, it is also central to Athanasius's position that Christ dwells in time and in particularity. Transcendence is not the inscrutable otherness of God, but it is a God who confronts us in all our particularity as a particular one who is infinitely other. This distance between humans and God is not overcome in God's proximity to us in drawing near in Christ, because the God who is revealed in coming near is revealed to be one who is beyond our possession or appropriation. God is one who is the veiled third walking beside us (Luke 24), always as one who will not be absorbed into our rendering of him.

For Arius, the guarantor of divine transcendence is divine unknowability. Christ could not be God because Christ was too familiar, too like us. There is within modern theology an analogous discomfit with Christology. Modern theology tends to treat the revelation of God in Jesus Christ as a partial revelation, because Christ in coming among us appears too parochial. If Jesus is only a partial or surface revelation of a hidden God, then we would appear better equipped to accommodate the claims of other religions. But this pluralism is won only by forgoing the affirmation that God is made known in Jesus Christ in whom the fullness of God is pleased to dwell. Yet the Athanasian view does not see divine condescension as finitude, but as an unfolding in which the word is revealed decisively through particular humanity.

In his own meditation on divine immanence and transcendence, Athanasius writes:

> For he was not, as might be imagined, circumscribed in the body nor, while yet present in the body, was He absent elsewhere; nor while he moved the body, was the universe left void of His working or Providence; but thing most marvellous, Word as he was, so far from being contained by anything contained all things in Himself, and just as while present in the whole of Creation, he is at once distinct in being from the universe, and present in all things by His own power—giving order to all things, and over all in all revealing His own providence, and giving life to each thing and all things, including the whole without being included, but being in His own Father alone wholly and in every respect--thus, even while present in a human body and Himself quickening it, He was, without inconsistency, quickening the universe as well, and was in every process of nature and was outside the whole and while known from the body by His works, He was none the less manifest from the workings as well.[36]

The Logos's presence within the body of Christ does not leave the world bereft of his involvement within creation. Although in the universe, he is not contained by it; on the contrary, the universe dwells in him and is quickened and contained by him. Therefore, the fear that God's special revelation within Jesus and within the church is a limitation of God does not take God's transcendence seriously enough. Christ draws near, we can faithfully assume, in a myriad of instances quickening his creation, while not being subsumed by it. At the same time the fullness of God dwells perfectly and completely within the Son so that humans may come to participate in divine fullness.

Such a view of creaturely life is not uniquely the domain of the Christian. All creatures are quickened by Christ, and no one community can boast of having Christ as its special possession. Human beings in particular share in divine life in being made in God's own image and in being regenerated in Christ. The word does not cease to dwell in creation in Jesus' condescension to humanity, nor does the word cease to dwell in those who do not confess him.

Yet, for Athanasius, God's transcendence in this sense does not mean that God is unapproachable. The church, in receiving the "first things" of revelation (not for its merit, but by virtue sheer gratuity), is enjoined to live in joyful and humble response to God's initiative. Athanasius is convinced that the life lived faithfully in worship and joyous response to God's work will bear much fruit, but it will be fruit of a certain kind. It will not be marked by boasting, but the humility and patience made known in Jesus Christ. It is not privilege or power that renders life in Christ manifest, but it is simplicity, renunciation, and Christ-like condescension. As Athanasius writes of St. Anthony: "We however make our proof 'not in the persuasive power of words of Greek wisdom,' as our teacher has it, but we persuade by the faith which manifestly precedes argumentative proof. . . . 'Believe, therefore, also yourselves, and you shall see that with us there is no trick of words, but faith through love which is wrought in us towards Christ. . . .'"[37] Belief is practical for Athanasius; it involves a turning of the will toward God, whose own turning toward the subject is prior; "it manifestly precedes argumentative proof." Thus Athanasius can write assuredly of the conversion of persons to Christ:

> But when they hear the teaching of Christ, forthwith they turn from fighting to farming, and instead of arming themselves with swords extend their hands in prayer. In a word, instead of fighting each other, they take up arms against the devils and the daemons, and overcome them by their self-command and their integrity of soul. These facts are proof of the Godhead of the Saviour, for he has taught men what they could never learn among the idols. It is also no small exposure of the weakness and nothingness of daemons and idols, for it was because they knew their own weakness that the daemons were always setting men to fight each other, fearing lest, if they ceased from mutual strife, they would learn to attack the daemons themselves. For in truth, the disciples of Christ, instead of fighting each other, stand arrayed against daemons by their virtuous actions, and chase them away and mock at their captain, the devil. Even in youth they are chaste, they endure in times of testing and persevere in toils. When they are insulted, they are patient, when they are robbed, they make light of it, and, marvellous to relate, they make light even of death itself, and become martyrs of Christ.[38]

Admittedly, this passage would seem an odd one to impress upon the reader the generosity of orthodox Christian faith. Athanasius is hardly concerned to find in his pagan opponent any sign of the movement of grace.[39] Yet, there are two things worthy of note here for our purposes. First is the inseparability of faith and morality, or inner piety and outward action, if you will. For Athanasius, idolatry issues in moral degeneracy, the corrosive power of idols exists not in their capacity to affront a jealous God but, rather, in their inevitable deprivation of those who would adhere to them. In them, there is no power by which they can offer creative possibilities beyond the endless replication of mimetic violence. In contrast, Christ awakens life and creative possibility beyond violence and moral degeneration. For Athanasius, this is not just on account of the teaching Christ bestows, but because of the efficacy of the gift that he gives humans through the Holy Spirit. Here, Athanasius gives us a clue to the deep meaning of James's maxim: "Faith without works is dead." This is not a moral lesson, as it is often read, but an ontological statement. For Athanasius, a faith that is alive is one that be compelled to spill over into righteous and charitable action.

Athanasius teaches us that Christian confession cannot coherently make the claim that Christ is a partial revelation of God, or that God somehow surpasses the disclosure of Jesus Christ. Christian confession gives rise to a profound appreciation for God's works, for God's goodness shines forth in men and women and creatures to the furthest reaches of creation. According to Athanasius, the revelation of God in Christ is a revelation that is fitting to our senses as Christ condescends to make himself known to human beings in time and in the flesh. Thus he "touches all parts of creation," and in so touching them, also sanctifies them, even in their lowliest and most broken parts. This is an argument that may not convince all non-Christians, but one that ought to give the Christian pause before diminishing its claim. For in denying the power attested to in Scripture about the redemption of creation by the Son, we are also denying the very blessing which the gospel claims that Christ has conferred upon humanity and creation, everywhere, including those parts of creation that do not know or confess him.

> How could he have called us if he had not been crucified, for it is only on a cross that a man dies with arms outstretched? Here, again, we see the fitness of his death and of those outstretched arms: it was that He might draw his ancient people with the one and the Gentiles with the other, and join both together in Himself. Even so, he foretold the manner of his redeeming death, "I, if I be lifted up, will draw all men unto Myself."[40]

Jesus signals in his death the unity to which we are called, but for him this unity is only by way of the cross, the way of death. It is not through coercion that the ancient people and Gentiles are brought together, but by God's outstretched and suffering hands for the sake of all people.

For Athanasius, this is perfect subjecthood. It is the posture of the one who loves the entire universe, but who refuses to appropriate by coercion. It is a pathic posture that is willing to allow human beings their freedom, even when that freedom is destructive. And it is a posture in which the grave and totalizing forces that hem us in are overcome in love. Such an alternate construal of human subjectivity is a profoundly different one from secular accounts of what it means to be human. To be human, according the Athanasius, is not to possess a sovereign will, but to be willing to risk suffering and even death in order to allow the other to be free.

Reflection upon Athanasius as a counterpoint to secular construals of the self points to several themes. For one, the question, Will non-Christians be saved? is a bad one, for it domesticates God's kenosis to a movement of capricious and arbitrary will to anoint only those who have heard the gospel and believed, and who have assented to the gospel in spite of its difficulty and its generally crummy heralds. For the way of Christ, although it proceeds through a narrow gate, surely has a wide reception area. Christ did not come to save Christians, but the world God so loved, a world that bears his image.

In his encyclical on mission, *Veritatis Splendor*, Pope John Paul II takes up Athanasian themes which tie creation and salvation in a way that is very congenial:

> The splendour of truth shines forth in all the works of the Creator and, in a special way, in man, created in the image and likeness of God (cf. *Gen* 1:26). Truth enlightens man's intelligence and shapes his freedom, leading him to know and love the Lord. Hence the Psalmist prays: "Let the light of your face shine on us, O Lord" (*Ps* 4:6). The light of God's face shines in all its beauty on the countenance of Jesus Christ, "the image of the invisible God" (*Col* 1:15), the "reflection of God's glory" (*Heb* 1:3), "full of grace and truth" (*Jn* 1:14). Christ is "the way, and the truth, and the life" (*Jn* 14:6). Consequently the decisive answer to every one of man's questions, his religious and moral questions in particular, is given by Jesus Christ, or rather is Jesus Christ himself, as the Second Vatican Council recalls: "In fact, *it is only in the mystery of the Word incarnate that light is shed on the mystery of man*. For Adam, the first man, was a figure of the future man, namely, of Christ the Lord. It is Christ, the last Adam, who fully discloses man to himself and unfolds his noble calling by revealing the mystery of the Father and the Father's love".[41]

To be human is to be Christ-like. All questions of the *humanum* are referred to the unique revelation that is found in Jesus Christ, God incarnate. There will be other claims about what it means to be human made by other religious faiths—some of them will be antagonistic to Christian claims; many of them, especially those of Judaism, will be congenial. Some of them will clarify Christian convictions of what it is to be human; some of them will confound them. In short, there can be no theory of religious unity; there can only be irreducible encounters with persons of various religious faiths, or those with none at all, whom we are obliged to encounter and to hold in the highest of regard, not despite Christian claims, but because of them.

The question becomes, If we cannot be said to believe the same thing, and if our differences are not merely trivial but are substantial, what then ought to be the Christian approach to the other religions? It seems to me that interreligious dialogue is not a virtue to be cultivated but a reality that is at hand. We live in a world in which there are persons of different faiths and an increasing number of no faith at all, and the vast majority of us whose faith is private and thus withering. It is generally quite likely that we share a bus seat, a classroom, an electoral district, or a hospital waiting room with a whole host of those who are not Christian. The dialogue that we share in public places is often regulated so as to invigilate against the other taking offense. This is not only because public policy has tended to disallow conversations about strong convictions, but also because we have internalized the rules of the game ourselves. But we ought to challenge these tacit assumptions, primarily because the Muslim or Jewish or Sikh or secular humanist neighbor is likely to be far more interesting than the official *Esperanto* speaker of secularism. This does not mean that we should insist on religious dialogue. One of the funny contradictions of the movement toward interreligious dialogue is that we assume that the neighbor wants to speak with us. Still, as Christians, we are compelled to engage the neighbor who is before us, and who presents anew to us God's gift.

And so, although it is ultimately rather unsatisfying, I find myself concluding that there can be no general theory of religious dialogue in advance of the face-to-face encounter with persons of other faiths, for to have a theory—pluralism, inclusivism, exclusivism, and the like—is to risk preempting the possibility of finding Christ veiled in the neighbor before me. It is to recognize that in that encounter with the other there is no foreclosure that is made for me in discovering anew the truth into which I have been drawn, that is, the truth of the incarnate one, Jesus Christ. This truth radiates to the whole world and its light is reflected not only by those within the church but also by those outside the church. As Athanasius has shown, all human beings participate in the world that is redeemed and sanctified by Christ, whether they know it or not,[42] and all human beings and creatures and the earth itself reflect his glory.

Love of the neighbor who is of another faith requires the capacity to assert religious conviction about the truth no less than the acknowledgment of other points of view. Otherwise, what one achieves is not dialogue but, rather, a cacophony of isolated monologues. Furthermore, if Christians were to retreat from advancing the claim that Jesus Christ is the unique mediator of salvation, it is not clear what they would have to offer to the world. Christians have no language to speak other than Christ, and so we hope that language will be spoken well. To speak the Christian faith well requires the self-knowledge and the patience to know when to catechize, when to repent, when to pray, when to testify, when to prophecy, and perhaps most of all, when to hold our tongues. Further, that confession for it to be true must cohere with our practices: which means that the best missionaries are the saints. Once again, the encyclical *Veritatis Splendor* puts it this way:

> Just as it does in proclaiming the truths of the faith, and even more so in presenting the foundations and content of Christian morality, the new evangelization will show its authenticity and unleash all its missionary force when it is carried out through the gift not only of the word proclaimed but also of the word lived. In particular, the life of holiness which is resplendent in so many members of the People of God, humble and often unseen, constitutes the simplest and most attractive way to perceive at once the beauty of truth, the liberating force of God's love, and the value of unconditional fidelity to all the demands of the Lord's law, even in the most difficult situations.[43]

CONCLUSION: CONFESSING THE CRUCIFIED ONE IN HUMILITY

To confess Christ as God in a pluralistic age is to confess the crucified one in humility.[44] To seek to baptize the nations in his name contains the profoundest of challenges, for such a baptism can never be the way of triumph, only of martyrdom, of the witness of suffering service. To confess Christ as God in a pluralistic age is to confess that the whole world has been healed by him, and thus to confess that the whole world shares, although partially, in his restored creation whether they believe in Christ or not. Christians are different only because they have received the good news first—and because of this they are perhaps far more likely to be in danger of God's judgment because this gift can be so easily squandered.[45]

Because Christians have received the gospel, they have the special task of not allowing the gospel to be reshaped to suit the demands of the fallen order. To confess Christ as God incarnate in a pluralistic age is to confess him boldly and publicly primarily to that fallen order, and to resist the kind of language that would water down the gospel's radical demands. To confess Christ as God in a pluralistic world is to confess the beauty of the individual in an order that subjugates the human to countless trivializations and distortions. It is this confession, not that of state-sanctioned pluralism, which prohibits Christian violation of the man or woman of other faiths.

Finally, to confess Christ as God incarnate is to refuse to participate in the world of fallen time, trying to measure our efficiency and our speed, and so to confess Christ as God incarnate is also to say that God has given us all the time in the world[46] to make disciples of the nations, for, behold, God is with us always, "to the end of the age" (Matt. 28:20).

In advocating a posture of humility and in celebrating the humble, Athanasius affirms that the form of the Christian faith is inextricably bound together with its content. We cannot proclaim the Prince of Peace in the violent rhetoric of colonialism, nor even of civil religion. The Christian word to the religious other must always be a word that is compellingly, and not compulsively, told. Such confession must also be willing to risk rejection, because it exists only to make room for the other to be free, and it knows that freedom is made possible in God alone, and will be made possible in God's own time.

By way of conclusion, I wish to return to Saba Mahmood, who offers an account of encounter that not only supports Athanasian calls to humility in our speech and in our action, but, like him, a prominent role for attendant waiting for a future that is not foreclosed by our political striving, but that remains open to transformative possibility:

> [W]hat I mean to gesture at is a mode of encountering the Other which does not assume that in the process of culturally translating other life-worlds one's own certainty about how the world should proceed can remain stable. This attitude requires the virtue of humility: a sense that one does not always know what one opposes and that a political vision at times has to admit its own finitude in order to even comprehend what it has sought to oppose.[47]

5

"HE WAS CRUCIFIED FOR US UNDER PONTIUS PILATE"

PROCLAIMING THE CROSS IN A VIOLENT WORLD

FOR MANY OF US WHO ARE PREACHERS, it has become exceedingly difficult to preach the meaning of Good Friday in ways that are intelligible. This is for a number of reasons. For one, the mood of the time is increasingly at odds with language of sin and sacrifice—there remains considerable truth to H. Richard Niebuhr's quip: "A God without wrath brought men without sin into a kingdom without judgment through the ministrations of a Christ without a cross."[1] A second and closely related difficulty is that, although we are by no means freed from the violence that characterized the societies in which a theology of the cross was articulated and defended, we believe ourselves to be. The kingdom that we have created here on earth, although certainly not without its problems, is good enough for us. At least this is what we affirm within the comfortable pews of North America. This is so because we immune ourselves to the harsh realities of our world through a variety of distractions. The scandal of the cross, for contemporary persons at least, is not the offense that God has suffered and has died, but the surprising fact that humans do. That suffering exists still in our progressive world requires no prayer for deliverance, only the mastery of technique so that we can more efficiently eradicate it.

And yet, in a global village, and in a context where the illusion of the inviolability of both our borders and our banks has been disrupted, perhaps the cross might have something new to say. And perhaps we who are preachers might find our congregations paying a little more attention when we preach on Good Friday than they might have been inclined to in years past.

Still, preaching Good Friday is a perilous task, and I am writing here more as the preacher and the pastor who has had to wrestle with the countless problems that my words which seek to "Lift High the Cross" can bring. How might we preach the cross in a violent world, and in a world in which preaching the cross has not given rise to resistance of the powers and principalities but, rather, has accommodated itself to those?

MODELS OF ATONEMENT

Many of us who have trained in Protestant seminaries have been trained to look at the cross in a certain way; specifically, as a problem to be solved—"Why did Jesus have to suffer and die upon the cross?"—as though the answer to the question of salvation were a kind of riddle to be solved in a distinct set of logical propositions. Gustav Aulén's famous book *Christus Victor* remains the classic text for answering such questions. Published in 1931 by the Swedish Lutheran bishop, we find in Aulén's writings the construction of a typology that would dominate theological texts and Western thinking about the cross to this very day. Aulén offers, according to his translator at least, a strictly historical and nontheological account of the atonement through three distinct types or models.[2]

The first model, which Aulén calls the "classical view of atonement," is *Christus Victor*, and regards Christ's cosmic triumph over the powers and principalities as *the* central moment of our redemption. As Aulén writes, "The Word of God, who is God Himself, has entered in under the conditions of sin and death, to take up the conflict with the powers of evil and carry it through to the decisive victory. This has brought to pass a new relationship between God and the world; atonement has been made."[3] Therefore, the reconciliation that is won by Christ is one that consists of the entire scope of his life. God condescends to the limits of humanity in order to "lift up" humanity toward the decisive victory, which is restored relationship with God. The distance between God and humanity is traversed in his condescension; just so, a new relationship between humans and God is established.

The second model of atonement laid out by Aulén is *satisfaction theory*. According to Aulén, although there are antecedents to his thought, it was Anselm who first developed the doctrine of atonement as satisfaction as a rational argument in his famous *Cur Deus Homo?* ("Why the God-man?"). This view, dubbed rather unfortunately by Aulén as the "Latin view," trades on metaphors of a penitential and feudal system, which is juridical in its innermost essence. According to it, humans owe God an infinite debt, which they cannot possibly pay. They therefore are without resort and unable to become reconciled to God, whose justice as Lord demands fitting recompense. It is for this reason that the God-man, Jesus, is sent to die in order to satisfy God's justice. Because of the boundlessness of Christ, it is only he who is able to satisfy the absolute demand of justice that our transgressions create. But because the sin is human sin, the ransom must be paid also by one who is also human. This theory, according to Aulén, gives rise to a penitential and sacramental system, and although it was later adopted by Protestant scholasticism, it was inimical to the teaching of Luther, who was representative of the classical *Christus Victor*, the view that Aulén espouses. As Aulén writes, Luther's teaching "can only be rightly understood as a revival of the old classic theme of the atonement as taught by the fathers, but with the greater depth of treatment."[4]

A third view, the *examplarist* model, is identified with medieval theologian Peter Abelard and offers a view of salvation that emphasizes the manner in which Christ functions as teacher and example, and who "arouses responsive love in men; this love is the basis on which reconciliation and forgiveness rest."[5]

As I have indicated, many of us have been raised with such various views of the atonement, and therefore have tended to wish to classify each of the theologies of the cross that we engage, and indeed each of the theologians that we encounter, as belonging to one of the types that Aulén has laid out for us. The problem with this is that these types are by no means mutually exclusive nor are they altogether accurate. For, like the Bible itself, we are presented in the writings of the Nicene teachers no neat theory of atonement. This is not to say that the weaving of images does not follow a pattern, but it is to say that the overdetermined and mutually exclusive character of Aulén's distinctions between Christ as paschal lamb, victor, and example is foreign to premodern theologies of the cross.

And yet, Aulén's typology has not only shaped our understandings of atonement within the church but has also been perpetuated in subsequent writings in the academy. This creates a nest of theological problems when thinking about the cross that needs to be sorted out. One of the problems is that most theologians who wrestle with the meaning of the cross do so simply by adopting Aulén's typology. Modern retrievals of *Christus Victor* as a model have tended simply to adopt Aulén's categories, and therefore subscribe to his position that the satisfaction theory is generally problematic, insofar as it divides God's mercy from God's judgment, pits the Father against the Son, and sets up a dichotomy between the incarnation and the crucifixion. According to Aulén's reading of the most notorious proponent of this view, Anselm of Canterbury (1033–1109), ". . . Anselm is saying, as clearly as words can express, that he is thinking of that which Christ accomplishes (i.e, his paying humanity's debt through the torture of his flesh and blood) as a man, of an offering made to God from man's side, from below."[6] This bloodthirsty and righteous God, according to Aulén, is not to be found in the Christian Scriptures, nor is this God to be found in the early church or in Luther's writings. Aulén appears to engage in some special pleading to distinguish Luther from the corruption of what Aulén refers to as Latin theology. Be that as it may, many followers of Aulén have been quick to castigate Anselm and to adopt the pure and nonviolent atonement that is identified with the model of *Christus Victor*.

DEMYSTIFYING THE CROSS

Chief among the contemporary critics of satisfaction theory is Mennonite theologian Denny Weaver, who repudiates any notion that God accomplishes anything through violence. Instead of seeing the cross as God's working out of salvation through a sacrificial cycle, God, in fact, puts an end to the cycle of sacrifice. Taking aim at all the various types of satisfaction theories from Anselm's to modern individual atonement theories within evangelicalism—penal substitution in which Christ pays the legal penalty that we owe on account of our sins—Weaver contends that each of these views is problematic because they depend upon the violent sacrifice of a victim for the purposes of salvation. As Weaver writes: "As long as the death of Jesus is aimed Godward, one cannot avoid the implication that death is the means through which God enables reconciliation, and thus God uses or sanctions a violent death, nor the implication that the powers which killed Jesus perform a service for God and are thus functioning within God's will."[7] To Weaver, God cannot possibly act out of violence, even if that violence has a purportedly peaceful end. Therefore, the cross is nothing other than the sum and total of Jesus' life of nonviolent resistance. As Weaver writes:

> From a position of apparent weakness, the reign of God as present in Jesus confronted and submitted to power. His nonviolent death was not a departure from the activist pattern of confronting the social order and making the reign of God visible. In the face of active or direct evil or violence, the refusal to respond in kind is a powerful, chosen act. . . . The outcome of Jesus' arrest and trial was that brute force killed him in what appeared to be a triumph for the powers of evil. Yet that triumph of evil was limited and momentary.[8]

In Weaver's view, there is no saving efficacy to be located in the cross. The cross represents merely the poverty and reality of violence in the face of love. There is nothing to be redeemed in the story of victimization; the cross is a place that stands outside of salvation history—it is absurd, a moment in which God's working through Christ is, as it were, suspended. Christian proclamation depends not on the cross, only on the life that precedes it and the life that follows it. Christian proclamation is a proclamation of life in the power of the resurrection. It is about the this-worldly overcoming of oppression and political strife through nonviolent means. As Weaver describes it, *Christus Victor* imagery has immediate political implications for us:

> The resurrection as the victory of the reign of God over the forces of evil constitutes an invitation to salvation, an invitation to submit to the rule of God. It is an invitation to enter a new life, a life transformed by the rule of God and no longer in bondage to the powers of evil that killed Jesus. For those who perceive the resurrection, the only option that makes sense is to submit to the reign of God. Christians, Christ-identified people, participate in the victory of the resurrection and demonstrate their freedom from bondage to the powers by living under the rule of God rather than continuing to live in the power of the evil that killed Jesus. Salvation is present when allegiances change and new life is lived "in Christ" under the rule of God.[9]

There is much to be commended in Weaver's correction to the doctrine of the atonement. For one, he points out the irreducibly political dimensions of the atonement. The atonement is not primarily about the overcoming of individual sin (as in many contemporary evangelical versions of penal substitution), nor is it simply about a *Deus ex Machina* God who sets everything aright through the power of the cross, so that we need not worry about our actions (cheap grace). Rather, the victory of God takes place in time and within a very real context of violent power that is Rome. Moreover, Weaver is surely right when he challenges a doctrine that would view God as the author of violence. Such a God is clearly inconsistent with the God of our Lord Jesus Christ, the Prince of Peace, and ends up turning God into a capricious and Janus-faced deity, orchestrating death instead of life, evil instead of good. Finally, Weaver is surely right to challenge those versions of the atonement that are based upon the settling of scores—a kind of retributive justice. He correctly points out that the economy of God is not one of exchange—an eye for an eye—but is one of forgiveness, one of pure and unmerited gift.

Weaver's desire to demystify the cross has been very helpful in these ways. However, what we often receive from Weaver and other political theologians in its stead is another form of mystification, as Christ's death upon the cross comes to serve a specific political end. Divested of its pietistic wallowing in suffering and pity, the cross serves no less a reified end in such theologies. The cross, according to this, although not salvific, represents a critical and activist theology. To this identification of Jesus with an "activist pattern of confronting the social order,"[10] several crucial question must be posed: Is Christ's death not substantively different from the death of countless victims, not because his death was more significant or more severe but because he opens up in his death a political possibility other than victimhood precisely because he is the firstborn of all creation (Col. 1:18)? In other words, is Christ's death not in some sense a sign of a new possibility, one might even say of a new order? Finally, is *Christus Victor* best exemplified not in glory—even if that glory is construed as nonviolent victory—but, rather, in defeat?

ATONEMENT AS RECAPITULATION

Perhaps the cross may be viewed as something greater than the sum total of a series of political infelicities. This is not to negate the specific political context in which Jesus was crucified. He truly suffered under Pontius Pilate; he was a particular Jewish victim of a particular political crime in a particularly pernicious moment in world history. Yet death was not merely symbolic, nor did it stand merely within an immanent plane in history. It was historical, yes, but it was also of cosmological significance. For it is here, at Golgotha, that the power of the seemingly untouchable courts and structures that try and crucify him is undone. It is on the cross that Christ's power is revealed. What Weaver does not appear to see is what his friend and mentor John Howard Yoder saw as the working out of the "the grain of the universe"[11] as peace begins to break forth even in seeming defeat. Such peace has the form not of victory, but of suffering servanthood. This is not just a political statement about what happens to pacifists in a violent world, but it is an ontological statement about the very form of God's power, of God's revolution, of God's salvation in a world of enmity and strife.[12]

The use of Aulén's typology by Weaver and others obscures several important features necessary to a biblical and orthodox theology of the cross. The remedy to this is not simply to say that *Christus Victor* must be complemented by the satisfaction and exemplarist theories, but to say, rather, that the categories are misleading and to dismiss them altogether. Christ's resurrected victory and glory was not *in spite of* Christ's abjection and humiliation on the cross, but the cross was the very form of God's glory, the very shape of God's power. This subtle distinction, between the victimhood and the godly and gracious agency displayed by Jesus even upon the cross (although not exclusively on it), was a point that was understood far better in the early centuries of the church than it is in contemporary theologies.

One of the oldest tropes for understanding the work of Jesus Christ, one that is often neglected in modern Christologies, is the theme of recapitulation, perhaps best interpreted and parsed out by St. Irenaeus of Lyons (c. 130–c. 200). Christ's identity represents a summary or a reheading of the main points of the story. The story that Jesus' life retells is that of creation. Christ, in "gathering all things up" (Eph. 1:7-10, 22-23), offers a summation

and a retelling of human history in such a way that the story of human disobedience is corrected and made new before God.

To read the atonement as a recapitulation is to read it in terms of the trajectory of creation and fall, in which Jesus Christ undoes the havoc wreaked upon
the world in the fall as a result of Adam's disobedience, and offers instead a prototype of perfect obedience. As Irenaeus puts it: "[W]hen He became incarnate,
and was made man, He commenced afresh the long line of human beings, and
furnished us, in a brief, comprehensive manner, with salvation; so that what we
had lost in Adam—namely, to be according to the image and likeness of God—
that we might recover in Christ Jesus."[13] In other words, Christ goes over again
the main points at which Adam failed, thus restoring humanity to the state of
affairs before sin existed. This is not to deny the other ways in which atonement
was understood, for it clearly has a great deal to do with substitution, but it is
to say that Jesus' substitution for us is not merely upon the cross in which he
bears our sins, but is the entire purpose and point of the incarnation. Read in
this way, that is, as a moment within salvation history that is entirely in keeping
with the motion of divine descent and ascent, we understand Christ's sacrifice
not as deriving from lack, but from a divine power that imbues him and remains with him, even in his condescension.[14]

Such a typological or figural renarration of Christ as the second Adam
is offered forcefully by Paul in Romans 5. In a clear juxtaposition of the
first and second Adam, Paul teaches us how to "read" the language of atonement—not as a system of sacrifice offered up to an angry God, not through
a *quid pro quo*, but always through the abundant and overflowing love of
God toward humanity in an infinite outpouring of love. This merit, this gift,
does not merely cancel out our debts, but exceeds them so abundantly that
righteousness is secured for posterity. This abundance is the logic of Christian
sacrifice:

> But the *free gift* is not like the trespass. For if the many died through
> the one man's trespass, much more surely have the grace of God and the
> free gift in the face of one man, *Jesus Christ, abounded for the many*. And
> the *free gift* is not like the effect of the one man's sin. For the judgment
> following one trespass brought condemnation, but the *free gift* following
> many trespasses brings justification. If, because of the one man's tres-
> pass, death exercised dominion through that one, *much more surely* will
> those who receive the abundance of grace and the *free gift* of righteous-
> ness exercise dominion in life through the one man. Therefore, just as
> one man's trespass led to the condemnation for all, so one man's act of
> righteousness leads to justification and life for all. For just as by the one
> man's disobedience the many were made sinners, so by the one man's
> obedience, many will be made righteous. (Rom. 5:15-19)

Christ, the second Adam, tells the story of God's creation of humanity aright. He is the second Adam for *he* offers what humanity after Adam's fall cannot, perfect justice. Christ is one who undoes Adam's trespass through a gesture of a different order, a free act of self-giving. As the firstborn of perfect humanity, Christ gives to his creatures an ever-abundant reserve of righteousness, mercy, and love, even in the face of torture and death. It is this Christ who is condemned, not by the judgment of the Father, but through the reckless momentum of sin arising from Adam, or from humanity's freedom turned in toward itself. And yet, the return to order does not require a sacrificial system of the *lex talionis*, an eye for an eye. Christ does not simply meet the demands of the one to whom humanity is enslaved on its own terms—that is, through violent retaliation—but breaks the bonds of death through the outpouring of his free gift. This gift is not only given on the cross; it is a renarration of an original gift—given in the foundations of the world, in the outpouring of the Father's love for the Son and the Son for the Father. And yet, this gift is in no way withheld or denied upon the cross; rather, the cross presents us again with the beginning of humanity's restoration.

When Irenaeus wrote "Against the Heresies," he was writing against Gnostic accounts of the identity of Jesus Christ that would reduce him to a spiritual and other-worldly teacher, sent down to impart a knowledge upon a portion of humanity. Against this, Irenaeus offers a theology that is at once historical and at the same time of cosmological significance. In the entire scope of Jesus' life, we see him electing as the second Adam an obedience that, because he is also God, has the effect of restoring the world from the fall. However, human activity is "summed up" not only in the negative sense, but in recapitulating humanity, Jesus also actively partakes in human suffering, in human temptation, and in human love:

> But in every respect, too, He is man, the formation of God; and thus he took up man into himself, and the invisible becoming visible, the incomprehensible being made comprehensible, the impassible becoming capable of suffering, and the Word being made man thus summing up all things in Himself. . . . He might draw all things to Himself at proper time.[15]

While Irenaeus is probably best known for articulating and defending the theology of recapitulation, it was a trope common among the ante-Nicene and Nicene theologians. The restoration of humankind depends crucially on Jesus Christ assuming our full humanity. Through this *katabasis*, or divine descent, he identifies fully in vulnerability and in brokenness with human nature, and through his *anabasis*, his ascent and return to the Father, restores humanity to its rightful place as those created in the image of God as he willfully displays human virtue and power as created in the image of God. This is the leading theme of the Nicene teachers in understanding cross and resurrection, and it is the thematic under which other tropes for salvation—atonement, substitution, ransom, exemplar, even victor—take their cue. The kenosis (or self-emptying) of the Son has the effect of not merely revealing a hidden God, but of revealing hidden humanity, a humanity that was disfigured and disguised by sin. Athanasius of Alexandria, taking up the theme of recapitulation, puts it this way:

> Now in truth this great work was peculiarly suited to God's goodness. For, if a king, having founded a house or city, if it be beset by bandits from the carelessness of its inmates, does not by any means neglect it, but avenges and reclaims it as his own work, having regard not to the carelessness of the inhabitants, but to what beseems himself; much more did God the Word of the all-good Father not neglect the race of men, His work, going to corruption: but, while He blotted out the death which had ensured by the offering of His own body, He corrected their neglect by his own teaching, restoring all that was man's by His own power.[16]

Humankind is thus redeemed not so much from an extrinsic source that holds them captive, much less by a God who seeks vengeance for their misdeeds, but by the mercy of God who calls human beings home in spite of the captivity that they have wreaked upon themselves. Thus the household has gone to waste because of bandits and careless inmates, but it is the king's own household. It is not divine punishment (the carelessness of the inmates) so much as it is a reclaiming of a property that is properly God's own. In overcoming death through divine offering of his own body, Christ simultaneously offers the efficacious teaching and restoration by which they receive what is the property of humankind.

Jesus' role in this redemption is not one that is alien to human beings, coming to take on our punishment in our stead, but is perfectly representative of it, and, in his representation of humanity before the Father, he gives himself as a sacrificial offering which is his death so that we may not die:

> [H]aving proved His Godhead by His works, He might offer the sacrifice on behalf of all, surrendering His own temple to death in place of all, to settle man's account with death and free him from the primal transgression. In the same act also He showed Himself mightier than death, displaying His own body incorruptible as the first-fruits of the resurrection.[17]

The cross here is identified entirely with the overarching purposes of God. Jesus, in assuming the priestly, sacrificial role, presents to the Father on our behalf, not for the sake of the satisfaction of an avenging God, but for the satisfaction of the sufferings in God—that is, in the referring of the sufferings to God so that they might be overcome. This is done through the assumption of the condemnation (death) by Jesus Christ. While this language seems very much in keeping with the atonement or penal substitution that Weaver decries, note how significant the incarnation is to its logic. Jesus is not merely the victim, but is also the high priest. He is not a scapegoat, but is the one who himself alone has within him the power to make such an offering. Here, Athanasius is drawing heavily on the letter to the Hebrews, in which Jesus is presented as one who "had to become like his brothers and sisters in every respect, so that he might be a merciful and faithful high priest in the service of God to make a sacrifice of atonement for the sins of the people. Because he was being tested by what he suffered, he was able to help those who are being tested" (Heb. 2:18-19). Here, Jesus' representative and sacramental function is made clear. In going over the testing under which men and women suffer, he is able to display an obedience in suffering that makes a way. He effects, therefore, a change in suffering even as he goes over it in his high priestly role. In going over the entire drama of human history, suffering, and recalcitrance, he effects a change in it by virtue of his divinity working through mortal life and transforming it from within. Christ's own sacrifice is effective in placing humans on a new trajectory that is no longer the tragic inevitability of despair and suffering. T. F. Torrance describes Christ's intrinsic transformation of the human condition thus: "[T]he work of atoning salvation does *not* take place *outside* of Christ, as something external to him, but takes place *within* him, *within* the incarnate constitution of his Person as Mediator."[18] Thus the transformation of humanity takes place through the hypostatic union between God and humans in Jesus as the life of God transfigures the life of humanity through humans' union with Christ.

Khaled Anatolios speaks of this as Christ's *appropriation* of humanity and reminds readers that the sacrifice of condescension to human life for Athanasius was not the subsumption of Christ into our ontological poverty, but was the assumption of our corruptibility by one who was incorruptible, and who thereby reverses it.

> Athanasius's emphasis in the loving "descent" of the Word does not entail any speculation in the direction of a kenoticism of the divine essence or a passible God. While modern speculation on the notion of divine passibility frequently concerns itself with the question of what happens to the divine essence when the Word has taken on human suffering, Athanasius's much more concrete perspective is preoccupied with what happens to human suffering and corruptibility when they

are assumed by the divine Word. The descent of the Word does not diminish the divine nature or amount to a reversal of divine sovereignty; rather, it is the negativities of the fallen human condition that are reversed by the Word's appropriation of them.[19]

Thus the sacrifice of Jesus upon the cross is a paradigmatic moment in the divine drama of appropriation of human nature to the point of abjection. This kenotic movement does not mean the absence of God but, rather, an identification of Jesus in the God-forsakenness of human life. Thus even the cry of dereliction points to the possibility of a new beginning, as God-forsakenness is taken up as an offering to the Father that it might be redeemed. David Bentley Hart sums it up well:

> The cross most definitely is not an instance of God submitting himself to an irresistible force so as to define himself in his struggle with nothingness or so as to be "rescued" from his impassibility by becoming our fellow sufferer; but neither is it a vehicle whereby God reconciles either himself or us to death. Rather he subverts death, and makes a way through it to a new life. The cross is thus a triumph of divine *apatheia*, limitless and immutable love sweeping us into itself, taking all suffering and death upon itself without being changed, modified, or defined by it, and so destroying its power and making us, by participation in Christ, "more than conquerors" (Romans 8.37).[20]

Thus Athanasius retains a sense of sacrifice not merely as ritual slaughter but as drawing near to God (*Korban*) that is consistent with the biblical witness.[21] On the cross, Jesus' blood is identified with the sprinkling of the altar, as human sin is removed through the sacrifice of Jesus (1 John 1:10). However, this sacrifice is not an act in which a finite life is given up for the sake of others, but it is a sacrifice in which the lamb is also the high priest. "He might offer Himself to the Father, and cleanse us all from sins in His own blood, and might rise from the dead."[22] Thus not merely victim, Christ is the one who effects a change in raising us up from our sinfulness. For Athanasius, the purification that Jesus effects is not a cultic appeasement to an angry God, but is an uplifting of God's own creation toward life eternal through the power of the one who came down from heaven. Again, the emphasis is not upon the slaughter, but of being raised up, thereby Christ "brings us near and offers to the Father those who approach him in faith, redeeming all and making expiation to God on behalf of all."[23] We find the twofold motion of *katabasis* and *anabasis*—descent and ascent—becoming the lens through which sacrificial language is interpreted in Athanasius, because this trajectory speaks to Christ's appropriation and transformation of human nature throughout the entirety of his life, death, and resurrection. Thus the language of sacrifice is not of ritual slaughter, but of the drawing near of humanity through the entirety of Christ's ministry, death, and resurrection that is, in fact, an offering or a lifting up of human life toward God.

One of the most consistent themes within a biblical understanding of sacrifice is prayer and self-offering to God the Father as a holy "living sacrifice" (Rom. 12:1). Thus sacrificial practice involves an offering up to the Father; however, what is offered is not death, but life, and abundant life at that. It is the proper and fitting gift that is to be made by God because atonement has been made "once and for all" by Christ, who, in suffering "outside the city gate," sanctifies people so that they, with him, may enter into the gates of the heavenly city. Here again, we see that the response to this life-giving death is not mimetic replication of his death, but prayer and praise, that death, too, has been taken up by God and so transformed in God. "Through him, then, let us continually offer a sacrifice of praise to God, that is, the fruit of lips that confess his name. Do not neglect to do good and to share what you have, for such sacrifices are pleasing to God" (Heb. 13:15-16). Sacrifices of praise become a form of personal recapitulation of what God has achieved in salvation history; thus worship, a gift of continuous praise, is the true nature of sacrificial action for human beings because of the one sacrifice, that is, the assumption of human flesh, to the point even of death, of Jesus Christ for our sakes. This sacrifice is not to be repeated because it is unrepeatable. It is unrepeatable because it is given by God, and therefore efficacious in change only in him: "[I]t belonged to none other to bring man back from the corruption which had begun, than the Word of God, Who had also made them from the beginning."[24] The proper response to this action is not repetition of this act, but praise for it. In a sacrifice of praise and worship, human beings approximate God's abundant and life-giving activity. Thus the sacrificial economy is broken as Christians are released from a life of mimetic violence toward right worship; "instead of arming their hands with weapons they raise them in prayer."[25]

Thus prayer is the form of sacrifice that represents Jesus' willful receptivity to the Father. Sarah Coakley writes of these spiritual disciplines beautifully:

> If . . . these traditions of Christian 'contemplation' are to be trusted, this rather special form of 'vulnerability' is not an invitation to be battered; nor is its silence a silencing. . . . By choosing to 'make space' in this way, one 'practises' the 'presence of God'—the subtle but enabling presence of a God who neither shouts nor forces, let alone 'obliterates'. . . . Thus the 'vulnerablity' that is its human condition is not about asking for unnecessary and unjust suffering (though increased self-knowledge can indeed be painful); nor is it . . . a 'self-abnegation'. On the contrary, this special 'self-emptying' is not a negation of self, but the place of the self's transformation and expansion into God.[26]

The cross provides a crack through which the light shines amidst the darkness and death. It offers in the midst of real political brutality neither retaliation nor resignation, but perfect obedience, which is perfect forgiveness, perfect grace. As John Howard Yoder puts it: "His very obedience unto death is not only the sign but also the firstfruits of an authentic restored humanity."[27] Yoder here presents a very different theology of the cross from that of his student, Weaver. More importantly, Yoder, I believe, is making an ontological claim about the power of the cross. The restoration of humanity is inaugurated in Jesus' obedience on the cross, an obedience that is not simply submission, but a kind of agency that works with "the grain of the universe" to make a way through the endless cycle of retribution, not through acquiescence, but through perfect forgiveness. Through the outpouring, the sacrifice of divine love in the face of death, God conquers it, and reveals the supposed power of those who sentence him to death—those trapped within a sacrificial order—to be naught.

In all of this, Jesus Christ is the "true human"—he alone, after the fall, remains as human beings were created to be, destined for immortal happiness. He alone does not need to die, but he elects to; he alone lives a life of perfect and abundant sacrifice to the Father. By this, I mean that he alone lives a life of love directed toward God, and he alone is able to love from a boundless reserve that does not succumb to resentment or manipulation. In all this, he does not depart from essential human nature but, rather, typifies it truly. In the cross, Christ shows his full humanity as the one who is both the image and likeness of God, who was able to do what Adam did not, that is, elect obedience over mastery, self-emptying over self-assertion, sheer gratuity over the calculations of cost. David Bentley Hart puts it this way:

> God simply continues to love freely, inexhaustibly, regardless of rejection. God gives and forgives; he fore-gives and gives again. There is no calculable economy in this Trinitarian discourse of love, to which creation is graciously admitted. There is only the gift and the restoration of the gift, the motion of a giving which is infinite, which comprehends every sacrifice made according to love, and which overcomes every sacrifice made for the sake of power.[28]

There is sacrifice in the divine life, but it is not the sacrifice of exchange or retribution; rather, it is one of abundant, generous, and inexhaustible love, which undermines all the sacrificial systems of this world. God's work upon the cross is not a perpetuation of the world's sacrificial system but the judgment of it, a judgment of the scores of crosses that lined the perimeters of Roman cities, a judgment of a sacrificial system that would attempt to create order and stability through the expulsion of the city's accursed ones.

It is not we who are judged by God upon the cross, except indirectly. It is God's mercy and God's love that is judged by us humans, and found to be a scandal and an offense, "scorned by others and despised by the people," and so it is crucified. And even in our revulsion toward him God does not break faith with us, but makes a way. This is the exchange that is made. It is the exchange that substitutes our rebellion, our disobedience, and our scorn for abounding love and mercy. The cross is the summary of human rebellion, hatred, and scorn, and even here God does not turn away in anger, but forgives.

Christ restores the likeness of God in humans by becoming fully human himself even to the point of abjection. In his taking on human flesh, he is condemned to bear the wrath, not of God, but of humanity's unrelenting cruelty. In the scourging, whipping, and stripping of this Jewish messiah, there is unfolded the entire story of violence in which Israel was caught up, and yet God keeps Israel as the apple of God's eye in the distilled and particular grace that was Christ.

The cross, therefore, represents the judgment of God not *directly* but *indirectly*: God "gives us up" (Rom. 1:24, 26, 28) to the consequences of our destructive desires and actions, which is the effect of freedom. It is this condition that Christ takes on in this life, and becomes the very victim of human freedom gone awry as we (with Judas) give him up. And still he knows no sin, only grace and mercy, which is perfect freedom, a humanity restored in its original nature. This original nature is a return to God, a union with the Father, that Christ calls us to participate in. More than simply calling, his invitation is always already present. Thus the reconciliation is not a moment in which Jesus overcomes the distance between God and humans, but a repetition of the motion of abundant gift. Such a view of the atonement is to blur the lines most forcefully between Christ as exemplar, victor, and substitute. What God has joined together, let no theologian rend asunder!

One is tempted to say that the doctrine of the hypostatic union ought to govern all that we say about the cross, for were we to separate out Christ's humanity from his divinity, we would in all likelihood have a theology that legitimates sacrificial violence. Were we to think simply of Christ's divinity to the exclusion of his humanity, it would be difficult to explain why or how he suffered for us, or why or how he suffered at all. The doctrine of recapitulation is doggedly hypostatic in its logic, for it speaks to a Savior who empties himself, taking the form of a slave, so that in that self-emptying humanity might be lifted toward God through the receptivity and the power that he displays.

To view the cross through the entire drama of Christ's life—a recapitulation of the human story—resists regarding the cross as merely an absence in the drama of salvation, as Weaver might have it. The cross itself becomes, through Jesus' sacrifice, a sign that subverts itself from within. Here, in the ultimate symbol of Roman power, the cross becomes in Jesus' death, and in Jesus' death only, the witness to God's unending love and power even in death, even in the furthest reaches of human agony. This is manifest in the capacity of Jesus to ask forgiveness for his assailants, to institute (Luke 23:34; Acts 7:60) and to pronounce salvation for the criminal crucified next to him (Luke 23:43). In short, this is not simply victimhood, but an efficacy of another kind. It is the very form of divine power that will not be touched by sacrificial violence.

CONCLUSION: GOD'S POWER IN SUFFERING

Therefore, to confess Christ as Savior in a violent world is to proclaim a victory in which the great and glorious kingdom that is expected and announced in the coming of the Messiah is unfolded in the unlikely mustard seed of Christ's death upon the cross. This is not a wallowing in sacrificial violence. It is, instead, the declaration of the end of sacrifice through the public and profound statement on the very form of God's power in its identification with human suffering and death that even these—especially these—may be taken up and redeemed in the triune God.

6

"TO JUDGE THE QUICK AND THE DEAD"

CHRIST AND THE REDEMPTION OF MEMORY

BIBLICAL FAITH UNDERMINES ORDINARY ASSUMPTIONS about time—about the sequential and cumulative character of past, present, and future. For Christians, as for Jews, the past must not be overcome; it must be in some sense *lived*. Within the last century, we have learned of the abiding significance of the past from Jewish thinkers who seek to live faithfully the memory of those killed in the Shoah. Writers such as Emil Fackenheim[1] and Elie Wiesel[2] sought to keep faith with those killed by not permitting the world to forget. Likewise, Christian theologians have sought to heed the call to remember, keeping ever mindful of the atrocities that humans have committed within the past century and the church's complicity within them.[3] Any theology that fails to remember the failure of humanity, and particularly of the churches, in the wake of massive human suffering is to be regarded as woefully irresponsible. Miroslav Volf challenges several of these commonplaces in his 2006 book *The End of Memory: Remembering Rightly in a Violent World.* Here Volf argues forcefully that we are enjoined, not to remembering, but to remembering *rightly*. According to Volf, remembering can often perpetuate rather than put an end to violence. Hence, in the most controversial argument of this book, Volf asserts that at times remembering rightly includes *forgetting* violence and suffering. In this chapter, I will engage Volf as my main conversation partner, but my own argument will be informed by drawing on another theologian of memory, Augustine of Hippo. Through Augustine, I hope to make a case for the significance of memory not only in responding to past evils, but also in understanding more fully the relation of memory to redemption in Christ.

Whereas the prophets of memory such as Elie Wiesel argue that "salvation, like redemption, can be found only in memory,"[4] Volf would issue a cautionary note. Volf asserts that memory in itself is not a form of salvation; after all,

all political and social goals seek to justify themselves in a particular kind of remembering. Therefore, the injunction to remember is vapid at best and lethal at worst, as our memories can be self-serving, ideological, or even vengeful. As Volf puts it:

> As victims seek to protect themselves they are not immune to becoming perpetrators. . . . The memory of their own persecution makes them see dangers lurking even where there are none; it leads them to exaggerate dangers that do exist and overreact with excessive violence or inappropriate preventative measures so as to ensure their own safety. Victims will often *become* perpetrators precisely *on account of* their own memories. It is because they remember past violence that they feel justified in committing present violence.[5]

Memory of past wrongs can inure victims to their own complicity and responsibility; further, it can goad them to violence in order to ensure that they will not be victims again. Christians enjoined to forgiveness are therefore to be cautious with memory; memory must give way to a higher end, which is not righteous anger or exclusion, but enemy love or embrace. This moral injunction is no mere platitude for Volf—he knows full well the difficulty of practicing costly forgiveness. Woven throughout *The End of Memory* are his own efforts to remember his past rightly, a past that involves real enemies—in particular Captain G., a military officer who subjected Volf to intense and constant scrutiny and interrogation during his mandatory year of military service within Yugoslavia's then-Communist army. Writes Volf: "What would it mean for me to remember Captain G. and his wrongdoing in the way I prayed to God to remember me and my wrongdoing? How should the one who *loves* remember the wrongdoer and the wrongdoing?"[6] Thus the end of memory is to so remember the wrongdoer that love for him is not impeded or restrained. Justice must always be predicated by its higher end, which is enemy love.

According to Volf, the command to love enemies requires an abbreviation of our exercise of memory because such memory thwarts reconciliation. In the concluding section of the book, Volf argues that we should, under certain conditions, aim to *let go* of our memories of wrong suffered because such letting go is the appropriate response to the very giftedness of the world God has created. Letting go is a thankful acknowledgment of God's "creation of the world of love."[7]

Love, the power at creation's center, seeks out the healing of perpetrator and victim alike, both of whom are trapped inside the cyclical and violent demands of setting accounts right. Thus remembering not only impedes the victim's ability to love the enemy, but also threatens to diminish her identity, offering her only a limited view of herself and her biography. Contrary to popular psychology, healing from past trauma ideally involves forgetting, or nonremembrance of past wrongs. This nonremembrance is not erasure, but a lack of presence of memory, as memories "fail to surface"[8] persistently in the consciousness of the wounded. As Volf writes: "Only non-remembering can end the lament over suffering which no thought can think away and no action can undo."[9]

This is not to say that Volf believes that forgetting can be achieved solely by an act of will. Forgetting in itself is not an ideal to be pursued as an independent project or therapy on the part of the victim, much less ought it to be a prescription offered to those who have suffered.[10] Instead, what Volf prefers to call the "not coming to mind" of past wrongs is an eschatological promise, the consequence of our restored relations in Jesus Christ, and can only be fully realized in the world to come. In the world to come, the victim and the perpetrator (imprecise as those words often are) will be reconciled to one another before nonremembrance is enacted. In the present world, such reconciliation can only be anticipated, for justice demands exposure of past sins. Hence, forgetting can only be gestured toward, but in that gesturing, there exists the real hope for memory's "own superfluity."[11] Thus the hope of the world to come, a hope in which the not coming to mind is the final moment in the reconciliation of enemies, can only be undertaken "partially and provisionally."[12] Yet, positively, this deferred hope also offers a great deal to those currently suffering from the wound of memory. For one, belief in erasure of past wrongs in the world to come prohibits any efforts to explain away suffering of the past or to attempt to uncover its meaning. For Volf, past suffering, especially memory of violence, will not be revealed as God's will, but will be set right in the world to come in God's judgment of perpetrators, honoring and healing of victims, and release of memories of suffering. Memories of wrong will "wither away like plants without water," because our minds will be rapt in the goodness of God.[13]

Because we await this final reconciliation in the world to come, Christians need not be overly concerned with creating meaning from personal suffering. Memory of past wrongs will not be elucidated in the world to come, much less in this world, by a neat theodicy; rather, the meaning of our lives will be rendered secure through the interpolation of another story, by another memory, which offers meaning—that is, the memory of Christ's reconciling act of love. Thus to remember rightly is to remember our life stories as "displaced," as "living outside the self" and to God.[14] To remember rightly is to remember the triumph over evil that is offered in Christ's redemption of humankind. Drawing on Martin Luther's *The Freedom of a Christian*, Volf argues that redemption involves a "wonderful exchange" between the believer and Christ, the bride and the bridegroom. In this exchange, the groom gratuitously takes on all the sin and infirmity of the bride through his "wedding ring of faith."[15] Through this union, the sins of the bride, even the scourge of death and hell, are "swallowed up"[16] by Christ, and she comes to take on a new identity of "eternal righteous-ness, life, and salvation."[17] To Volf, such a promise is profoundly hopeful for those who have been trapped in their memories.

Thus meaning is not to be found in the suffering of humans, but in the specific suffering of Jesus Christ, who takes on our sins once and for all. Volf is thus careful to distinguish between the efficacy of Christ's sacrificial death and the sacrifice of victims. Only Christ's death has the power to free us from sin, and as such, Jesus' sacrifice, not that of others, is the means through which a new relationship between God and humans and among humans is attained. In this sacrifice, Christ sets us free from the power of sin and death, and, by exten-sion, the tyranny of past suffering. We are not justified by our memories, but by grace alone. It is grace that wipes away the suffering of the past to point us in the direction of a new future. Thus Volf asserts that "being in God frees our lives from the tyranny the unalterable past exercises with the iron fist of time's irreversibility."[18]

This orientation toward the future is true also of Christ's own suffering. Christ offers reconciliation in the Passion through the nonremembrance of his assailants' offenses and, through the power of the resurrection, inaugurates a new world freed from a past of sins and sorrow. The cross is thus viewed as "a stage on the road to resurrection and exaltation" and, as such, it is "a stage that can be left in the past even if its effects last for eternity."[19] Because enmity has been overcome at the cross, the cross can fade into oblivion.[20] The cross becomes superfluous because Christ does not need to bear our wounds perpetu-ally. As Volf challenges, "If Christ was not the Crucified One before creation, why would he have to be the 'Crucified One' after redemption has been com-pletely and unassailably secured in the world to come?"[21] The cross effects its own withdrawal from the world, and becomes redundant in its very efficacy.

Throughout his account, Volf presents a soteriology that is cast temporally in distinct and exclusive occasions. First suffering and enmity, then memory, then sin's defeat at the cross, then judgment, next reconciliation, next forget-ting. Moreover, these stages of salvation are also rather neatly divided between the historical (sin, memory, the cross) and the eschatological (judgment, heal-ing, reconciliation, and forgetting). Finally, there is a deep fissure between jus-tice (judgment) and love (healing, reconciliation, forgetting), with love always surpassing justice as the future goal of history and the character of the world to come. What is lost in such a construal of time is the manner in which the kingdom of God is inflected throughout the grammar of historical time and memory. This is to say that the reign of Christ is not simply a past event or a future hope, but a present reality, although only partially available to us. What is also lost is the manner in which love and justice are inexorably linked in both this world and in the world to come; they are bound together on earth as in heaven. As Augustine shows, God's abiding presence is to be known, not in a flight from memory or time, but in memory's recapitulation in Christ, through memory's just ordering. A return to Augustine on memory, I believe, offers a way forward for the very important problems that Volf presents.

AUGUSTINE AND THE GIFT OF MEMORY

In his *Confessions*, Augustine writes a narrative that also places memory at the center of his theological reflection. It is *theological* reflection because, as Augustine shows, one's life, even one's life as it is caught up in sin, reflects the story of God's love and mercy. Even through the messy and recalcitrant matter that is our lives, God is at work. Thus "confession" takes on a double meaning: it is at once the "true confessions"—a penitent account of Augustine's life of waywardness and homecoming—while it is also confession of the Christian, in the recounting of the story of salvation in Jesus Christ.

Augustine regards memory as recollection of a kind in which the self is present to itself through reflection as though upon an object. To come into the mind's presence, for Augustine, is to possess an awareness of the self not in the past, but in the present. Thus Augustine celebrates the power of memory,[22] even at its natural, material level, such as the sensible images carried in the mind, a faculty that even the beasts share with humans. Memory also has the capacity to grasp and retain objects of knowledge.[23] Further, human memory is able to contemplate the abstract, such as emotions that were once suffered, but which are now recollected in tranquility. Finally, memory retains vestiges of joy, as it endlessly seeks out the soul's happiness. It is here that the power of human memory or the human mind falls short, for while it seeks out joy, it cannot attain it, and without the grace of God, the soul is likely to fall into error as it seeks out those things that are finite as the objects of its love.

In spite of its fallen nature, memory is a gift from God through and through. It is both a source of wisdom, while it also offers the soul an awareness of its own finitude. Like the knowledge derived from the philosophers, memory can only lead Augustine to an awareness of the finitude of the mind, but this awareness also is the occasion for the recognition that there exists beyond the mind that which is infinite. Augustine realizes this in contemplating forgetting. The phenomenon of forgetting actually displays the power of memory, for forgetting is not the absence of memory but its faultiness, for we are not by nature compelled to forget, but to remember, as evidenced by the nagging persistence with which the mind seeks out that which it has forgotten. Such seeking for something that is lost is a purposive activity of memory, and it is an activity that is especially significant in humans as they seek joy. Memory of joy is retained in the mind, even among those who have not experienced joy. And yet joy is not fully known in the mind, nor in the human grasping to attain those images; such joy is only known as it is received. Such joy is only received in the eternal and excessive gift that is grace. However great the power of human memory, it alone is insufficient to contemplate eternal things for which it yearns, for God transcends not only what is to be known but also the mind itself.

Thus Augustine concludes that while God dwells in the memory, God also exceeds the memory. God is "Lord God of the mind"[24] and seeks out the pilgrim even within memory, and thus works on the mind/memory to transform one's desires into God's own. Here we have the first and most fundamental difference between Volf and Augustine. For Augustine, memory, although fallen and often given over to partial ends, is not to be subordinated or overcome, for it is the home of God's very self-communication. This is so because the minds of humans have been healed in the incarnation, as Jesus the Physician[25] reconciles us to God even in our wounded knowledge. Thus our memory is a place of tremendous possibility, for it is in the memory that God draws near and takes up our memory into God's own telling. Like the thief crucified next to Jesus, we are remembered as we remember God (Luke 23:42). We remember rightly, according to Augustine, through God's self-communication in the Son who redeems and restores memory, as he redeems and restores time. God's redemption of the world does not impose a kind of Docetic eternity but, as the *Confessions* amply displays, works through the reconciliation of fallen time, and hence of fallen memory.

Similarly, in his treatment of memory in *On the Trinity*, Augustine understands the mind's working as an analogy, a vestige of God's very being, impressed upon the mind, and accommodated to human capacities as memory, understanding, and will. These three faculties, like the Trinity, work together in complementary ways, drawing upon each one simultaneously.

Thus the linear relationship of God's salvation—of the distinct moments of past, present, and future—is disrupted profoundly in memory. Remembering is not simply the remembering of past events in one's own biography; it is properly the present awareness of the self's home, which is found in a God who is, as Augustine describes, "not far from every one of us."[26] Remembering is also inexorably linked and contingent upon a future destination, as our narrative gains its meaning and purpose in the eternal purposes of God. As Rowan Williams writes: "What we do not and cannot know about our past, present, and future is given over to God, who will draw out of us cries and aspirations that more and more clearly give voice to what is hidden in us, knowing that all this elusive human agenda unrecognized within us is embraced in the incarnation and may be employed by Christ in his work."[27] There is a heuristic structure to memory. Augustine is no less concerned than Volf with remembering rightly but, for Augustine, right remembering will follow a very different pattern of redemption. The human narrative is not to be overcome or displaced for it is itself an outworking of the logic of grace, although that grace remains largely hidden. Thus all of the human being, all of our "elusive human agenda," is given over to God for God's eternal purposes.

Here we see a related difference between Volf's account of memory and that of Augustine: for Augustine, grace involves not merely the displacement of the self, but a *coming to the self*, which is now seen as the theatre of divine purposive activity. And yet, grace awakens not only the knowledge that the self has been addressed and arrested by God, but that this grace has always been at work upon one's personal narrative, even when one (here, Augustine) was unaware. Thus the story of the soul's redemption as set forth in the *Confessions* is, in fact, a parable of the redemption of the entire created order. It is a recollection of the fragmented and wayward creature and an invitation to her to participate in God's redemptive purposes. This divine remembering does not abjure suffering and sin, but works through these in its giving, forgiving, and fore-giving. As Augustine writes most beautifully:

> Late have I loved Thee, O Beauty so ancient and so new; late have I loved Thee! For behold Thou wert within me, and I outside and I sought Thee outside and in my unloveliness fell upon those lovely things that Thou has made. Thou wert with me and I was not with Thee. I was kept from Thee by those things, yet had they not been in Thee, they would not have been at all. Thou didst call and cry to me and break open my deafness: and Thou didst send forth Thy beams and shine upon me and chase away my blindness: Thou didst breath fragrance upon me, and I drew in my breath and do now pant for Thee: I tasted Thee, and now hunger and thirst for Thee: Thou didst touch me, and I have burned for Thy peace.

What role, then, does memory of sin and suffering have in the course of redemption? Is it the case that Augustine concurs, as Volf claims, that the forgetting of past sin is intrinsic to remembering rightly?[28] The memory of oneself as a sinner is essential to redemption, not only of the individual soul, but also of the properly ordered city, as the political virtue most to be desired in the earthly city is humility.[29] The *Confessions* is an account of the soul's proper ordering as Augustine comes to know and love Christ. Its subject is the recalcitrant and messy matter that is human life. And yet, Augustine's God has deigned to work through even our weak and frail natures, and restore these into God's goodness. Christ is not, as it were, frozen in time, but offers this grace and mercy preveniently, persistently, and repeatedly through the particular time and narrative in which we participate. Thus Augustine can write in the *Confessions* of

Christ's reconciliation at work even in the petty and banal boyhood theft of the pears:

> What fruit therefore had I (in my vileness) in those things of which I am now ashamed? Especially in that piece of thieving, in which I loved nothing except the thievery—though that in itself was no thing and I only the more wretched for it. Now—as I think back on the state of my mind then—I am altogether certain that I would not have done it alone. Perhaps then what I really loved was companionship of those with whom I did it. If so, can I still say that I loved nothing over and above the thievery? Surely I can; that companionship was nothing over and above, because it was nothing. What is the truth of it? *Who shall show me, unless He that illumines my heart and brings light into its dark places?*[30]

In this sense, the remembering of the past sins of Augustine and his companions is requisite to understanding his need for the grace of illumination. More than merely instrumental to illumination, the confession of sin for Augustine is simultaneous with the redemption of memory.

The soul's redemption takes place in the movement from confession to forgiveness through the mediating activity of Christ persistently upon the pilgrim. Such a mediating activity is not merely a stepping in of Christ on behalf of the disciples so much as it is a restoration of their wills through the power of the crucifixion and resurrection, as the disciples themselves participate in the economy of salvation—they die with Christ and rise again with him to a restoration of relations. In a wonderful exposition of the resurrection encounters between Jesus and his disciples, Rowan Williams notes that the salvation that is offered at Easter is not a whitewashing of the disciples' past sins; rather, it is a rectification of the past. Thus resurrection is fulfilled in the disciples' own participation in the risen Christ. As Williams reflects upon Peter's encounter with the risen Christ:

> Peter's fellowship with the Lord is not over, not ruined, it still exists, and is alive because Jesus invites him to explore it further. Here the past is returned within a lived relationship that is evidently moving and growing. To know that Jesus still invites is to know that he accepts, forgives, bears and absorbs the hurt done: to hear the invitation is to know oneself forgiven and *vice versa*.[31]

Divine forgiveness involves not merely an overcoming of past sin through the power of the cross, but a setting right of the past. It is a setting right of the past because, in God's time, the past, even past marred by sin, is not exhausted of possibility. This does not mean that the past can be revised through an historical sleight of hand, but it does mean that it can be corrected through its public renunciation, through its confession, and through its referral to a new trajectory of hope. There still exists, within God's purposes and time, the possibility of redemption of memory, not through its annulment, but through its *metanoia*. Confession provides the occasion for the soul to acknowledge its own need of God, precisely through the acknowledgment of past sins. Without such acknowledgment, the soul remains cut off from grace's future working upon it. While Volf would in no way wish to deny the importance of repentance, its capacity to restore past relations seems to be understated. That is to say, the soul's turning away from sin involves a changed relationship to the past, in which the past sin becomes in a sense open to new possibility. Thus the past can itself be visited upon by transfiguring grace and, as such, its memory ought never be squandered. John Milbank puts it well: ". . . it is not that forgiveness nihilistically pretends to obliterate past evidence, but rather that this past existence is itself preserved, developed and altered through re-narration. In this re-narration one comes to understand why oneself or others made errors, in terms of the delusions that arise through mistaking lesser goods for the greater . . ."[32]

So while memory is not squandered, it also does not remain stable in its redemption. Augustine therefore makes a stark distinction between memory and the affections that accompany it. He would disagree strongly with Volf's assertion that memory is authentic insofar as it is preserves its original "sensibilities."[33] As Volf argues, "Memories of suffering unaccompanied by corresponding feelings of pain inevitably involve forgetting."[34] For Augustine, the transfiguration of memory through charity involves not forgetting the sensibilities, but disciplining them through properly ordered desire. Contemplation of memory through love of Christ permits a transfiguration of memory from passion to continence. Christ's tutelage of memory, a tutelage that involves prayer and the mediation of the church, evokes charity, which dissolves not the memory, but transforms passions that accompany trauma, prominently anger, the desire for revenge, the sense of futility or hopelessness.

What then of memory of evil? As Volf rightly argues, evil is deprived of permanency—it will fade into oblivion. While evil has no final permanency, memory of loss, or the homelessness of the soul, remains characteristic of knowledge of God itself.[35] Understanding oneself as being visited upon and endowed with grace involves an awareness of the corruptible power of sin. Thus the human sojourner finds herself, by grace, capable of reading her own narrative as the story of God's purposive activity. Such a renarration of her story does not involve a blotting out of memory of personal transgression, or of transgressions against her, but, rather, an acute awareness of them. Further, this is not simply an awareness of Christ's redemption overcoming all the instances of sin and waywardness in one divine fiat; instead, for Augustine, such memory of one's own propensity to sin involves a steady and patient vigilance. This is not to say that Augustine envisages no restoration of the soul, but that restoration takes place over time, in the patient and durable practice of confession and supplicant prayer—practices of humility that give rise to the soul's and the city's proper ordering.

THE PROBLEMATIC NATURE OF FORGIVENESS

As we have seen, for Volf, the cross can fade away, even though its effects are eternal; for Augustine, on the other hand, the cross is to be remembered not as a surd—that is, not as an interruption of the story of salvation—but the extension of the divine gift even at the farthest reach of human agony and desolation. This gift is not only given on the cross; it is a renarration of an original gift—given in the foundations of the world, in the outpouring of the Father's love for the Son and the Son for the Father. And yet, this gift is in no way withheld or denied upon the cross. The cross provides a crack through which the light shines amidst the darkness and death. It offers, in the midst of violence, neither retaliation nor resignation, but perfect humility, which is perfect forgiveness, perfect peace. Through the outpouring of love, even in the midst of violence, Christ reveals the supposed power of those who sentence him to death to be naught, as he reveals the hidden power of God at work. As Augustine writes:

> For He was not stripped of the flesh by obligation of any authority, but He stripped Himself. For doubtless He who was able not to die, if He would not, did die because He would; and so he made a show of the principalities and powers, openly triumphing over them and in Himself. For whereas by His death the one and most real sacrifice was offered up for us, whatever fault there was, whence principalities and powers held fast as of right to pay its penalty, He cleansed, abolished, extinguished; and by His own resurrection He also called us whom he predestinated to a new life, and whom He called, them He justified, and whom He justified, them He glorified. And so that devil, in that very death of the flesh, lost man . . .[36]

While Christ breaks the hold of the powers and principalities, at the same moment he calls us to a new life; he restores us. Whereas in Volf we see Christ's triumph over past sins that held us in bondage, we see in Augustine not only the loosening of bonds, but also the glorification of those set free by the power of the divine and eternal gift from one "not able to die" who nevertheless "did die because he would."

Like Volf, Augustine considers forgiveness a divine gift that is rendered possible through the cross of Jesus Christ. However, the divine gift that Augustine emphasizes is also one in which we are called personally and collectively to participate. Whereas for Volf we are set free from the forces of enmity by the cross, which makes way for a new future beyond retribution, for Augustine the future is inextricably bound to the past, a past that requires the setting right of past sins through justice before its bonds are loosened, before liberation can occur. Christ provides not the substitute for humanity in his forgiveness and reconciliation upon the cross; rather, he becomes the prototype of the human possibility of forgiveness and reconcilation.

Forgiveness is not merely an acquiescence in spite of the wrong committed; it is not a truce; instead, forgiveness is a gift given in excess; it is exceeding the measure of justice by allowing the perpetrator to be released from the bondage of the debt that she owes. Just so, because forgiveness requires the personal resourcefulness, capacity, and grace of one who has been wronged, it cannot be demanded, coerced, or legislated.

A critical voice sounding warning about the human capacity to forgive is that of Jacques Derrida. Derrida find an *aporia* intrinsic to forgiveness: it be vicariously offered by states or citizens on behalf of history's victims, and it cannot compensate for violence of any magnitude.[37] By rational standards many acts are "unforgiveable." According to Derrida, "genuine forgiveness must engage two singularities: the guilty and the victim. As soon as a third party intervenes, one can again speak of amnesty, reconciliation, reparation, etc., but certainly not of forgiveness in the strict sense."[38] Genuine forgiveness, according to Derrida, can only occur when there is a face-to-face encounter between guilty and forgiven. Anything short of this encounter is a partial form of reconciliation, or amnesty perhaps, and where legal and religious power oversee the process the two singularities become, at best, secondary agents in the process of reconciliation. Far too often this will let the perpetrator off the hook instead of being confronted directly by the victim, and thwarts the possibility of the victim receiving any form of direct justice from the perpetrator.

Forgiveness as a concept also contains within itself, according to Derrida, the question of limits. One can easily forgive the minor offense, but it is the major violations—particularly the collective atrocities that the past century has witnessed[39]—that expose the very problematic nature of forgiveness. Thus forgiveness contains within it two poles: the "irrational" granting of a perpetrator release from her obligation without restriction—including from unforgiveable acts—and the partial sense in which forgiveness is worked out juridically and conditionally:

It is important to analyse at its base the tension at the heart of a heritage between, on the one side, the idea which is also a demand for the unconditioned, gracious, infinite, aneconomic forgiveness granted to the guilty as guilty, without counterpart, even to those who do not repent or ask for forgiveness, and on the other side, as a great number of texts testify through many semantic refinements and difficulties, a conditional forgiveness proportionate to the recognition of the fault, to repentance, to the transformation of the sinner who then explicitly asks for forgiveness.[40]

To say that it is impossible to forgive is not to say that it should not be valued or esteemed. It is to say, rather, that pure forgiveness is impossible, just as a pure gift is impossible for Derrida, because it will always degenerate into the habit of exchange, of expectation of return. Partial forgiveness is always of a qualitatively different order from the ideal that haunts it: it is a half-measure of forgiveness, performed vicariously, or manipulated as compromise, or it engenders in the giver a *ressentiment* and is always given over to the possibility of betrayal or continued violence:

Forgiveness then becomes a relation of power, the establishment of sovereignty of self over another or over itself: "If I am conscious that I forgive, then I not only recognize myself but I thank myself, or I am waiting for the other to thank me, which is already the inscription of forgiveness into an economy of exchange and hence the annihilation of forgiveness."[41]

In a fundamental way, Derrida names the problematics that inhere in Volf's account of forgiveness. For Volf, Derrida's argument is affirmed by the central role of forgetting in his account. Forgiveness, for Volf, cannot restore the dead or make right the past, so the best that it can do is to provide a truce with it. This partial forgiveness requires forgetting the full extent of the fault, or presumes to expiate it in a manner adequate to the memory of the pardoner, rather than to the transgression itself—a pardoner who may well be a third party. In both cases, there is an annulment of memory for the greater good of reconciliation and justice.

THE ECONOMY OF FORGIVENESS

Augustine has neither the naïveté of Volf in the efficacy of forgetting nor the pessimism of Derrida, for whom forgiveness always involves a kind of violence, particularly a violence to memory. For Augustine, judgment of the past and its perpetrators is a fraught thing: one cannot say with full confidence that one has forgiven or been forgiven with finality in this life. Augustine's notion of judgment is profoundly eschatological; forgiveness is partial for Augustine, as it is for Derrida, but it is also anticipatory of its perfection. For Augustine, both forgiving and remembering the past are possible, and indeed are necessary, in the seeking of justice. Although on this side of the eschaton forgiveness often falls short of the direct aneconomic ideal that is necessary for the forgiveness of sin, he nevertheless believes that precisely such excessive forgiveness can be won on earth as in heaven. This is because Augustine changes the subject of forgiveness substantially. First, as we have amply seen, Augustine does not have a dualistic anthropology in which perpetrator and victim are easily parsed out. He concedes that all individuals, like the social body, are a *corpus mixtum*, fragmented and given over to sinfulness. Therefore, forgiveness as a human possibility is conditional upon one's own recognition of the self as wayward and in need of healing. This is not to level sin, or to blur the lines between perpetrator and victim, but it is to recognize the offended as one who is also in need of forgiveness. We can forgive only because we have been forgiven. Here is an economy, yes, but it is an economy in which gift exchange is not merely between two finite parties. We can see something of this trajectory in Augustine's pastoral exhortation: as pastoral advice, Augustine enjoins the hearers of his sermons to be mindful of the grace that they have received so that they might forgive: "So there is hope in God's mercy, if our misery is not so barren as to yield no work of mercy. What do you want from the Lord? Mercy. Give, and it shall be given to you. What do you want from the Lord? Pardon. Forgive and you will be forgiven."[42]

So while Augustine problematizes the notions of pardoner and pardoned by pointing out that we all stand in need of God's mercy and pardon, so, too, does he problematize the concept of agency. In Augustine, being forgiven and the act of forgiving are, in an important sense, impossible acts, just as Derrida describes them. But Augustine does not believe that we are alone in our acting. Christ, who is mediator and physician, overcomes the injury between persons; as one who is both human and divine, he offers the gift of an impossible and abundant grace, an unconditional forgiveness from above. Yet he also offers forgiveness as a human betrayed and handed over to torture and to death.

Forgiveness therefore becomes possible for persons (although it cannot be not demanded) precisely because the forgiver is a sinner, too, and has received the loving forgiveness first from God as pure, unmerited gift. Such is a gift that keeps on giving because it is a gift that cannot be put to death. Forgiveness involves remembering sin, not so as to create a cycle of retribution, but so as to work upon sin's eradication. Divine forgiveness is a gift that is given in excess. It is also a gift that does not seek to domesticate evil either by explaining it away or by letting go of its memory, but it is a gift that looks at the evil of those who have sentenced him to die, and proclaims still, "Father, forgive them, for they know not what they do" (Luke 23:34). It is a gift that remembers an entire history of human recalcitrance and malice and yet pronounces blessing.

Forgiveness among humans is not so much willed as it is received. It is a gift that is made possible through memory of the working of God's grace upon the one who is forgiving. The bestowal of forgiveness by the forgiver is thus an active memory, one that remembers one's own past sins, that attends truthfully to perpetrator's wrongs, and that beseeches God's active restoration of the past. It is for this reason that Augustine refers to Christ as Mediator. Not simply because Christ overcomes a gulf between God and humans, but because he conjoins the human and divine, and therefore presents the appropriate posture of human relations, which points us to neighbor love in excess. Because Christ has interceded by assuming and overcoming human frailty, we are bound to surpass the measure of distributive justice. Thus, while the past cannot be simply revised, it can be renarrated through the participation of memory in the divine gift. Such a gift does not eradicate a past of suffering, but it mediates it, and thus it mitigates its hold and thwarts its replication.

This is true, for Augustine, even when the victims are no longer present. Unlike Derrida, Augustine believes that the past exerts a force that demands conversion still. There is still, for Augustine, the possibility of unfinished business even when the parties can no longer be brought together. One cannot simply, therefore, forget or concede a priori that there can be no reconciliation with the past once the victims are dead. The forgetting of history's victims has a palpable presence, according to Augustine. It is not merely a privation or lack or absence. This is because, even in our confused and bewildered minds, according to Augustine, there remain traces (*vestigia*) of the Triune God that invite us to participate in God. In participating in the divine mind, through contemplation and prayer, we learn that the memories that are partial in us are somehow retained in a mind, in a Logos, that transcends ours. This retention has everything to do with the fact that the Triune God in whose image we have been made knows no lack, no absence, and therefore no forgetting. Such a perfect Trinity does not merely stand in opposition to our partial and faulty knowledge, but it draws us toward it so that our minds might be transformed as we participate in God. There are thus, according to Augustine, always traces, vestigial remainders that require our attention. These cannot be brought into the present by willful recollection alone; memory of things past, and our reconciliation with it, must again be received. And its reception is not merely a deliberate noetic return, but is facilitated and occasioned in embodied practices.

MEMORY AND CHARITY

In the *Confessions*, Augustine draws our attention to the manner in which the faculty of memory is a complex and "awe-inspiring mystery."[43] Even as he attempts to parse out its many features, he recognizes his limitations in comprehending it. In seeking that which is forgotten, the mind is indeed remembering, according to Augustine, and that memory is evidence of the existence of the thing in the past. This seeking is related to desire. In the longing for the lost thing, including happiness or joy, we seek to recover it, to return to it. Therefore, desire for happiness is not seeking novelty, but something that was known once to us, something to which we long to return. The sheer universality of the desire for happiness, even among the afflicted whom have never experienced it, is a sign that happiness is something that we know even in our natures.

The problem of memory is not merely a problem of the self; it is also a problem of history and cosmology. Central to Augustine's analysis is his Christology. Because the infinite word of God becomes flesh and dwells in time, therefore time, flesh, history, and memory are redeemed. Not only in Christ's coming, but in all human flesh, time, and history, because we have, by the power of the Holy Spirit, become united with him. Such a healing of history, such a healing of time and of memory requires our response—that is, to respond in time to the eternal gift of God. John Milbank puts it this way:

> Augustine seems to insist on *remaining* in time to get to God. *Intention* and *distention* appear to be resolved *christologically*. One only intends God via Christ, thus if the answer to what is time is 'self', then the answer to 'what is self' is not simply dispersal *or* inattention, but, rather, the receiving back of our true self from Christ via the church. Hence, Christ has restored the process of time; Christ *is* time, and in receiving Christ . . . we discover that we are to 'comprehend' time as the mystery of the possibility of charity, of giving and co-inherence. Hence, the only graspable meaning of time is an ethical one; time is the time of *cura* (care) . . . [44]

The restoration of our soul in Christ that we participate in (albeit partially) through memory gives rise not merely to increased capacities but, rather, to increased attentiveness to memory and to the singularities of history that demand our attention. Such attentiveness is not a mere calling to mind, but bids us to a return of the gift that we have received in God: it bids us to charity. We are prompted by love to be united with love. The mind, ignited by desire, seeks to know God, yet that mind does not merely rest in knowledge, but inflects the will with its light, as the human knower seeks to make what is known manifest in the world.

MEMORY AND EUCHARIST

In the sacraments, Christ becomes tangible and present through the memorial reenactment of his last supper with the disciples, a memorial in which past, present, and future intersect. And through the participation in the sacraments, in the identification of believers with the body of Christ, believers are promised transformation. This transformation occurs through the rousing of the pilgrim in the beauty of the liturgy, in the partaking of the sacraments, and in the participation in the communal meal.

Thus the liturgy stirs our desire so that we come to will the very virtue that it embodies. As Michael Hanby points out, Augustine "conflates *voluntas* with the *dilectio* that binds us to the objects of our delight."[45] It is not that we choose to pursue what we desire so much as our desire for a particular object forms our will. Even this description is too causal for what Augustine has in mind: for him, desiring is also willing: "being at once moved by the objects of our delight and the principle by which we move ourselves." Thus prayer and the sacraments are essential for the cultivation of properly ordered desire and hence virtue. As Augustine writes:

> When I first came to know you, you raised me up to make me see that what I saw is Being. And you gave a shock to the weakness of my sight by the strong radiance of your rays, and I trembled in love and awe. And I found myself far from you 'in the region of dissimilarity', and heard as it were your voice from on high: 'I am the food of the fully grown; grow and you will feed on me. And you will not change me into you like the food your flesh eats, but you will change into me.'[46]

In coming to remember and to remember God, Augustine finds himself increasingly drawn toward God, and in that drawing forth comes to participate more and more fully in God. Through this transfiguration, his mind and his will, in remembering the truth of God and of his own being, are given the gifts of continence. No longer is his will at war with itself. As remembering, understanding, and willing are drawn toward God, they receive their proper ordering. This proper ordering is also enacted on a collective scale in the church where the body of Christ is built up in the nonsacrificial economy of the Eucharist: "This is the sacrifice of Christians, who are 'many, making up one body in Christ'. This is the sacrifice which the Church continually celebrates in the sacrament of the altar, a sacrament well-known to the faithful where it is shown to the Church that she herself is offered in the offering which she presents to God."[47] Because we remember and participate in the Eucharist in a giving and receiving that knows no measure, members of the body of Christ become trained in the virtues of self-donation for others. We come, in the Eucharist, to love the neighbor: to experience her not as mimetic rival, but as an irreducible part of the body of Christ. To learn to love this member is also to learn to allow our wills to be shaped by the needs of the person before us. This process of self-donation begins with the active remembering and desiring of one who comes "in the form of a slave" (Phil. 2:7).

The life of the world to come is a social life for Augustine. It is a life in which the body is ordered harmoniously so that each distinct voice is heard, and no voice is sacrificed or drowned out. This body is not the same as the church. The church, as the empire, is yet the comingling of two cities, of Rome and Jerusalem. It is not until the end times that the wheat will be separated from the chaff. True, Augustine somewhat notoriously held to the belief in a consummate justice that included the relegation of the damned to eternal perdition, and yet his belief in the open-ended nature of history caused him to shun any speculation on who might be damned or saved, nor was he willing to foreclose history in order to identify those movements that would be most agreeable to him. For him, such judgment is to be left to God alone.

Yet Augustine is willing to hazard to name, if not the citizens, then certainly the rewards that the citizens enjoy in heaven, and he identifies this with certain attributes that he has already developed in his account of the mind, which retains the image of God. That image is perfected in the heavenly city, and Augustine can only deduce from Scripture that the life of the world to come is one that is inherently social. Here social life is not a curse but beatitude, because here, our originally blessed state, a state in which our wills are not at enmity with God or neighbor, is so perfectly disciplined that its desires are the same as the desires of the neighbor. That desire is to love God. It is not that the memory, knowledge, and the will will be rendered obsolete, but that they will be perfected because they participate in the light of God. Thus memory, that faculty which keeps us mindful of the good, the true, and the beautiful, is not obliterated. Not even memory of sin is obliterated but, rather, the saints gaze upon the past world of sin with continence, remembering it as a far country, gladly traversed, a traversal for which they "now sing the mercies of the Lord for all eternity."[48] In this final sabbath there will be thanksgiving for sin and suffering overcome, for release that has been enjoyed, and for the restoration of the world from the grips of death and enmity: "There we shall be still and see; we shall see and we shall love; we shall love and we shall praise. Behold what will be, in the end without end! For what is our end but to reach the kingdom which has no end?"[49]

Volf concludes *The End of Memory* with a reflection upon his own (successful) efforts at overcoming enmity. An Augustinian analysis would support Volf's premises that Captain G.'s petty taunts and intimidations are not permanently replicated because they themselves constitute nothing—they only signal repetitive, banal, and noncreative acts, and thus cannot but dissolve into oblivion. And yet the memory of this suffering can become the occasion (although not the cause) of God's creative purposes. The work that is *The End of Memory* itself is a testimony to this possibility. The objectification of violent acts in memory, when recollected through the mediating power of Christ, becomes an occasion for lament over a world that longs for God's justice and mercy; it can also, by grace, become transfigured from lament to charity. For Augustine, the work of justice does not involve remembering past sins primarily for the distribution of reward and punishment but, instead, justice involves the visitation of Christ's grace even at the farthest reaches of personal agony. In the justice that God commands of the church, nothing in this life can fall outside that cannot be brought back to God to be healed. There is no caducity within the world that God created and redeemed.

THE ETERNAL AND THE MUNDANE

Christ appears to his beloved disciples not as a healed and perfect body, but as a body that bears still the marks of his crucifixion, although these are no longer bleeding wounds. The glorious resurrected Christ invites Thomas to probe those wounds, and Thomas finds in this physical memory of torture not something that is repugnant, but something that is worthy of adoration: "Thomas said to him: 'My Lord and My God'" (John 20:28). Just so, our memories of pain and suffering (even, we might say, the very suffering we have caused, for surely Jesus' wounds are also this) also carry with them the potential to become signs through which God's glory is revealed. To change the idiom somewhat, consider Catherine Pickstock's wonderful reflections on Augustine's musical aesthetic:

> This redemptive process most of all fulfills Augustine's contention that nothing falls outside the harmony of the cosmic poem. Hence his Christian account of music introduces the new aesthetic idea that every apparent discord can, in the course of musical time, be granted its concordant place. Indeed, for Augustine, in a fallen world, true harmony can resound via this passage only through discordant noise which nonetheless ceases to be mere noise.[50]

Augustine's vision of a consummate harmony is not a totalizing one. Discordant voices are not sacrificed for the sake of creating perfect music. Likewise, memory of suffering is not erased for the sake of the whole. Here is a profoundly different kind of ordering from that of contemporary politics. Here is a profoundly different justice. Justice is not to be won through the distribution of time-specific punishment and amnesty, but in the preservation of even the discordant and the afflicted. Indeed, the notes of discord and of suffering are utterly essential to this music. Nothing can be squandered in this justice. It must all be referred to God, who is "all in all." (1 Cor. 15:28). For Augustine, time and eternity are not opposites, but earthly time is folded into eternity. From the vantage of earthly time, eternity is hidden, but not remote. There remain signs of the eternal punctuated throughout the mundane. The task of confession is to seek out these signs, even within the fragmented narrative of the self. In such self-recollection, in spite of the dangers that inhere in writing one's own story, the confessor is to find God at work, restoring the soul, working upon it, as the soul seeks to work upon itself. This promise of self-understanding comes only through the practice of confession, only through personal humility, and through the advertence of one's story to the Story of God's working in time as recounted in Scripture. Progress through time is not the enemy of attaining unity with God, but the very condition for it.[51]

Hence, the subjects of one's narrative—for the life of pilgrimage is always a social life—are irreducible and unsubstitutable agents within one's story, to the degree that the other, whose desires and actions confront, confound, and complement my own. This is to say that human beings, like God, cannot be reduced to an abstraction. They are always mysterious, even to themselves. As Augustine writes: "(and yet there is something in man that not even the spirit of man itself knows, which is [nevertheless] in him, but you, O Lord, you know all of him [man], for you made him)" (*Confessions* 10.5.7). The undisclosed and ineffable nature of the other does not necessarily produce a theory that is amenable to contemporary accounts of alterity such as that of Derrida, nor is the other included necessarily in the embrace that overcomes enmity as in Volf. The other remains mysterious to the human sojourner, at once a source of delight, while also one who might be spurned and/or abandoned because, as with Augustine's unnamed concubine, is nonconducive to his moral and spiritual progress. Here we have no final account of the significance of the other in relation to the self. In the flux of time, human relations, too, are partial, and we do not find our rest in others, in spite of our persistent longings. The stability of relations to Augustine, and the capacity of other humans to reveal the grace of God, is compromised in this life. Nevertheless, there are those within this life, and there are those moments within this life, whose singular nature penetrates even into our confounded hearts. Such is the vision that Augustine shares with Monica—notice how his mother is one of the few characters in his narrative that is named—in her last days in Ostia. It is there that Augustine and she receive a foretaste of the rest that is promised to the human sojourner on the seventh day. It is here that her identity is rendered more transparent to Augustine, as she takes her rest in God. The vehicle for such a vision is memory as they "entered into their own minds."[52] Monica's response to this vision is instructive for our purposes. Although she has no anxieties concerning death, and welcomes her repose, she nevertheless enjoins her son to "remember" her "at the altar of the Lord, wherever [he] may be."[53]

The vision of Ostia was a foretaste for Augustine and Monica of their true identities, still "hidden with Christ in God," which involved an overcoming of their longing for the things of the world. Yet such a longing does not include a rejection of the self. Rather, the restfulness obtained in God, a restfulness that reconciled Monica to the deterioration of her body to the ravages of time, did not connote an obliteration of her memory, but its remaining. It is a remaining in the remembering of her at the altar of the Lord. Such remembering transcended circumstance and even death. This is so because such remembering, in being offered to God, is gathered up by God and retained in a God who blesses earthly life and earthly love. At the conclusion of the *Confessions*, Augustine offers the final word, *Aperietur*, meaning, "It shall be opened." I take this to mean that, as for Monica and Augustine, the life that we now experience will be, in the end, opened to its fullness in such a way that our memories will not be finally lost, but will be conferred with its proper significance as it is gathered up in Christ.

CONCLUSION: MEMORY AND THE FUTURE

Perhaps the prophets of memory such as Elie Wiesel, Emil Fackenheim, and others—those for whom time has not erased the memories of their people's suffering—are not far from Augustine's remembering. Like them, he refuses to yield the memories of victims to any kind of future in which they are not present, in which they are not, in some sense, restored. While it is true that the keeping of memory can become a weapon in the world of fallen time, it is no less true that letting go can far too easily become a shield which obscures the future to which we are called, and to which their memories and their witness beckon. In the Talmud, it is written, "Attend to three things, and you will not come into the hands of transgression. Know what is above you: an eye sees, an ear hears, and all of your deeds are written in a book."[54] Augustine has shown us how this eye and ear are not only above, but also within, and that the book is not only a book of judgment, but also a book of life.

CONCLUSION
"INVENTORY THE HERITAGE"—
CHRISTOLOGY AND CRITIQUE

THE THRUST OF THE ARGUMENT that I have presented here in many different ways is that confession of Christ connotes a certain ontology which concerns the goodness of the world and its overwhelming orientation, in spite of the fall, toward peace. This view engenders a positive assessment of the political life, and it deems that political life is indeed essential to Christian witness. However, it is a certain kind of politics that is affirmed in each of the ancient writers we have explored. It is a politics that is not of this world; that is, it is a politics that is based upon the incursion of peace into the world in the coming of Jesus Christ in time and in flesh. Throughout this book, we have seen several affirmations of God's peace as uttered at the very foundation of the world, and uttered again with particular and abundant clarity in the coming of Christ, which will have profound implications for our life together. It is also toward this peace that the world, in spite of its many contradictions, is bound. This peace, given again and again by God, and uniquely and fully in God's becoming human in Christ, knows no limits. It is a fundamental and eternal yes that is spoken to the world through the word made flesh.

Such a view is a challenge to the dominant mode of theological inquiry that arises from the critical disciplines of nineteenth-century biblical and twentieth-century social criticism. According to those biblical critics, the chief concern of interpretation was to uncover the social and cultural needs of a community that animated a certain interpretation. Subsequent theological interpretations of texts were also highly influenced by ideology criticism that sought not merely to uncover the hidden needs and desires of a community, but also the ways in which those needs and desires were coercive. Thus critical interpreters became intent on uncovering the hidden agenda of a community or forces within it toward dominance and repression. A theology which begins with critique often takes for granted that the hidden desires of a community are bound to be oppressive and even violent. Religious language is a powerful force in propping up the power of oppressive forces within a community.

It is this affirmation that compels me to recommend not critique, but a form of receptivity, as the starting point of theology, and also compels me to challenge those forms of theology that begin with negation. To move toward a postcritical theology is not to abandon or deny critique, but it is to frame critique within a theology that begins with the presumption of and for the good. It is therefore a kind of receptivity that ought to characterize our engagement with religious texts, traditions, and communities. Jesus Christ displays such receptivity toward the Father, but also toward human sojourners as he is willing to engage this receptivity in all its messiness, in all its recalcitrance, but not to be determined by it. Through the power of the incarnation, we share in Christ's creative capacities, which do not blindly replicate the patterns of this world, but may, through grace, come to transform such powers in Christ.

By receptively dwelling within the Christian narrative, our minds and wills may be so moved that it becomes the central modality of our political engagement.[1] This is not to abandon critique, but it is to claim that the capaciousness which has been found within the religious narrative is sufficiently broad that it can also be a source of internal criticism, a criticism that has enormous possibilities for those committed to the church, but who nevertheless are wary of its internal incoherence and oppressive practices. Just as Jesus and the prophets were able to point out the internal contradictions within the religious ideologies of their communities and times, we may also appeal to a tradition that is broader than its preferred current manifestations to point out distortions to its witness. We have seen many examples of such prophetic work in the writings surveyed here: Athanasius's refutation of the Arians, McFague's challenge to a wooden literalism, Weaver's challenge to piety based upon sacrificial violence. Such work is key to the critical task as an internally generated endeavor that does not understand its role as merely negation. In some cases, however, I have argued that such internal critics of Christian theological doctrine did not go far enough in their assessment; that there are sources within the Christian tradition which are uniquely helpful in any reconstruction of theology. They are uniquely helpful because our foremothers and forefathers also wrestled with the same problems as they sought to make sense of the evangel within a broken world. True, Basil was not concerned explicitly with helping to save the earth from environmental ruin; Augustine did not share a feminist hermeneutic of suspicion about language. Yet both were concerned to write about the nature of the creative and eternal word being made flesh within fallen time and within a creation still groaning in anticipation of its delivery. To my mind, these concerns are deeply in keeping with the aspirations and longings of McFague, Cixous, Weaver, Smith, Ruether, and the other critical thinkers with whom I have conversed.

POSTCRITICAL, NOT UNCRITICAL

Critique is often most effective (and interesting) when it is internally generated, largely because it then arises from a reader who knows the texts well. They
know the texts not merely in the abstract and detached sense, but they know
the texts within the communities in which texts have been received. A posture
like that of ethnographer Saba Mahmood is compelling here: let's resist for a
moment our fear and anxieties over this group of pious Muslim women and let's
find within them and among them something of the moral and social force of
their position. Postcritical is not uncritical;[2] but the criticism arises from within
the desires and principles of the communities themselves rather than from an
extrinsic source. It will engage, therefore, religious texts and communities with
an aim to understand the meaning of religious language within the community's own frame of reference. Rather than bracketing out religious meaning,
postcritical theology will seek to understand a text or a religious community in
relation to its commitment to and trust in the living God, without whom the
text or community would make no sense. As Jewish scholar Peter Ochs puts it,
postcriticism "resituates criticism in its appropriately social and hermeneuti-
cal setting."[3] Thus the postcritical reader is not merely the solitary investigator
standing detached from the world of religious meaning; instead, she herself
stands within a community, within a tradition that seeks to makes sense of the
community.

Of course, none of this is new as a methodological vantage. The postmodern theologian has been telling us for a generation at least that there is no
neutral Archimedean point from which we might stand as judge over theology or the Bible. "Il n'y a pas d'hors-texte" ("there is no outside-the-text"),[4]
Jacques Derrida has reminded. Yet the deconstructive impulse within reading
from multiple sites within the text also has had the effect of rendering the text
unstable and unusable or at least secondary to the complex method that sought
to deconstruct it. A return to the "text"—whether that be the Bible or foundational theological writings—need not be a naïve return to their unquestioned
authority, but may take its cues from the complexities of the texts themselves,
realizing that their interglossing, self-critical, and often even dialectical natures
may be a lively source for engagement with the political concerns of our time.

This is not to say that this is the only manner in which theology or religious
studies might be undertaken. There is much knowledge also to be gained by the
critical disciplines in biblical studies and theology, but it is to aver that a postcritical form of inquiry from within a community and a tradition is a legitimate
one, and one that is particularly suited to theology at a time in which knowledge of the tradition seems ever more tenuous. It is also a way of knowing particularly suited to theology, for theology claims that the knowledge in which it

is invested is not merely personal knowledge or the knowledge of a community, but is a knowledge that is animated, infused, and directed by a God who wills, through the fragmented words of men and women in texts and in a tradition, that the word might be known.

This brings us to the second part of Ricoeur's injunction to us, quoted in the introduction to this book. We must not only pay the debt, we must also "inventory the heritage." To inventory something is to recognize it as one's property, but it is a property that is somewhat unfamiliar, because it is not fully or immediately within view. To inventory is to go over the heritage, to recapitulate it with specific headings, to examine and weigh, to appraise it and take stock of it. Implicitly, it is also to recognize something as an asset, especially when the extent or value of that asset is under dispute.

This book has suggested that "thinking Christ" through the insights of the Nicene teachers opens up possibilities for imagining the world as not only in dire need of salvation, but as a world in which such transfiguration is already taking place. This is so because God has come among us, conforming the divine self, but also transcending our actions and our capacities, and thereby restoring them in God. This realistic transfiguration of the human heritage makes the process of inventorying it an ongoing one: compelling us to treat ancient figures of the past as living sources whose values are not yet fully determined. It also urges us to engage our contemporary world with an understanding that the dilemmas that we face are neither insurmountable nor final, but that they, too, are addressed and transfigured by the word who comes among us and by a word that invites human initiative.

This book has also suggested that the process of inventorying a heritage is not a one-way effort. While we have considered some words of ancient and modern commentators alike, we should remember that we, too, are part of the heritage that is being inventoried. We may be right to fear that our contributions will be paltry in comparison, that the dross of our prejudices and preoccupations will obscure some hidden gold concealed by our own erring. But, ultimately, the inventory that is taken is not our own; it is judged by a mind that is infinitely more discerning and more compassionate. For it is in Christ's "thinking" us—the ambiguous and unwieldy stock that is the Christian heritage—that we are secured and brought toward our proper end.

NOTES

INTRODUCTION

1. See Francis Mading Deng, "Human Rights among the Dinka," in *Human Rights in Africa: Cross-Cultural Perspective*, ed. Francis Deng (Washington, D.C.: Brookings Institution Press, 1990), 269.

2. Elizabeth L. Eisentein, *The Printing Press as an Agent of Change* (Cambridge: Cambridge University Press, 1979), 295.

3. Batoche was the battle that suppressed the Métis and indigenous North-West Rebellion in western Canada in 1872. Three days after its conclusion, its leader, Louis Riel, surrendered and was hanged for treason later that year. I evoke it here as a symbol of Canada's dark colonial history.

4. Hannah Arendt compels us to be more judicious in our assessment of the past and our identification of its concrete perpetrators. Commenting on the collective guilt in post-War Germany that let war criminals off the hook, she wrote: ". . . where all are guilty, then no one is." Hannah Arendt, *Responsibility and Judgment* (New York: Random House, 2003), 28.

5. Paul Ricoeur, *Memory, History, Forgetting*, trans. Kathleen Blamey and David Pellauer (Chicago: University of Chicago Press, 2004), 89.

6. I have argued elsewhere—following George Lindbeck—for regulative principles as those soteriological affirmations that guide theology, particularly the reading of Scripture. In this book, I am particularly concerned with the christological principles of Christ's historical specificity and of his consubstantiality with the Father. See my *Lord, Giver of Life: Toward a Pnueumatological Complement to George Lindbeck's Theory of Doctrine* (Waterloo, Ont.: Wilfrid Laurier University Press, 2006), 4–8; and George Lindbeck, *The Nature of Doctrine: Religion and Theology in a Post-liberal Age* (Louisville, K.y.: Westminster John Knox, 1984).

7. Only Athanasius would qualify if this were the criterion. Athanasius was a participant at Nicaea in 325 CE. Basil of Caesarea died two years before the Council of Constantinople, although his teachings on the Holy Spirit were clearly influential to it. Augustine belonged to a generation after the "Cappadocians." In "reading" Augustine as a Nicene figure, I am indebted to Lewis Ayres's work, which offers a salutary rapprochement beyond the tired polemics between Eastern and Western patristic theology, which he demonstrates to be a modern construct. In his reading of Augustine as "pro-Nicene," he argues that Augustine's mature trinitarian theology is an exemplary instance of a working out of Nicene trinitarian grammar

of unity and distinction of the Godhead through the overarching trope of divine simplicity. See Lewis Ayres, *Nicaea and Its Legacy: An Approach to Fourth-Century Trinitarian Theology* (Oxford: Oxford University Press, 2004), esp. ch. 15, "The Grammar of Augustine's Trinitarian Theology," 364–81.

8. See J. N. D. Kelly, *Early Christian Creeds*, 3rd ed. (New York: Longman, 1972), chs. 1–8.

9. As Rowan Williams points out, the ascription of Arianism to a theological position was a movement that rendered theological opponents in the position of "other," both in ancient and in contemporary theological discourse. See introduction, "Images of a Heresy," in *Arius: History and Tradition* (London: SCM, 2001).

10. As Jaroslav Pelikan points out, the defenders of Nicene orthodoxy did not tire of noting incoherence of Arian worship (in glorifying the Son) with their confession of faith in him as created by the Father. Arguments based upon the common liturgical practice of the church were powerful means in this period of exposing theological inconsistency and point to a desire within theological debates of the time to reflect and uphold the common confession of the church—or the sensus fidelium. See Jaroslav Pelikan, *The Emergence of the Catholic Tradition* (100–600) (Chicago: University of Chicago Press, 1971), 238.

11. Charles Taylor, "What's Wrong with Negative Liberty?," in *Freedom: A Philosophical Anthology*, ed. Ian Carter, Matthew H. Kramer, and Hillel Steiner (Malden, Mass.: Blackwell, 2007), 154.

12. John David Dawson, "Figural Reading and the Fashioning of Christian Identity in Boyarin, Auerbach and Frei," *Modern Theology* 14, no. 2 (April 1998): 187–88.

13. David Bentley Hart, *The Beauty of the Infinite: The Aesthetics of Christian Truth* (Grand Rapids, Mich.: Eerdmans, 2003), 151.

14. Gregory Baum, "Critical Theology: Replies to Ray Morrow," in *Essays in Critical Theology* (Kansas City, Mo.: Sheed & Ward, 1994), 7.

15. David Bentley Hart offers a quite wonderful exposition of the posture of the Christian "reader" of culture. Judging by the writing of Mahmood, Cixous, Hardt, and Negri, it is not only Christians who negate "negating." "Christian thought expects to find in every cultural coding a fundamental violence . . . but, perhaps fantastically, it treats this pervasive violence, inscribed upon being's fabric, as a palimpsest, obscuring another text that is still written (all created being is 'written') but in the style of a letter declaring love." Hart, *The Beauty of the Infinite*, 55.

16. Baum, *Essays in Critical Theology*, 10.

17. The classic essay that raises this point is Joanne Carlson Brown and Rebecca Parker, "For God So Loved the World": "Divine child abuse is paraded as salvific and the child who suffers 'without even raising a voice' is lauded as the hope of the world. Those whose lives have been deeply shaped by the Christian tradition feel that self-sacrifice and obedience are not only virtues but the definition of a faithful

identity." In *Violence against Women and Children: A Christian Theological Sourcebook*, ed. Carol Adams and Marie Fortune (New York: Lexington, 1995), 37.

18. Ricoeur, *Memory, History, Forgetting*, 89.

CHAPTER 1

1. See, for example, Richard Horsley, ed., *Paul and Empire: Religion and Power in Roman Imperial Society* (Harrisburg: Trinity Press International, 1997); idem, *Jesus and Empire: The Kingdom of God and the New World Disorder* (Minneapolis: Fortress Press, 2003); Neil Elliott, *Liberating Paul: The Justice of God and the Politics of the Apostle* (Minneapolis: Fortress Press, 2006); idem, *The Arrogance of Nations: Reading Romans in the Shadow of Empire, Paul and Critical Contexts* (Minneapolis: Fortress Press, 2010); John Dominic Crossan, *God and Empire: Jesus against Rome, Then and Now* (New York: HarperCollins, 2008); and Joerg Rieger, *Christ and Empire: From Paul to Postcolonial Times* (Minneapolis: Fortress Press, 2007).

2. Edward W. Said, *Culture and Imperialism* (New York: Vintage, 1994), 10.

3. On postcolonial biblical interpretation, see, for example, Fernando F. Segovia, *Decolonizing Biblical Studies: A View from the Margins* (Maryknoll, N.Y.: Orbis, 2000); R. S. Sugirtharajah, *Asian Biblical Hermeneutics and Postcolonialism: Contesting the Interpretations* (Maryknoll, N.Y.: Orbis, 1998); idem, *The Bible and the Third World: Precolonial, Colonial, and Postcolonial Encounters* (Cambridge: Cambridge University Press, 2001); idem, *Postcolonial Criticism and Biblical Interpretation* (New York: Oxford University Press, 2002); idem, *Postcolonial Reconfigurations: An Alternative Way of Reading the Bible and Doing Theology* (St. Louis: Chalice, 2003). Also see collections from the Bible and Postcolonialism series: R. S. Sugirtharajah, ed., *The Postcolonial Bible* (Sheffield: Sheffield Academic Press, 1998), R. S. Sugirtharajah, ed., *Vernacular Hermeneutics* (Sheffield: Sheffield Academic Press, 1999); Fernando F. Segovia, ed., *Interpreting beyond Borders* (Sheffield: Sheffield Academic Press, 2000); Roland Boer, ed., *Last Stop before Antarctica: The Bible and Postcolonialism in Australia* (Sheffield: Sheffield Academic Press, 2001); Musa W. Dube and Jeffrey L. Staley, eds., *John and Postcolonialism: Travel, Space, and Power* (London: Continuum, 2002); and Stephen D. Moore and Fernando F. Segovia, eds., *Postcolonial Biblical Criticism: Interdisciplinary Intersections* (London: T & T Clark International, 2005). For the establishment of postcolonial theory, most refer to the work of Edward W. Said, *Orientalism*, rev. ed., with new preface and afterword (New York: Vintage, 1994); idem, *Culture and Imperialism*; Gayatri Chakravorty Spivak, *In Other Worlds: Essays in Cultural Politics* (New York: Routledge, 1988); idem, *The Postcolonial Critic: Interviews, Strategies, Dialogues*, ed. Sarah Harasym (New York: Routledge, 1990); idem, *A Critique of Postcolonial Reason: Toward a History of the Vanishing Present* (Cambridge, Mass.: Harvard University Press, 1999); and Homi K. Bhabha, *The Location of Culture* (London: Routledge, 1994). For biblical and theological analyses of empire, see Horsley, ed., *Paul and Empire*; Richard A. Horsley, ed., *Paul and Politics: Ekklesia, Israel, Imperium, Interpretation; Essays in Honor of Krister Stendahl* (Harrisburg: Trinity Press International, 2000); idem, ed., *Paul and the Roman Imperial Order* (Harrisburg: Trinity Press International, 2004); and idem, ed., *Hidden Transcripts and the Arts of Resistance: Applying the Work of*

James C. Scott to Jesus and Paul, Semeia Studies 48 (Atlanta: Society of Biblical Literature, 2004); Richard A. Horsley, "Submerged Biblical Histories and Imperial Biblical Studies," in *Postcolonial Bible*, 152–73; idem, "Feminist Scholarship and Postcolonial Criticism: Subverting Imperial Discourse and Reclaiming Submerged Histories," in *Walk in the Ways of Wisdom: Essays in Honor of Elisabeth Schüssler Fiorenza*, ed. Shelly Matthews, Cynthia Briggs Kittredge, and Melanie Johnson-DeBaufre (Harrisburg: Trinity Press International, 2003); Sze-kar Wan, "Collection for the Saints as Anticolonial Act: Implications of Paul's Ethnic Reconstruction," in *Paul and Politics*, 191–215; idem, "Does Diaspora Identity Imply Some Sort of Universality? An Asian-American Reading of Galatians," in *Interpreting beyond Borders*, 107–31; and Abraham Smith, "'Unmasking the Powers': Toward a Postcolonial Analysis of 1 Thessalonians," in *Paul and the Roman Imperial Order*, 47–66.

4.   Michael Hardt and Antonio Negri, *Empire* (Cambridge, Mass.: Harvard University Press, 2000). Hardt and Negri's analysis is strongly influenced by Seattle and the other anti-globalization movements of the turn of the millennium. As philosopher Slavoj Žižek writes, "What makes Empire and Multitude such a refreshing reading . . . is that we are dealing with books which refer to and function as the moment of theoretical reflection of—one is almost tempted to say: are embedded in—an actual global movement of anti-capitalist resistance: one can sense, behind the written lines, the smells and sounds of Seattle, Genoa and Zapatistas. So their theoretical limitation is simultaneously the limitation of the actual movement." Slavoj Žižek, *"Objet a* as Inherent Limit to Capitalism: On Michael Hardt and Antonio Negri," http://www.lacan.com/zizmultitude.htm.

5.   Hardt and Negri, *Empire*, 34.

6.   Antonio Negri with Danilo Zolo, "A Conversation about Empire," in *Antonio Negri, Reflections on Empire*, trans. Ed Emery (Cambridge, UK: Polity, 2008), 16.

7.   Ibid., 52.

8.   Michael Hardt and Antonio Negri, *Multitude: War and Democracy in the Age of Empire* (Harmondsworth, UK: Penguin, 2005).

9.   Michael Hardt and Antonio Negri, "Adventures of the Multitude," *Re-Thinking Marxism* 13, nos. 3/4 (Fall/Winter 2001): 243.

10.   Michael Hardt and Antonio Negri, "Arabs Are Democracy's New Pioneers: The Leaderless Middle East Uprisings Can Inspire Freedom Movements as Latin America Did Before." http://www.guardian.co.uk/commentisfree/2011/feb/24/arabs-democracy-latin-america.

11.   Hardt and Negri, *Empire*, 396.

12.   Ibid., 400.

13.   Ibid., 361–62.

14.   Elizabeth A. Clark, "On Not Retracting the Unconfessed," in *Augustine and Postmodernism: Confessions and Circumfession*, ed. John D. Caputo and Michael Scanlon (Bloomington: Indiana University Press, 2005), 233.

15.   Carol Harrison, *Augustine: Christian Truth and Fractured Humanity* (New York: Oxford University Press, 2000), 60.

16.   Augustine was cozy enough with imperial powers that he could call on imperial coercion to quell the Donatists in spite of his initial reticence in doing so. In *Theology and Social Theory*, John Milbank makes an apologia of sorts in Augustine's defense. In particular, Milbank wishes to defend Augustine's conception of religious faith as participation within a political entity, which is the church, against the Donatist tendency toward private faith, which to Augustine is a privation that has the capacity to distort the whole. See John Milbank, *Theology and Social Theory: Beyond Secular Reason* (Malden, Mass.: Blackwell, 1990), 402–3.

17.   Robert Dodaro, "Loose Canons: Augustine and Derrida on Their Selves," in John D. Caputo and Michael J. Scanlon, eds., *God, the Gift, and Postmodernism* (Bloomington: Indiana University Press, 1999), 97–98.

18.   It is important to note, however, that Augustine does not reject the writings of Roman historians, but reinterprets them in a distinctly Christian key. Although he draws liberally from the Roman historian Sallust, even appropriating his term *libido dominandi*, by which he characterizes the temperament of later Roman leaders, he parts company with them in his denial of a golden age of antiquity whereby the earthly city offers an ideal of justice. In bringing together the Romulus and Remus story with that of Cain and Abel, Augustine sounds his judgment on the ubiquity of violence within earthly political life.

19.   Michael Hanby, "Democracy and Its Demons," in *Augustine and Politics*, ed. John Doody, Kevin Hughes, and Kim Pattensworth (Oxford, UK: Lexington, 2005), 124.

20.   Augustine, *City of God*, trans. Marcus Dods, in *Nicene and Post-Nicene Fathers*, vol. 2, ed. Philip Schaff (Peabody, Mass.: Hendrickson, 2004), Book V, ch. 20, 102.

21.   James K. A. Smith questions Hardt and Negri for precisely such a move. In the face of such accounts, it might seem like a "foundationalist" hangover to ask for reasons to resist. But on the other hand, if we are to avoid the kind of relativism that Hardt and Negri rightly criticize, as well as a naïve empiricism, it seems legitimate to find criteria for opposition, particularly since they also want to construct a "real alternative." It would seem that the articulation of an alternative demands concrete formulation of the criteria that would spell out both what's wrong with the regime of empire and then provide the basis for configuring an "alternative." James K. A. Smith, "The Gospel of Freedom, or Another Gospel? Augustinian Reflections on Empire and American Foreign Policy," *Political Theology* 10, no. 3 (2009): 513–36, at 530.

22.   See Book III of the *City of God* for Augustine's inventory of these within Roman civilization.

23.   For example, in Kenya's Kakuma (literally "nowhere") refugee camp, refugees were refused the right to leave the camp without a permit. They were not permitted to engage in employment or grow their own food, and were subject to surveillance from UN policymakers intent to monitor their every movement.

24.   Hannah Arendt's dissertation was on love as a political virtue in Augustine. Many political theorists have also seen Augustine's abiding influence upon Arendt's political theory in her subsequent writings as well. See Hannah Arendt, *Love and St. Augustine*, ed. Joanna Vechiarelli Scott and Judith Chelius Stark (Chicago: University of Chicago Press, 1996).

25.   Hannah Arendt, "We Refugees," in *The Jewish Writings*, ed. Jerome Kohn and Ron H. Feldman (New York: Schocken, 2008), 271.

26.   Hanby, "Democracy and Its Demons," 119.

27.   Žižek exposes the dynamics of mimetic violence inherent within the Multitude this way: "This is also why Negri and Hardt's reference to Bakhtin's notion of carnival as the model for the protest movement of the multitude—they are carnevalesque not only in their form and atmosphere (theatrical performances, chants, humorous songs), but also in their non-centralized organization—is deeply problematic: is late capitalist social reality itself not already carnevalesque? Furthermore, is "carnival" not also the name for the obscene underside of power—from gang rapes to mass lynchings? Let us not forget that Bakhtin developed the notion of carnival in his book on Rabelais written in the 1930s, as a direct reply to the carnival of the Stalinist purges." Žižek, "*Objet a* as Inherent Limit to Capitalism" (see n.4, above).

28.   Hardt and Negri, *Multitude*, 413.

29.   Augustine, *City of God*, Book XIX, ch. 21, 881.

30.   Ibid., 882.

31.   John von Heyking puts it well: "This reformulation reflects Augustine's understanding of political representation in that it corresponds to his view that human beings seek to become like or to imitate the objects they love or prize. Just as one becomes more godlike by imitating Christ, and just as one's soul is dispersed into the flux of the world when one inordinately pursues worldly goods, so too do political societies become more like the objects their people love." John von Heyking, *Augustine and Politics as Longing in the World* (Columbia: University of Missouri Press, 2001), 83.

32.   See Eph. 1:22-23: "And he has put all things under his feet and has made him the head over all things for the church which is his body, the fullness of him who fills all in all." Eph. 3:18-19: "I pray that you may have the power to comprehend, with all the saints, what is the breadth and length and height and depth, and to know the love of Christ that surpasses all knowledge so that you might be filled with all the fullness of God." Col. 1:19: "For in him the fullness of God was pleased to dwell . . ." Col. 2:9-10: "For in him the whole fullness of deity dwells bodily, and you have come to fullness in him, who is the head of every ruler and authority."

33.   Augustine, *City of God*, Book VII, ch. 2.

34.   Graham Ward, *Cities of God* (New York: Routledge, 2000), 77.

35.   Milbank, *Theology and Social Theory*, 411, cited in Michael J. Hollerich, "Milbank and Augustine," in *History, Apocalypse, and the Secular Imagination: New Essays*

of Augustine's City of God (Bowling Green: Bowling Green State University, 1999), 325.

36. Augustine, *City of God*, trans. Henry Bettenson (Harmondsworth, UK: Penguin, 1972), Book IX, ch. 20, 366.

37. Michael Hanby, *Augustine and Modernity* (London: Routledge, 2003), 63.

38. Augustine, *Concerning the City of God against the Pagans*, trans. Henry Bettenson (London: Penguin, 2003), Book XIV, ch. 13, 573.

39. Ibid., Book XIX, ch. 26, 892.

40. "Thus even the Heavenly City in her pilgrimage here on earth makes use of the earthly peace and demands and seeks the compromise between human wills in respect of the provisions relevant to the mortal nature of man, so far as may be permitted without detriment to true religion and piety. In fact, that City refers the earthly peace to the heavenly peace, which is so truly peaceful that it should be regarded as the only peace deserving the name, in least in respect of the rational creation; for this peace is the perfectly ordered and completely harmonious fellowship in the enjoyment of God, and of each other in God." Augustine, *City of God*, trans. Henry Bettenson, Book XIX, ch. 17, 878.

41. Robert Markus captures this self-critical aspect to Augustine's thought; however, he tends to frame it as a primarily existential commitment, and therefore perhaps one that, in my judgment, loses its political edge: "The characteristically Christian assessment of all human values is structured in an eschatological perspective. This is what defines the peculiarity of Augustine's 'pilgrim city' in this world: its members, unlike those of the earthly city, who are fully at home in their temporal concerns, refer these concerns to the enjoyment of 'early peace.' . . . Thus when a Christian, from such an eschatological perspective, affirms some secular value, some human enterprise or achievement, his affirmation will not be simple self-identification. His peculiar posture in the world precludes identifying himself with its values without some reservation. The fullest endorsement of secular value is tinged with criticism. What others may affirm simply as 'good' must survive the more deeply penetrating questioning from an eschatological perspective." Robert A. Markus, *Saeculum: History and Society in the Theology of St. Augustine* (Cambridge: Cambridge University Press), 168.

42. Hanby, "Democracy and Its Demons," 132–33.

43. Augustine, *City of God*, trans. Henry Bettenson, Book XXII, ch. 30, 1088.

CHAPTER 2

1. Wendell Berry, "Christianity and the Survival of Creation," *Cross Currents* 43, no. 2 (Summer 1993): 149–63, http://www.crosscurrents.org/berry.htm.

2. Sallie McFague, *Life Abundant: Rethinking Theology and Economy for a Planet in Peril* (Minneapolis: Fortress Press, 2000).

3. Ibid, 158.

4. Ibid.

5. Ibid.

6. Ibid., 163.

7. While there is no way of measuring this, it would appear that the scale of continued violation of human bodies and the scale of human indifference to it are unprecedented in history. According to the Nobel Women's Initiative: "In the last twenty years—from Bosnia to Rwanda, from Colombia to the Democratic Republic of Congo—sexual violence against women, and sometimes against men, has become a strategic military tactic designed to humiliate victims and shatter enemy societies." Jina Moore, "Confronting War as a War Crime: Will a New U.N. Campaign Have Any Impact?," *CQ Global Researcher: Exploring International Perspectives* 4, no. 5 (May 2010), http://www.nobelwomensinitiative.org/images/stories/women_new_security/CQ_Press_women_in_war.pdf.

8. The sacramental, according to McFague, ought to be complemented by the disruptive power of the prophetic for a truly ecological economic Christology.

9. McFague, *Life Abundant*, 169.

10. Ibid.

11. Ibid., 169–70.

12. According to McFague, "Jesus points beyond himself to the source of love and power in the universe." Ibid., 178.

13. The *Hexaemeron* is hardly a systematic treatise. Rather than developing a theology of humans as creatures, Basil's coda to the ninth homily becomes an occasion for defending the consubstantial unity of Father and Son, clearly occasioned by a lingering of the Arian controversy.

14. See, for example, I. P. Sheldon-Williams, "The Cappadocians," in A. H. Armstrong, *The Cambridge History of Later Greek and Early Medieval Philosophy* (Cambridge: Cambridge University Press, 1967), 432–38.

15. See, for example, the very important work of Denis Edwards, who writes, "When the various sciences look at an atom, at a galaxy, or the most complex thing we know, the human brain, they find patterns of relationships." *How God Acts: Creation, Redemption and Special Divine Action, Theology and the Sciences* (Minneapolis: Fortress Press, 2010), 5.

16. Basil of Caesarea, Homily V, in *The Hexaemeron*, trans. Blomfield Jackson, in *Nicene and Post-Nicene Fathers*, second series, vol. 8, *Basil: Letters and Selected Works*, ed. Philip Schaff and Henry Wace (Peabody, Mass.: Hendrickson, 2004), 7:79.

17. *Hexameron*, Homily VII, 4:93.

18. Ibid., 4:97.

19. *Hexaemeron*, Homily II, 2:59.

20. *Hexaemeron*, Homily IX, 3:103.

21. Basil of Caesarea, *On the Human Condition*, trans. Nonna Verna Harrison (Crestwood, N.Y.: St. Vladimir's Seminary Press, 2005), 43–44.

22. Ibid., 44.

23. Ibid.

24. Lewis Ayres, *Nicaea and Its Legacy: An Approach to Fourth-Century Trinitarian Theology* (New York: Oxford University Press, 2006), 219.

25. Basil also presciently argues, in spite of the prevailing science of his time, that the heavenly bodies—moon, sun, planets—are also temporal, and have a beginning and an end (*Hexaemeron*, Homily I, 3:53).

26. Sallie McFague, *Models of God: Theology for an Ecological, Nuclear Age* (Minneapolis: Fortress Press, 1987), 67.

27. Again, rather surprisingly, McFague elaborates a heavily anthropocentric theory of metaphor: "We are not naming ourselves, one another, and our earth, in ways commensurate with our own times." Ibid., 3.

28. David Bentley Hart, *The Beauty of the Infinite: The Aesthetics of Christian Truth* (Grand Rapids: Eerdmans, 2004), 25.

29. Although I am sympathetic with the line of reasoning within theodical arguments that it is human beings that have aggravated natural disasters, and therefore they are a product of human will, I do not buy into it entirely. For one, it is naïve and a romantic view of nature that views it as perennially good. The violences within it are just too extravagant to say that creation is beneficent. Second, it is also a naïve and romantic picture of the world that extricates humans and their technologies entirely from nature. It is also an unfortunate gesture to separate humans from the natural world, in a world in which many hubristically assume that they are above nature.

30. *Hexaemeron*, Homily IX, 1:101.

31. Jaroslav Pelikan, *Christianity and Classical Culture: The Metamorphosis of Natural Theology in the Christian Encounter with Hellenism* (New Haven: Yale University Press, 1993), 93.

32. Rowan Williams, *Wrestling with Angels: Conversations in Modern Theology* (Grand Rapids: Eerdmans, 2007), 80.

33. Robert Stillman, *Philip Sidney and the Poetics of Renaissance Cosmopolitanism* (Aldershot, UK: Ashgate, 2008), 85.

34. *Hexaemeron*, Homily VIII, 8:101.

35. Sallie McFague, *A New Climate for Theology: God, the World, and Global Warming* (Minneapolis: Fortress Press, 2008), 117.

36. Hart, *The Beauty of the Infinite*, 328.

37. Nonna Verna Harrison, "Introduction," in Basil of Caesarea, *The Human Condition*, 28.

38. Ayres, *Nicaea and Its Legacy*, 196.

39. *Hexaemeron*, Homily V, 3:77.

40. Basil of Caesarea, Homily 6.2, cited in Brian E. Daley, S.J., "Building a New City: The Cappadocian Fathers and the Rhetoric of Piety," *Journal of Early Christian Studies* 7, no. 3 (Fall 1999): 443.

41. Basil of Caesarea, Letter XXIII, "To a Solitary," in *Basil: Letters and Selected Works*, 130.

42. See also John Meyendorff, *Christ in Eastern Thought* (Crestwood, N.Y.: St. Vladimir's Seminary Press, 1975): "This transformation—the aim of asceticism and of all spiritual life—does not imply the acquisition of supernatural or extrinsic virtues but the re-integration of those virtues that were our own from the time of creation" (150).

43. Basil of Caesarea, "To A Solitary," 150.

44. Basil of Caesarea, Homily on Deuteronomy in *Basil: Letters and Selected Works* XV, 9:lv.

45. Basil of Caesarea, Homily 8, cited in Daley, "Building a New City," 447.

46. As Brian E. Daley points out, the ecosystem was fragile indeed during his tenure as presbyter. In 369 CE, a drought swept through Cappadocia, causing widespread famine. Basil's sermons of that summer consist of a set of powerful biddings to the elite classes to share their resources with the poor. It is in this context that Basil set up his hospices and soup kitchens.

47. Harrison, "Introduction," in Basil of Caesarea, *The Human Condition*, 27.

48. Basil of Caesarea, "On the Spirit," in *Basil: Letters and Selected Works*, VIII, 11.

CHAPTER 3

1. Rosemary Radford Ruether, *Sexism and God-Talk: Toward a Feminist Theology* (Boston: Beacon, 1983), xiv.

2. Ibid., 18.

3. Ibid., 19.

4. Rosemary Radford Ruether, *Womanguides* (Boston: Beacon, 1985), xi.

5. Ruether, *Sexism and God-Talk*, 125.

6. Ibid.

7. Ibid.

8. For a brief treatment of Rosemary Radford Ruether's use of Marxism as a theological strategy, see D. Stephen Long, *Divine Economy: Theology and the Market* (New York: Routledge, 2000), 108–11.

9. Terry Eagleton, *Ideology: An Introduction* (London: Verso, 1991), 6.

10. Ruether is by no means unique in her quest for a usable language in feminist theology. In her landmark book, *Human Liberation in a Feminist Perspective: A*

Theology, Letty Russell writes ". . . the language at our disposal frequently presents problems of communication" (Philadelphia: Westminster, 1974), 93.

11. Hélène Cixous, "Laugh of the Medusa," trans. Keith Cohen and Paula Cohen, *Signs: Journal of Women in Culture and Society* 1, no. 4 (1976): 882.

12. Jacques Derrida endorses the book as her most important work in its foreword: "*Stigmata* is henceforth a great classic. It can be read as the best introduction to Hélène Cixous's entire corpus whose strokes of genius it heralds and collects together as the becoming-literary of her life." In Hélène Cixous, *Stigmata: Escaping Texts* (New York: Routledge, 2005), x.

13. Ibid., xiii.

14. Ibid., xii.

15. Ibid.

16. Ibid.

17. Ibid., xvi.

18. Hélène Cixous, "Coming to Writing," in *Coming to Writing and Other Essays,* ed. Deborah Jenson (Cambridge, Mass.: Harvard University Press, 1991), 11.

19. Cixous, *Stigmata,* 198.

20. Cixous, "Coming to Writing," 4.

21. Graham Ward. *Theology and Contemporary Critical Theory* (New York: St. Martin's, 1996), 145.

22. Muriel Rukeyser, "Käthe Kollwitz," in *Out of Silence: Selected Poems,* ed. Kate Daniels (Evanston, Ill.: Northwestern University Press, 2000), 131.

23. Cixous, *Stigmata,* Kindle edition, location 333, retrieved from Amazon.ca.

24. Ibid. "David is outside. It is the hour. (He is) the ordinance-giver." This sentence also has resonance verbally to *David est l'or* ("David is gold") and that he is *l'hors donnateur* ("the giver on the outside," or "the giver of the outside"). In all these textual layers, allusions, and word plays, Bathsheba's desire is highlighted.

25. See, for example, when Augustine speaks of his seduction by skilled oratory: "See how the human soul lies weak and prostrate when it is not yet attached to the sold rock of truth. The winds of gossip blow from the chest of people ventilating their opinions, so the soul is carried about and turned, twisted back again. The light is obscured from it by a cloud, the truth is not perceived. Yet look, it lies before us." Augustine, *Confessions,* trans. Henry Chadwick (New York: Oxford University Press, 2008), Book IV, xv, 23 (66).

26. Peter Brown, *Augustine of Hippo: A Biography* (Berkeley: University of California Press, 2000), 259.

27. Augustine, *On Christian Doctrine,* trans. J. F. Shaw, in *Nicene and Post-Nicene Fathers,* first series, ed. Philip Schaff (Peabody, Mass.: Hendrickson, 2004), Book I, ch. 2, 523.

28. See Oliver O'Donovan, "Usus and Fruitio in Augustine, De Doctrina Christiana 1," *Journal of Theological Studies* 33 (1982): 45–62; and Hannah Arendt, *Love and Saint Augustine, ed. Joanna Vercchiarelli Scott and Judith Chelius Stark* (Chicago: University of Chicago Press, 1996), 31–34.

29. Unfortunately, Paul writes this in relation to slavery. Yet this is not slavery's justification. On the contrary! In making use of our condition, even slavery, we afford it no ontological justification. Slavery is not to be considered one's purpose and being; it is relativized because it is considered a mere way station on the way to one's proper destiny, which is the knowing and being known by God (1 Cor. 8:3). In writing of the *Haustafeln* texts, such as 1 Corinthians 7, John Howard Yoder argues that within Paul's complacent household codes, there is, in fact, a revolutionary contradiction that unfolds: "The one thing the Haustafeln cannot have meant originally . . . is to reinforce extant authority structures as divinely willed for their own sake." John Howard Yoder, *The Politics of Jesus* (Grand Rapids: Eerdmans, 1994), 190.

30. Augustine, *On Christian Doctrine*, Book I, ch. 4.

31. Rowan Williams, *The Truce of God* (Grand Rapids: Eerdmans, 2005), 90.

32. Ruether has stated baldly that "Paul's position was unquestionably that of anti-Judaism." Rosemary Radford Ruether, *Faith and Fratricide: The Theological Roots of Anti-Semitism* (New York: Crossroad, 1979), 104.

33. Augustine, *On Christian Doctrine*, Book 1, ch. 7.

34. See, for example, Domna C. Stanton, "Difference on Trial: A Critique of the Maternal Metaphor in Cixous, Irigaray, and Kristeva," in *The Poetics of Gender*, ed. Nancy K. Miller (New York: Columbia University Press, 1986), 157–82.

35. Augustine, *Confessions*, Book I, ch. 1, 3.

36. Augustine, *On Christian Doctrine*, Book I, ch. 10.

37. Ibid.

38. Augustine, *Confessions*, Book III, ch. 2, 2.

39. Augustine, *On Christian Doctrine*, Book I, ch. 10.

40. The parallels with Derrida, Cixous's research partner and friend, are striking here. In a wonderful analysis of Derrida's "Circumfession," John D. Caputo writes: "The fifty-nine periphrases of 'Circumfession' are so many words cut by the wound of circumcision, that wound I have never seen (Circ. 66/66), a 'virtual,' 'unmemorable' and 'indecipherable' wound (Circ. 271/293), which strikes down the proud heart, which circumcises the heart and the word, the ear and the tongue." John D. Caputo, "Shedding Tears beyond Being: Derrida's Confession of Prayer," in John D. Caputo and Michael J. Scanlon, eds., *Augustine and Postmodernism: Confessions and Circumfession* (Bloomington: Indiana University Press, 2005), 104.

41. Lewis Ayres, *Nicaea and Its Legacy: An Approach to Fourth-Century Trinitarian Theology* (New York: Oxford University Press, 2006), 116.

42. Lewis Ayres, "Augustine's Trinitarian Theology," in *Augustine and His Critics: Essays in Honour of Gerald Bonner*, ed. Robert Dodaro and George Lawless (New York: Routledge, 2002), 57.

43. Augustine, *Confessions*, Book VIII, xii, 29 (152).

44. Helmut David Baer, "The Fruit of Charity: Using the Neighbor in *De Doctrina Christiana*," *Journal of Religious Ethics* 24, no. 1 (Spring 1996): 47–64.

45. Augustine, *On Christian Doctrine*, Book I, ch. 1, 522.

46. Ibid., 523.

47. Rowan Williams, "Language, Reality and Desire in Augustine's *De Doctrina Christiana*," *Journal of Literature and Theology* 3, no. 2 (July 1989): 142.

48. John Milbank, *Being Reconciled: Ontology and Pardon* (New York: Routledge, 2003), 181.

49. Ibid., 182.

CHAPTER 4

1. John Hick, *An Interpretation of Religion* (New Haven: Yale University Press, 1989), 374 (italics mine).

2. Wilfrid Cantwell Smith, *The Meaning and End of Religion* (San Francisco: Harper & Row, 1978), 29.

3. Ibid., 189.

4. Ibid., 169.

5. Ibid., 76.

6. Ibid., 168.

7. Ibid., 171.

8. Ibid., 190.

9. Ibid., 5.

10. See Slavoj Žižek's insightful analysis of this: "Fetishist 'reification' is thus double: not only are 'relations between people' reified in 'relations between things' (so that critical analysis must penetrate the reified surface and discern beneath it the 'relations between people' which actually animate it)—an ever more tricky 'fetishist reification' is at work when we (mis)perceive the situation as simply involving 'relations between people', and fail to take into account the invisible symbolic structure which regulates these relations. An everyday bourgeois subject not only (mis)perceives money as a material object with the 'magic' property as functioning as the equivalent of all commodities; in his everyday consciousness, such a subject is usually well aware that money is a mere sign guaranteeing its owner the right to have at his disposal a part of the social product, and so on. What an everyday bourgeois subject effectively fails to perceive at a much more fundamental level, is the fact that money is precisely not merely a token of interpersonal relations but emerges as the

materialization of the symbolic institution in so far as this institution is irreducible to direct interaction between 'concrete individuals.'" Slavoj Žižek, *The Plague of Fantasies* (New York: Verso, 1997), 101.

11. Peter Slater is much more incisive on this weakness in Smith: "[Smith] is so eager to affirm such transcendence that he loosens ties to the Christ figure and risks disembodying the Christian faith completely. Ironically, this move reflects a more, not less, parochial outlook on Christianity, enshrining a classical Protestant mistrust of sacramental religion. Despite the drift of his recent work towards theology, Smith's weakness here is that he is not theological enough." Peter Slater, "Review Essay: Three Views of Christianity," *Journal of the American Academy of Religion* 50, no. 1 (1982): 97–109, at 99.

12. Smith, *The Meaning and End of Religion*, 85.

13. Ibid., 108.

14. This is the title of ch. 4 of *The Meaning and End of Religion*.

15. Talal Asad, "Reading a Modern Classic: W. C. Smith's *The Meaning and End of Religion*," *History of Religions* 40, no. 4 (2001): 205–222, at 214.

16. "Operation Enduring Freedom," a military offense against Afghanistan, was launched on October 7, 2001, by the United States and Great Britain under the umbrella of what Bush declared the "Global War on Terror."

17. George W. Bush, White House Archives, http://georgewbush-whitehouse .archives .gov/news/releases/2001/11/20011119-14.html.

18. See Saba Mahmood and Charles Hirschkind, "Feminism, the Taliban and the Politics of Counterinsurgency," Fathom Archive, http://fathom.lib.uchicago .edu/1/777777190136/. It is odd how the increasing public discussion of U.S. involvement in the civil war in Afghanistan has not altered the neat circuit of women's oppression, Taliban evil, and Islamic fundamentalism. Again, we might recall a little of this stunning history. U.S. interests were first stirred in what was until then a neglected part of southwest Asia when the Soviet Union invaded Afghanistan in 1979. President Jimmy Carter signed a directive to begin covert operations in Afghanistan in order to harass the Soviet occupying forces by supplying funds, weapons, and other forms of support to the Afghan fighters known as the mujahideen. By 1986, under the Reagan administration, this project had mushroomed into the largest covert operation in U.S. history since World War II. Overall, the United States funneled more than $3 billion to the mujahideen, and Saudi Arabia, one of the staunchest U.S. allies, provided as much financial support, if not more.

19. Melanie McAlister, *Epic Encounters: Culture, Media, and U.S. Interests in the Middle East, 1945–2000* (Berkeley: University of California Press, 2005), 281–82.

20. Cited in Christine McCarthy McMorris, "Grappling with Islam: Bush and the Burqa," *Religion in the News* 5, no. 2 (Spring 2002), http://www.trincoll.edu/depts/ csrpl/RINVol5No1/Bush%20burqa.htm.

21. In April 2011, France banned the burqa and niqab for its citizens and visitors, with a penalty of a fine of 150 euros. In August 2011, Belgium followed suit with a slightly lesser fine.

22. Mahmood and Hirschkind, "Feminism, the Taliban, and the Politics of Counterinsurgency" (see n. 18, above).

23. Saba Mahmood, "Secularism, Politics and Empire: The Politics of Islamic Reformation," *Public Culture* 18, no. 2 (2006): 323.

24. Athanasius, *On the Incarnation*, trans. Archibald Robertson (London: D. Nutt, 1885), 54:3.

25. Khaled Anatolios, *Athanasius: The Coherence of His Thought* (New York: Routledge, 1998), 2.

26. Charles Taylor has been the most articulate critic of an ethics of inarticulacy; that is, of an ethics that is not based upon a conception of the good. As Fergus Kerr summarizes Taylor's project: "There are two moves here. . . . The first is the move being the question of what we ought to do, to the question of what it is good for human beings to be. The second is the move beyond the question of what a good life for humans might be, to the consideration of a good which would be beyond life, in the sense that its goodness cannot be entirely or exhaustively explained in terms of its contributing to a fuller, better, richer, more satisfying life." Fergus Kerr, "Taylor's Moral Ontology," in *Charles Taylor*, ed. Ruth Abbey (Cambridge: Cambridge University Press, 2004), 91.

27. This would date the treatise to before 318 when the official condemnation of the Arians was given. The most notable modern scholar to defend an early dating is E. P. Meijring, in *Athanasius: Contra Gentes: Introduction, Translation, and Commentary* (Leiden: E. J. Brill, 1984).

28. Timothy Barnes, *Athanasius and Constantius: Theology and Politics in the Constantinian Empire* (Cambridge, Mass.: Harvard University Press, 1993), 32.

29. Khaled Anatolios, "'When Was God without Wisdom?' Trinitarian Hermeneutics and Rhetorical Strategy," in "Orientialia: Clement, Origen, Athanasius, The Cappadocians, Chrystostom," *Studia Patristica* XLI, ed. Frances Young, M. Edwards, P. Parvis (Louvain: Peeters, 2006), 122.

30. Athanasius, *On the Incarnation of the Word*, trans. Archibald Robertson, in *Nicene and Post-Nicene Fathers*, vol. 4, *Athanasius: Select Works and Letters* (Peabody, Mass.: Hendrickson, 2004), §3.3, 37.

31. Ibid.

32. Ibid., §3.4.

33. Ibid., §9.4, 41.

34. Ibid. §45, 61.

35. Anatolios, *Athanasius*.

36. Athanasius, *On the Incarnation of the Word*, 2004 ed., §17, 45.

37. Athanasius, *Life of Anthony*, trans. Archibald Robertson, in *Nicene and Post-Nicene Fathers*, vol. 4, *Athanasius: Select Works and Letters*, 217.

38. St. Athanasius, *On the Incarnation: The Treatise De Incarnatione Verbi Dei*, (Crestwood, N.Y.: St. Vladimir's Seminary Press, 1993), 91.

39. A comment by Khaled Anatolios helps to clarify: "It is striking, for example, that a typical modern complaint about Athanasius lays special stress on his intransigence, his undeniable aura of being sure of himself and his position. But this complaint has its own culturally bound history, having at least as much to do with the Western post-Kantian construction of the virtue of epistemological humility as it does with Athanasius himself. For his closer contemporaries, this 'intransigence' was interpreted as a courageous steadfastness and an inspired perception of what was radically at stake. Moreover, his withering ridicule of his opponent and sometimes bombastic rhetoric, objectionable (though far from non-existent) according to the academic standards of our day, was rather standard fare for the times. Above all, a judicious evaluation of Athanasius's character must give due weight to the undeniable fact, conceded even by the most vehement of his modern critics, that he eventually gained the overwhelming support and admiration of his own people." Anatolios, Athanasius, *The Early Church Fathers* (New York: Routledge, 2004), 34–35.

40. Athanasius, *On the Incarnation of the Word*, 2004 ed., §25, 48–49.

41. Pope John Paul II, "Veritatis Splendor—The Splendour of Truth," *Papal Encyclical*, August 1993, The Vatican Archives, http://www.vatican.va/holy_father/john_paul_ii/encyclicals/documents/hf_jp-ii_enc_06081993_veritatis-splendor_ en.html.

42. One might argue that this position is akin to Karl Rahner's "anonymous Christian," because I am making the case that the Christian faith is not an identity to be appropriated but an objective reality which is not contingent upon human assent. My concern with Rahner is that he attaches Christ's coming too closely with "Christianity." This objectification has the effect of setting up the Christian church as an exemplar of morality that defies, in my judgment, any empirical evidence!

43. Ibid.

44. In spite of my criticism of the pluralism of a Wilfred Cantwell Smith, I do wish to acknowledge his deep appreciation of the precisely Christian imperative toward humility: "[Exclusivism] is intolerable from merely human standards. It is doubly so from Christian ones. Any position that antagonizes and alienates rather than reconciles, that is arrogant rather than humble, that promotes segregation rather than brotherhood, that is unlovely, is ipso facto un-Christian." Wilfred Cantwell Smith, *The Faith of Other Men* (New York: Harper Torchbooks, 1972), 131.

45. See George A. Lindbeck: "One can say that the situation of the Christian is, in some respects more, not less, perilous than that of the non-Christian. Judgment begins in the house of the Lord (I Peter 4:17), and many of the first shall be last, and the last first (Matt 19:30). When one considers these and related passages,

one sometimes gets the impression that the Bible balances Cyprian's claim that there is no salvation outside the church (extra ecclesia nulla salus) with an at least equally emphatic insistence that the beginning of damnation, of deliberate opposition to God, is possible only within the church, within the people of God: Jesus pronounced his woes (and wept) it will be recalled, over the cities of Israel, not those of the Gentiles. On this view, there is no damnation, just as there is no salvation, outside the church." *The Nature of Doctrine: Religion and Theology in a Postliberal Age* (Philadelphia: Westminster, 1984), 59.

46.   Many will know that these words are a blatant repetition of one of Stanley Hauerwas's well-crafted turns of phrase. By it, I take him to mean that time has been redeemed in Jesus Christ, and thus is not ours to possess or manage. Thus the church is free to make inefficient use of its time as it participates already (although partially) in God's eternity. See, for example, Stanley Hauerwas, *The State of the University: Academic Knowledges and the Knowledge of God* (Malden, Mass.: Blackwell, 2007), 136.

47.   Saba Mahmood, *Politics of Piety: The Islamic Revival and the Feminist Subject* (Princeton: Princeton University Press, 2005), 199.

CHAPTER 5

1. H. Richard Niebuhr, *The Kingdom of God in America* (New York: Harper & Row, 1959), 193.

2. A. G. Hebert, "Translator's Preface," in Gustav Aulén, *Christus Victor: An Historical Study of the Three Main Types of the Idea of the Atonement* (London: SPCK, 1953), i.

3. Aulén, *Christus Victor*, 49.

4. Ibid. 119.

5. Ibid., 112.

6. Ibid., 104.

7. J. Denny Weaver, *The Nonviolent Atonement*, 2nd ed. (Grand Rapids: Eerdmans, 2011), 261.

8. Ibid., 42.

9. Ibid., 47.

10. Ibid., 42.

11. "[P]eople who bear crosses are working with the grain of the universe . . ." This oft-cited phrase of John Howard Yoder was given special prominence by Stanley Hauerwas, who used it as the title of his 2001 *Gifford Lectures* (Grand Rapids: Brazos, 2001). The original phrase comes from John Howard Yoder, "Armaments and Eschatology," *Studies in Christian Ethics* 1, no. 1 (1998): 43–61.

12. P. Travis Kroeker describes the realistic thrust of Yoder's Christology thus: "This crucified Messiah even now exercises real, living, cosmic sovereignty, a rule

displayed not in the exercise of juridical authority or state power but in the pattern of life displayed in the slain Lamb and imitated in the community of disciples that follow him, identified by Paul as the 'messianic body' or 'body of Christ.'" P. Travis Kroeker, "Is a Messianic Political Ethic Possible? Recent Work by and about John Howard Yoder," *Journal of Religious Ethics* 33 (2005): 144.

13. Irenaeus, *Against Heresies*, in *The Ante-Nicene Fathers*, vol. 1: *Apostolic Fathers, Justin Martyr, Irenaeus*, ed. Alexander Roberts and James Donaldson (Peabody, Mass.: Hendrickson, 2004), Book III, ch. 18.1, 446.

14. In his work on Athanasius, T. F. Torrance puts it this way: "The whole life of Christ is understood as a continuous sacrifice and oblation which, as such is indivisible, for everything he assumed for us is organically united in his one Person and work as saviour and Mediator." *The Trinitarian Faith* (New York: Continuum, 1991), 152.

15. Irenaeus, *Against Heresies*, Book III, ch. 16.6, 443.

16. Athanasius, *On the Incarnation* (Peabody, Mass.: Hendrickson, 2004), §10, 41.

17. Ibid., §20, 47.

18. Torrance, *The Trinitarian Faith*, 155.

19. Khaled Anatolios, *Athanasius* (London: Routledge, 2004), 56.

20. David Bentley Hart, *The Doors of the Sea: Where Was God in the Tsunami?* (Grand Rapids: Eerdmans, 2005), 80–81.

21. See, for example, Christian A. Eberhart on Levitical sacrifices, which include cereal offerings as equally efficacious, and of the importance of a burnt offering. Neither the Hebrew nor the Greek term [for scrifices] stresses or alludes to animalslaughter. Instead, both express the inherent dynamics of a sacrificial ritual which, throughout its performance, 'moves' toward the most holy altar, thus 'approaching' God who resides in the sanctuary. Therefore a first conclusion of this survey of the sacrificial cult in the HB/OT is that the slaughter of animals is rather insignificant." Christian Eberhart, *Hebrews: Contemporary Methods, New Insights* (Leiden: Brill, 2005), 44.

22. Athanasius, *Four Discourses against the Arians*, trans. Archibald Robertson, in *Nicene and Post-Nicene Fathers*, vol. 4, *Athanasius: Select Works and Letters* (Peabody, Mass.: Hendrickson, 2004), 2, 7, 352.

23. Ibid.

24. Athanasius, *On the Incarnation*, §10, 3.41.

25. Ibid., §52.3, 64.

26. Sarah Coakley, *Powers and Submissions: Spirituality, Philosophy and Gender* (Malden, Mass.: Blackwell, 2002), 35–36.

27. John Howard Yoder, *The Politics of Jesus*, 2nd ed. (Grand Rapids: Eerdmans, 1994), 147.

28. David Bentley Hart, *The Beauty of the Infinite: The Aesthetics of Christian Truth* (Grand Rapids: Eerdmans), 351.

CHAPTER 6

1. In his famous "614th commandment," Emil Fackenheim urges that Jews not hand Hitler a posthumous victory. "We are, first, commanded to survive as Jews, lest the Jewish people perish. We are commanded, secondly, to remember in our very guts and bones the martyrs of the Holocaust, lest their memory perish. We are forbidden, thirdly, to deny or despair of God, however much we may have to contend with him or with belief in him, lest Judaism perish. We are forbidden, finally, to despair of the world as the place which is to become the kingdom of God, lest we help make it a meaningless place in which God is dead or irrelevant and everything is permitted. To abandon any of these imperatives, in response to Hitler's victory at Auschwitz, would be to hand him yet other, posthumous victories." Emil Fackenheim, *To Mend the World: Foundations of Post-Holocaust Jewish Thought* (New York: Schocken, 1994), 213.

2. See also Elie Wiesel's Nobel Peace Prize lecture: "Remembering is a noble and necessary act. The call of memory, the call to memory, reaches us from the very dawn of history. No commandment figures so frequently, so insistently, in the Bible. It is incumbent upon us to remember the good we have received, and the evil we have suffered. New Year's Day, Rosh Hashana, is also called Yom Hazikaron, the day of memory. On that day, the day of universal judgment, man appeals to God to remember: our salvation depends on it. If God wishes to remember our suffering, all will be well; if He refuses, all will be lost. Thus, the rejection of memory becomes a divine curse, one that would doom us to repeat past disasters, past wars." Elie Wiesel, "Hope, Despair and Memory," December 11, 1986, http://http://www.nobelprize.org/nobel_prizes/peace/laureates/1986/wiesel-lecture.html.

3. See, for example, "We Remember: A Reflection on the Shoah," a document of the Vatican's Commission for Religious Relations with the Jews. "Before this horrible genocide, which the leaders of nations and Jewish communities themselves found hard to believe at the very moment when it was being mercilessly put into effect, no one can remain indifferent, least of all the Church, by reason of her very close bonds of spiritual kinship with the Jewish people and her remembrance of the injustices of the past. The Church's relationship to the Jewish people is unlike the one she shares with any other religion. However, it is not only a question of recalling the past. The common future of Jews and Christians demands that we remember, for 'there is no future without memory.' History itself is memoria futuri." http://www.vatican.va/roman_curia/pontifical_councils/chrstuni/documents/rc_pc_chrstuni_doc_16031998_shoah_en.html.

4. Elie Wiesel, *From the Kingdom of Memory: Reminiscences* (New York: Summit, 1990), 201, cited in Miroslav Volf, *The End of Memory: Remembering Rightly in a Violent World* (Grand Rapids: Eerdmans, 2006), 19.

5. Volf, *The End of Memory*, 33.

6. Ibid., 9.

7. Ibid., 147.

8. Ibid., 145.

9. Miroslav Volf, *Exclusion and Embrace: A Theological Exploration of Identity, Otherness, and Reconciliation* (Nashville: Abingdon, 1996), 135.

10. Volf, *The End of Memory*, 146.

11. Ibid., 150.

12. Ibid., 151.

13. Ibid., 214.

14. Ibid., 198.

15. Ibid., 187.

16. Ibid., 188

17. Ibid.

18. Ibid., 201.

19. Ibid., 191.

20. Ibid., 190.

21. Ibid.

22. See *Confessions*, Book X, ch. 17: "Great is the power of memory, a thing, O my God, to be in awe of, a profound and immeasurable multiplicity; and this thing is my mind, this thing am I. What then am I, O my God? What nature am I? A life powerfully various and manifold and immeasurable. In the innumerable kinds of things, present either by their images, as are all bodies, or in themselves as our our mental capacities, or by certain notions or awarenesses, like the affections of the mind—for even when the mind is not experiencing them, although whatever is in the memory is in the mind too—in and through all these does my mind range, and I move swiftly from one to another and I penetrate them deeply as I can, but find no end. So great is the force of memory, so great the force of life even when man lives under the sentence of death here." Augustine, *The Confessions*, trans. F. J. Sheed (New York: Sheed & Ward, 1942), 186.

23. Ibid., ch. 12, 182.

24. Ibid., ch. 25, 192.

25. Ibid., ch. 28, 193.

26. Ibid., 192.

27. Rowan Williams, "*Augustine* and the *Psalms*," *Interpretation* 58 (2004): 19.

28. See Volf's treatment of Augustine as a defender of forgetting in *The End of Memory*, 22–24, 133.

29. See Jane Barter Moulaison, "Lord of Two Cities: Political or Christological Realism in Augustine's City of God?" in *From Logos to Christos: Essays in Honour of Joanne McWilliam* (Waterloo, Ont.: Wilfrid Laurier University Press, 2010), 229–44.

30. Augustine, *Confessions*, Book II, ch. 8, 30 (italics mine).

31. Rowan Williams, *Resurrection: Interpreting the Easter Gospel* (Cleveland: Pilgrim, 2003), 30.

32. John Milbank, *Being Reconciled: Ontology and Pardon* (London: Routledge, 2003), 53.

33. Volf, *The End of Memory*, 23.

34. Ibid.

35. See Augustine, *City of God*, trans. Marcus Dods, in *Nicene and Post-Nicene Fathers*, first series, volume 2, ed. Philip Schaff (Peabody, Mass.: Hendrickson, 2004), Book XXII, ch. 30, 510–11.

36. Augustine, *On the Holy Trinity*, trans. Arthur West Haddan, in *Nicene and Post-Nicene Fathers*, first series, volume 3, Book IV, ch. 13, 78.

37. As a Winnipeger, this argument hits close to home as we were the inaugural city for the hearings of Canada's Truth and Reconciliation Commission on "Indian Residential Schools." Derrida's arguments raise legitimate concerns about what such commissions might be expected to achieve. They cannot manufacture forgiveness, but they can set in place a process whereby public testimony and reparations allow for the possibility of a fuller, more genuine reconciliation, while also offering the measure of justice of the kind that states can hope to assure for posterity.

38. Jacques Derrida, *On Cosmopolitanism and Forgiveness* (London: Routledge, 2001), 42.

39. Derrida asks, "Did forgiveness die in the death camps?" By this, Derrida challenges the aneconomic ideal of forgiveness—one in which there is no possibility for restoration of the victims because of the sheer magnitude of the affront. For him, the ideal of forgiveness further compounds victims' suffering (or, in this case, the suffering of their Jewish representatives who survived) as the victims (now the representatives) are asked to pardon the unpardonable.

40. Ibid., xi.

41. Ibid., 53.

42. Augustine, Sermon 179A, *Sermons 148–183 on the New Testament*, trans. Edmund Hill, ed. John Rotelle (New York: New City Press, 1992), 306.

43. Augustine, *Confessions*, Book X, ch. 18, para. 26, 194.

44. John Milbank, "Augustine and the Indo-European Soul," in *Augustine and His Critics: Essays in Honour of Gerald Bonner*, ed. Robert Dodaro and George Lawless (London: Routledge, 2002), 101–2 n.61.

45. Michael Hanby, "Augustine and Descartes: An Overlooked Chapter in the Story of Modern Origins," *Modern Theology* 19, no. 4 (October 2003): 463.

46. Augustine, *Confessions*, Book VII, ch. 10, para. 16, 123–24.

47. Augustine, *City of God*, Book X, ch. 6, 380.

48. Ibid., Book XXII, ch. 30, 1090.

49. Ibid., 1091.

50. Catherine Pickstock, "Music: Soul, City, Cosmos after Augustine," in *Radical Orthodoxy: A New Theology* (London: Routledge, 1999), 265.

51. I owe this way of putting it to Robert Kennedy's analysis of Augustine's understanding of scripture as the perfect embodiment of time and eternity: "The very fact that the words of Scripture are both temporal and yet the perfect expression of God's eternal will shows that the incomparability of time and eternity does not imply any opposition between them." Robert Peter Kennedy, "Book Eleven: The Confessions as Eschatological Narrative," in *A Reader's Companion to Augustine*, ed. Kim Paffenroth and Robert Kennedy (Louisville: Westminster John Knox, 2003), 183.

52. Augustine, *Confessions*, Book IX, ch. 10, para. 24, 171.

53. Ibid., ch. 11, para. 27, 173.

54. Avot 2:1, cited in *The Cambridge Companion to the Talmud and Rabbinic Literature*, ed. Charlotte Elisheva Fonrobert and Martin S. Jaffee (Cambridge: Cambridge University Press, 2006), 325.

CONCLUSION

1. Many readers will be familiar with this trajectory—from story to world, not world to story—from postliberal theology, a theology with which I am certainly sympathetic. However, I find the term *postcritical* more helpful because it lacks the connotation of a political life; viz., the church that is set at odds against the life of the polis within modernity. It seems to me that Augustine does not permit us to draw so sharp a demarcation between story and world, church and polis, as George Lindbeck might. Postcriticism does not wish to abandon the liberal project of reforming the world through, in part, the operations of the "state." Instead, it questions the state as it is commonly conceived in contemporary society as a modality for securing individual rights. Critique as shaped by the logic of the state and of the market cannot but help looking like profiteering for one party's interest. This is not to critique criticism altogether, but it is to indicate that criticism as a first principle within contemporary society is likely to be invested heavily in market ideologies invested in certain models of individual freedom and choice.

2. See, for example, feminist types of postcritical analyses: "In a place where there is no innocent discourse of liberation, my hope has been to use both our internal contradictions and our differences across one another to refigure community, to include ways of disagreeing productively among ourselves

. . ." Patti Lather, "Post-Critical Pedagogies," in *Feminisms and Critical Pedagogies* (London: Taylor and Francis, 1992), 132.

3. Peter Ochs, *The Return to Scripture in Judaism and Christianity: Essays in Post-critical Scriptural Interpretation* (Mahwah, N.J.: Paulist, 1993), 44.

4. See Jacques Derrida, *Of Grammatology*, trans. Gayatri Chakavorty Spivak (Baltimore: Johns Hopkins University Press, 1976), 158–59.

BIBLIOGRAPHY

ARTICLES AND BOOK CHAPTERS

Anatolios, Khaled. "'When Was God without Wisdom?' Trinitarian Hermeneutics and Rhetorical Strategy." In *Studia Patristica: Orientialia, Clement, Origen, Athanasius, The Cappadocians, Chrystostom*, ed. Frances Young, M. Edwards and P. Parvis, 41:117–23. Leuven: Peters, 2006.

Arendt, Hannah. "We Refugees." In *The Jewish Writings*, ed. Jerome Kohn and Ron H. Feldman, 264–74. New York: Schocken, 2007.

Asad, Talal. "Reading a Modern Classic: W. C. Smith's 'The Meaning and End of Religion'." *History of Religions* 40, no. 3 (Feb. 2001): 205–22.

Ayres, Lewis. "The Fundamental Grammar of Augustine's Trinitarian Theology." In *Augustine and His Critics: Essays in Honour of Gerald Bonner*, ed. Robert Dodaro and George Lawless, 51–76. New York: Routledge, 2000.

Baer, Helmut David. "The Fruit of Charity: Using the Neighbor in *De Doctrina Christiana*." *Journal of Religious Ethics* 24, no. 1 (Spring 1996): 47–64.

Barter Moulaison, Jane. "Lord of Two Cities: Political or Christological Realism in Augustine's City of God?" *From Logos to Christos: Essays in Honour of Joanne McWilliam*, ed. Ellen Leonard and Kate Merriman, 229–44. Waterloo, Ont.: Wilfrid Laurier University Press, 2010.

Baum, Gregory. "Critical Theology: Replies to Ray Morrow." In *Essays in Critical Theology*, ed. Gregory Baum, 3–34. Kansas City: Sheed & Ward, 1994.

Behr, John. "Irenaeus on the Word of God." In *Studia Patristica: Critica et Philologica, Nachleben, First Two Centuries, Tertullian to Arnobius, Egypt before Nicaea, Athanasius and His Opponents*, ed. M. F. Wiles and E. J. Yarnold, 36:163–67. Leuven: Peeters. 2001.

Behr, John, Roland Flamini, Sarah Glazer, Robert Kiener, Barbara Mantel, and Jennifer Weeks. "Confronting Rape as a War Crime: Will a New U.N. Campaign Have any Impact?" *CQ Global Researcher* 4, no. 5 (May 2010): 105–30. http://www.nobelwomensinitiative.org/images/stories/women_new_security/ CQ_Press_women_in_war.pdf.

Bell Jr., Daniel. "'The Fragile Brilliance of Glass'; Empire, Multitude and the Coming Community." *Political Theology* 11, no. 1 (2010): 61–76.

Berry, Wendell. "Christianity and the Survival of Creation." *Cross Currents* 43, no. 2 (Summer 1993): 149–63. http://www.crosscurrents.org/berry.htm.

Bush, George W. "President Hosts *Iftar*." White House Archives. http://george wbush-whitehouse.archives.gov/news/releases/2001/11/20011119-14 .html.

Caputo, John D. "Shedding Tears beyond Being: Derrida's Confession of Prayer." In *Augustine and Postmodernism: Confessions and Circumfession*, ed. John D. Caputo and Michael J. Scanlon, 95–114. Bloomington: Indiana University Press, 2005.

Carlson Brown, Joanne, and Rebecca Parker. "For God So Loved the World?" in *Violence against Women and Children: A Christian Theological Sourcebook*, 36–59. New York: Lexington, 1995.

Cixous, Hélène. "Coming to Writing." In *Coming to Writing and Other Essays,* ed. Deborah Jenson, 1–58. Cambridge, Mass.: Harvard University Press, 1991.

———. "The Laugh of the Medusa." 1975. Trans. Keith Cohen and Paula Cohen. *Signs* 1 (1976): 875–93.

Clark, Elizabeth A. "On Not Retracting the Unconfessed." In *Augustine and Postmodernism: Confessions and Circumfession*, ed. John D. Caputo and Michael Scanlon, 222–43. Bloomington: Indiana University Press, 2005.

Commission for Religious Relations with the Jews. "We Remember: A Reflection on the Shoah." The Roman Curia. http://www.vatican.va/roman_curia/pontifical_councils /chrstuni/documents/rc_pc_chrstuni_doc_16031998_shoah_ en.html.

Dawson, David. "Figural Reading and the Fashioning of Christian Identity in Boyarin, Auerbach and Frei." *Modern Theology* 14, no. 2 (April 1998): 181–96.

———. "Transcendence as Embodiment: Augustine's Domestication of Gnosis." *Modern Theology* 10, no. 1 (January 1994): 1–26.

Deng, Francis Mading. "Human Rights among the Dinka." In *Human Rights in Africa: Cross-Cultural Perspective*, ed. Francis Deng, 261–89. Washington, D.C.: Brookings Institution Press, 1990.

Dodaro, Robert. "Loose Canons: Augustine and Derrida on Their Selves." In *God, the Gift, and Postmodernism*, ed. John Caputo and Michael J. Scanlon, 79–112. Bloomington: Indiana University Press, 1999.

Fredriksen, Paula. "*Secundum Carnem*: History and Israel in the Theology of St. Augustine." In *The Limits of Ancient Christianity: Essays on Late Antique Thought and Culture in Honor of R. A. Markus*, ed. William E. Clingshirn and Mark Vessey, 26–41. Ann Arbor: University of Michigan Press, 1999.

Hanby, Michael. "Augustine and Descartes: An Overlooked Chapter in the Story of Modern Origins." *Modern Theology* 19, no. 4 (October 2003): 455–82.

———. "Democracy and Its Demons." In *Augustine and Politics*, ed. John Doody, Kevin Hughes, and Kim Pattensworth, 117–44. Oxford, UK: Lexington, 2005.

———. "Desire: Augustine beyond Western Subjectivity." In *Radical Orthodoxy: A New Theology*, ed. John Milbank, Catherine Pickstock, and Graham Ward, 109–28. London: Routledge, 1999.

Hardt, Michael, and Antonio Negri. "Adventures of the Multitude: Response of the Authors." *Re-Thinking Marxism* 13, no. 3/4 (Fall/Winter 2001): 236–43.

———. "Arabs Are Democracy's New Pioneers: The Leaderless Middle East Uprisings Can Inspire Freedom Movements as Latin America Did Before." *The Guardian*, February 4, 2011, http://www.guardian.co.uk/commentisfree/2011/feb/24/arabs-democracy-latin-america.

Horsley, Richard A. "Feminist Scholarship and Postcolonial Criticism: Subverting Imperial Discourse and Reclaiming Submerged Histories." In *Walk in the Ways of Wisdom: Essays in Honor of Elisabeth Schüssler Fiorenza*, ed. Shelly Matthews, Cynthia Briggs Kittredge, and Melanie Johnson-DeBaufre, 297–317. Harrisburg, Pa.: Trinity Press International, 2003.

Kennedy, Robert Peter. "Book Eleven: The Confessions as Eschatological Narrative." In *A Reader's Companion to Augustine's Confessions*, ed. Kim Pattenforth and Robert Kennedy, 167–84. Louisville: Westminster John Knox, 2003.

Kerr, Fergus. "Taylor's Moral Ontology." Cited in *Charles Taylor*, ed. Ruth Abbey, 84–104. Cambridge: Cambridge University Press, 2004.

Kroeker, P. Travis. "Is a Messianic Political Ethic Possible? Recent Work by and about John Howard Yoder." *Journal of Religious Ethics* 33 (2005): 139–74.

Kurz, Joel R. "The Gifts of Creation and the Consummation of Humanity: Irenaeus of Lyons' Recapitulation Theology of the Eucharist." *Worship* 83, no. 2 (March 2009): 112–32.

Lather, Patti. "Post-Critical Pedagogies: A Feminist Reading." In *Feminisms and Critical Pedagogy*, ed. Carmen Luke and Jennifer Gore, 120–37. London: Taylor and Francis, 1992.

Mahmood, Saba. "Secularism, Politics and Empire: The Politics of Islamic Reformation." *Public Culture* 18, no. 2 (2006): 323–47.

Mahmood, Saba, and Charles Hirschkind. "Feminism, the Taliban and the Politics of Counterinsurgency." Fathom Archive, http://fathom.lib.uchicago.edu/1777777190136/.

Markus, Robert. "'Tempora Christiana' Revisited." In *Augustine and His Critics: Essays in Honour of Gerald Bonner*, ed. Robert Dodaro and George Lawless, 199–212. London: Routledge, 2000.

McFague, Sallie. "An Ecological Christology: Does Christianity Have It?" In *Christianity and Ecology*, ed. Dieter Hessel and Rosemary Radford Ruether, 29–45. Cambridge: Harvard University Press, 2000.

McMoris, Christine McCarthy. "Grappling with Islam: Bush and the Burqa." *Religion in the News* 5, no. 1 (Spring 2005), http://www.trincoll.edu/depts/csrpl/RINVol5No1/Bush%20burqa.htm.

Milbank, John. "Sacred Trials: Augustine and the Indo-European Soul." In *Augustine and His Critics: Essays in Honour of Gerald Bonner*, ed. Robert Dodaro and George Lawless, 77–102. New York: Routledge, 2000.

Negri, Antonio, with Danilo Zolo. "A Conversation about Empire." In *Reflections on Empire*, ed. Antonio Negri, Michael Hardt, and Danilo Zolo, 11–31. Trans. Ed Emery. Cambridge: Polity, 2008.

O'Donovan, Oliver. "*Usus* and *Fruitio* in Augustine, *De Doctrina Christiana* 1.*" *Journal of Theological Studies* 33 (1982): 361–97.

Pickstock, Catherine. "Music: Soul, City, Cosmos after Augustine." In *Radical Orthodoxy: A New Theology*, ed. Catherine Pickstock, Graham Ward, and John Milbank, 243–76. London: Routledge, 1999.

Pope John Paul II. *Veritatis Splendor/ The Splendour of Truth*. Papal Encyclical, August 1993. The Vatican Archives, http://www.vatican.va/holy_father/john_paul_ii/encyclicals/documents/hf_jp-ii_enc_06081993_veritatis-splendor_en.html.

Rukeyser, Muriel. "Käthe Kollwitz." In *Out of Silence: Selected Poems*, ed. Kate Daniels, 129–32. Evanston, Ill.: Northwestern University Press, 2000.

Sheldon-Williams, I. P. "The Cappadocians." In *The Cambridge History of Later Greek and Early Medieval Philosophy*, ed. A. H. Armstrong, 432–57. Cambridge: Cambridge University Press, 1967.

Slater, Peter. "Review Essay: Three Views of Christianity." *Journal of the American Academy of Religion* 50, no. 1 (1982): 97–109.

Smith, Abraham. "'Unmasking the Powers': Toward a Postcolonial Analysis of 1 Thessalonians." In *Paul and the Roman Imperial Order*, ed. Richard A. Horsley, 47–66. Harrisburg, Pa.: Trinity Press International, 2004.

Smith, James K. A. "The Gospel of Freedom or Another Gospel? Augustinian Reflections on Empire and American Foreign Policy." *Political Theology* 10, no. 3 (July 2009): 513–36.

Surin, Kenneth. "A Certain 'Politics of Speech': 'Religious Pluralism' in the Age of the McDonald's Hamburger." *Modern Theology* 7, no. 1 (October 1990): 67–100.

Taylor, Charles. "What's Wrong with Negative Liberty?" In *Freedom: A Philosophical Anthology*, ed. Ian Carter, Matthew H. Kramer, and Hillel Steiner, 153–62. Malden, Mass.: Blackwell, 2007.

Wan, Sze-kar. "Collection for the Saints as Anticolonial Act: Implications of Paul's Ethnic Reconstruction." In *Paul and Politics: Ekklesia, Israel, Imperium, Interpretation; Essays in Honor of Krister Stendahl*, 191–215. Harrisburg, Pa.: Trinity Press International, 2000.

———. "Does Diaspora Identity Imply Some Sort of Universality? An Asian-American Reading of Galatians." In *Interpreting beyond Borders*, ed. Fernando F. Segovia, 107–31. *Bible and Postcolonialism*, vol. 3. Sheffield: Sheffield Academic Press, 2000.

Wiesel, Elie. "Hope, Despair and Memory." Nobel lecture. The Nobel Foundation. http://nobelprize.org/nobel_prizes/peace/laureates/1986/wiesel-lecture.html.

Williams, Rowan. *"Augustine* and the *Psalms." Interpretation* 58 (2004): 17–27.

———. "On Being Creatures." In *On Christian Theology*, 63–78. Challenges in Contemporary Theology. Malden, Mass.: Blackwell, 2000.

Yoder, John Howard. "Armaments and Eschatology." *Studies in Christian Ethics* 1, no. 1 (1998): 43–61.

Žižek, Slavoj. *"Objet a* as Inherent Limit to Capitalism. In Michael Hardt and Antonio Negri." http://www.lacan.com/zizmultitude.htm.

BOOKS

Anatolios, Khaled. *Athanasius: The Coherence of His Thought.* New York: Routledge, 1998.

———. *Athanasius.* New York: Routledge, 2004.

Arendt, Hannah. *Love and Saint Augustine.* Ed. Joanna Vercchiarelli Scott and Judith Chelius Stark. Chicago: University of Chicago Press, 1996.

———. *Responsibility and Judgment.* Ed. Jerome Kohn and Ron H. Feldman. New York: Random House, 2003.

Athanasius. *Contra Gentes.* Introduction, Translation, and Commentary by E. P. Meijering. Leiden: Brill, 1984.

———. *Life of Anthony.* Trans. Archibald Robertson. In *Nicene and Post-Nicene Fathers*, vol. 4, *Athanasius: Select Works and Letters.* Peabody, Mass.: Hendrickson, 2004.

———. *On the Incarnation: The Treatise De Incarnatione Verbi Dei.* Crestwood, N.Y.: Saint Vladimir's Seminary Press, 1993.

———. *On the Incarnation.* Trans. Archibald Robertson. London: D. Nutt, 1885.

———. "On the Incarnation of the Word." Trans. Archibald Robertson. In *Nicene and Post-Nicene Fathers*, vol. 4, *Athanasius: Select Works and Letters.* Peabody, Mass.: Hendrickson, 2004.

Augustine. *Confessions.* Trans. F. J. Sheed. New York: Sheed & Ward, 1942.

———. *Confessions.* Trans. Henry Chadwick. Oxford: Oxford University Press, 2008.

———. *City of God.* Trans. Marcus Dods. *Nicene and Post-Nicene Fathers,* vol. 2, ed. Philip Schaff. Peabody, Mass.: Hendrickson, 2004.

———. *Concerning the City of God against the Pagans.* Trans. Henry Bettenson. London: Penguin Books, 2003.

———. *On Christian Doctrine.* Trans. J. F. Shaw. *Nicene and Post-Nicene Fathers,* first series, ed. Philip Schaff. Peabody, Mass.: Hendrickson, 2004.

———. *On The Holy Trinity.* Trans. Arthur West Haddan. *Nicene and Post-Nicene Fathers,* vol. 3, ed. Philip Schaff. Peabody, Mass.: Hendrickson, 2004.

Ayres, Lewis. *Nicaea and Its Legacy: An Approach to Fourth-Century Trinitarian Theology*. Oxford: Oxford University Press, 2004.

Barnes, Timothy. *Athanasius and Constantius: Theology and Politics in the Constantinian Empire*. Cambridge, Mass.: Harvard University Press, 1993.

Barter Moulaison, Jane. *Lord, Giver of Life: Toward a Pneumatological Complement to George Lindbeck's Theory of Doctrine*. Waterloo, Ont.: Wilfrid Laurier University Press, 2007.

Basil of Caesarea. *The Hexaemeron*. Trans. Blomfield Jackson. In *Nicene and Post-Nicene Fathers*, second series, vol. 8, *Basil: Letters and Selected Works*, ed. Philip Schaff and Henry Wace. Peabody, Mass.: Hendrickson, 2004.

———. Homily 6.2. Quoted in Brian E. Daley, S.J., "Building a New City: The Cappadocian Fathers and the Rhetoric of Piety." *Journal of Early Christian Studies* 7, no. 3 (Fall 1999): 431–61.

———. Letter XXIII, "To a Solitary." Trans. Blomfield Jackson. In *Nicene and Post-Nicene Fathers*, second series, vol. 8, *Basil: Letters and Selected Works,* ed. Philip Schaff and Henry Wace. Peabody, Mass.: Hendrickson, 2004.

———. *On the Human Condition*. Trans. Verna Harrison. Crestwood, N.Y.: St. Vladimir's Seminary Press, 2005.

———. "On the Spirit," Trans. Blomfield Jackson. In *Nicene and Post-Nicene Fathers*, second series, vol. 8, *Basil: Letters and Selected Works*, ed. Philip Schaff and Henry Wace. Peabody, Mass.: Hendrickson, 2004.

Bhabha, Homi K. *The Location of Culture*. London: Routledge, 1994.

Boer, Roland, ed. *Last Stop before Antarctica: The Bible and Postcolonialism in Australia*. Sheffield: Sheffield Academic Press, 2001.

Brown, Peter. *Augustine of Hippo: A Biography*. Berkeley: University of California Press, 1967.

Cixous, Hélène. *Stigmata: Escaping Texts*. New York: Routledge, 2005.

———. *Stigmata: Escaping Texts.* 2005. Kindle ed., downloaded from Amazon.ca.

Coakley, Sarah. *Powers and Submissions: Spirituality, Philosophy, and Gender* (Malden, Mass.: Blackwell, 2002.

Crossan, John Dominic. *God and Empire: Jesus against Rome, Then and Now*. New York: HarperCollins, 2008.

Derrida, Jacques. Foreword to Hélène Cixous, *Stigmata: Escaping Texts*. New York: Routledge, 2005.

———. *On Cosmopolitanism and Forgiveness*. London: Routledge, 2001.

Dube, Musa W., and Jeffrey L. Staley, eds. *John and Postcolonialism: Travel, Space, and Power.* London: Continuum, 2002.

Dunn, James D. G. *The Theology of Paul the Apostle*. Grand Rapids: Eerdmans, 1998.

Eagleton, Terry. *Ideology: An Introduction*. London: Verso, 1991.

Eberhart, Christian. *Hebrews: Contemporary Methods, New Insights.* Leiden: Brill, 2005.

Edwards, Denis. *How God Acts: Creation, Redemption and Special Divine Action.* Minneapolis: Fortress Press, 2010.

———. *Jesus the Wisdom of God: An Ecological Theology.* Maryknoll, N.Y.: Orbis, 1995.

Eisentein, Elizabeth L. *The Printing Press as an Agent of Change.* Cambridge: Cambridge University Press, 1979.

Elliot, Neil. *The Arrogance of Nations: Reading Romans in the Shadow of Empire.* Paul in Critical Contexts. Minneapolis: Fortress Press, 2010.

———. *Liberating Paul: The Justice of God and the Politics of the Apostle.* Minneapolis: Fortress Press, 2006.

Fackenheim, Emil. *To Mend the World: Foundations of Post-Holocaust Jewish Thought.* New York: Schocken, 1994.

Fonrobert, Charlotte Elisheva, and Martin S Jaffee, eds. *The Cambridge Companion to the Talmud and Rabbinic Literature.* Cambridge: Cambridge University Press, 2006.

Fredriksen, Paula. *Augustine and the Jews: A Christian Defense of Jews and Judaism.* New York: Doubleday, 2008.

Hardt, Michael, and Antonio Negri. *Multitude: War and Democracy in the Age of Empire.* Harmondsworth, UK: Penguin, 2005.

Harrison, Carol. *Augustine: Christian Truth and Fractured Humanity.* New York: Oxford University Press, 2000.

Harrison, N. H., trans. Introduction to Basil of Caesarea, *On the Human Condition.* Crestwood, N.Y.: St. Vladimir's Seminary Press, 2005.

Hart, David Bentley. *The Beauty of the Infinite: The Aesthetics of Christian Truth.* Grand Rapids: Eerdmans, 2003.

———. *The Doors of the Sea: Where Was God in the Tsunami?* Grand Rapids: Eerdmans, 2005.

Hauerwas, Stanley. *The State of the University: Academic Knowledges and the Knowledge of God.* Malden, Mass.: Blackwell, 2007.

Herbert, A. G., trans. Translator's preface to Gustav Aulén, *Christus Victor: An Historical Study of the Three Main Types of the Idea of Atonement.* Eugene, Ore.: Wipf and Stock, 2003.

Hick, John. *An Interpretation of Religion: Human Responses to the Transcendent.* New Haven: Yale University Press, 1989.

Horsley, Richard A., ed. *Hidden Transcripts and the Arts of Resistance: Applying the Work of James C. Scott to Jesus and Paul.* Semeia Studies 48. Atlanta: Society of Biblical Literature, 2004.

———. *Jesus and Empire: The Kingdom of God and the New World Disorder.* Minneapolis: Fortress Press, 2003.

————, ed. *Paul and Empire: Religion and Power in Roman Imperial Society*. Harrisburg, Penn.: Trinity Press International, 1997.

————, ed. *Paul and Politics: Ekklesia, Israel, Imperium, Interpretation; Essays in Honor of Krister Stendahl*. Harrisburg, Pa.: Trinity Press International, 2000.

————, ed. *Paul and the Roman Imperial Order*. Harrisburg, Penn.: Trinity Press International, 2004.

Irenaeus of Lyons. In *The Ante-Nicene Fathers*, vol. 1, *Apostolic Fathers, Justin Martyr, Irenaeus*. Ed. Alexander Roberts and James Donaldson. Peabody, Mass.: Hendrickson, 2004.

Johnson, Lawrence J. *Worship in the Early Church: An Anthology of Historical Sources*. Collegeville, Minn.: Liturgical, 2009.

Lindbeck, George A. *The Nature of Doctrine: Religion and Theology in a Postliberal Age*. Louisville: Westminster John Knox, 1984.

Kelly, J. N. D. *Early Christian Creeds*. 3rd ed. New York: Longman Group, 1972.

Long, Stephen. *Divine Economy: Theology and the Market*. New York, N.Y., Routledge, 2000.

Markus, Robert A. *Saeculum: History and Society in the Theology of St. Augustine*. Cambridge: Cambridge University Press, 1989.

McAlister, Melanie. *Epic Encounters: Culture, Media, and U.S. Interests in the Middle East, 1945–2000*. Berkeley: University of California Press, 2005.

McFague, Sallie. *The Body of God: An Ecological Theology*. Minneapolis: Fortress Press, 1993.

————. *Life Abundant: Rethinking Theology and Economy for a Planet in Peril*. Minneapolis: Fortress Press, 2001.

————. *Models of God: Theology for an Ecological, Nuclear Age*. Philadelphia: Fortress Press, 1987.

————. *A New Climate for Theology: God, the World and Global Warming*. Minneapolis: Fortress Press, 2008.

Meijering, E. P., trans. *Athanasius: Contra Gentes: Introduction, Translation and Commentary*. Leiden: Brill, 1984.

Meyendorff, John. *Christ in Eastern Thought*. Crestwood, N.Y.: St. Vladimir's Seminary Press, 1975.

Milbank, John. *Being Reconciled: Ontology and Pardon*. London: Routledge, 2003.

————. *Theology and Social Theory: Beyond Secular Reason*. Malden, Mass.: Blackwell, 1990.

Moore, Stephen D., and Fernando F. Segovia, eds. *Postcolonial Biblical Criticism: Interdisciplinary Intersections*. London: T&T Clark, 2005.

Niebuhr, H. Richard. *The Kingdom of God in America*. New York: Harper & Row, 1959.

Ochs, Peter. *The Return to Scripture in Judaism and Christianity: Essays in Postcritical Scriptural Interpretation*. Mahwah, N.J.: Paulist, 1993.

Pelikan, Jaroslav. *Christianity and Classical Culture: The Metamorphosis of Natural Theology in the Christian Encounter with Hellenism*. New Haven: Yale University Press, 1993.

——. *The Emergence of the Catholic Tradition*. Chicago: University of Chicago Press, 1971.

Ricoeur, Paul. *Memory, History, Forgetting*. Trans. Kathleen Blamey and David Pellauer. Chicago: University of Chicago Press, 2004.

Rieger, Jeorg. *Christ and Empire: From Paul to Postcolonial Times*. Minneapolis: Fortress Press, 2007.

Ruether, Rosemary Radford. *Faith and Fratricide: The Theological Roots of Anti-Semitism*. New York: Crossroad, 1979.

——. *Sexism and God-Talk: Toward a Feminist Theology*. Boston, Mass.: Beacon, 1983.

——. *Womanguides: Readings toward a Feminist Theology*. Boston, Mass.: Beacon, 1985.

Russell, Letty. *Human Liberation in a Feminist Perspective: A Theology*. Philadelphia: Westminster, 1974.

Said, Edward W. *Culture and Imperialism*. New York: Vintage, 1994.

——. *Orientalism*. Rev. ed. New York: Vintage, 1994.

Sanders, E. P. *Paul and Palestinian Judaism: A Comparison of Patterns of Religion*. Philadelphia: Fortress Press, 1977.

Segovia, Fernando F. *Decolonizing Biblical Studies: A View from the Margins*. Maryknoll, N.Y.: Orbis, 2000.

——, ed. *Interpreting beyond Borders*. Bible and Postcolonialism, vol. 3. Sheffield: Sheffield Academic Press, 2000.

Smith, Wilfrid Cantwell. *The Faith of Other Men*. New York: Harper Torchbooks, 1972.

——. *The Meaning and End of Religion*. San Francisco: Harper & Row, 1978.

Spivak, Gayatri Chakravorty. *A Critique of Postcolonial Reason: Toward a History of the Vanishing Present*. Cambridge: Harvard University Press, 1999.

——. *Other Worlds: Essays in Cultural Politics*. New York: Routledge, 1988.

——. *The Postcolonial Critic: Interviews, Strategies, Dialogues*. Ed. Sarah Harasym. New York: Routledge, 1990.

Stendahl, Krister. *Paul among the Jews and Gentiles and Other Essays*. Philadelphia: Fortress Press, 1976.

Stillman, Robert. *Philip Sidney and the Poetics of Renaissance Cosmopolitanism*. Aldershot, UK: Ashgate, 2008.

Sugirtharajah, R. S. *Asian Biblical Hermeneutics and Postcolonialism: Contesting the Interpretations*. Maryknoll, N.Y.: Orbis, 1998.

———. *The Bible and the Third World: Precolonial, Colonial, and Postcolonial Encounters*. Cambridge: Cambridge University Press, 2001.

———. *Postcolonial Criticism and Biblical Interpretation*. New York: Oxford University Press, 2002.

———. *Postcolonial Reconfigurations: An Alternative Way of Reading the Bible and Doing Theology*. St. Louis: Chalice, 2003.

Torrance, T. F. *The Trinitarian Faith*. New York: Continuum, 1991.

Unterseher, Lisa A. *The Mark of Cain and the Jews: Augustine's Theology of Jews and Judaism*. Piscataway, N.J.: Gorgias, 2009.

Volf, Miroslav. *The End of Memory: Remembering Rightly in a Violent World*. Grand Rapids: Eerdmans, 2006.

———. *Exclusion and Embrace: A Theological Exploration of Identity, Otherness, and Reconciliation*. Nashville: Abingdon, 1996.

von Heyking, John. *Augustine and Politics as Longing in the World*. Columbia: University of Missouri Press, 2001.

Ward, Graham. *Cities of God*. New York: Routledge, 2000.

———. *Theology and Contemporary Critical Theory*. New York: St. Martin's, 1996.

Weaver, J. Denny. *The Nonviolent Atonement*. 2nd ed. Grand Rapids: Eerdmans, 2011.

Wiesel, Elie. *From the Kingdom of Memory: Reminiscences*. New York: Summit, 1990. Cited in Miroslav Volf, *The End of Memory: Remembering Rightly in a Violent World*. Grand Rapids: Eerdmans, 2006.

Williams, Rowan. *Arius: History and Tradition*. London: SCM, 2001.

———. *Resurrection: Interpreting the Easter Gospel*. Cleveland: Pilgrim, 2003.

———. *The Truce of God*. Grand Rapids: Eerdmans, 2005.

———. *The Wound of Knowledge: Christian Spirituality from the New Testament to Saint John of the Cross*. 2nd ed. Cambridge: Cowley, 1990.

———. *Wrestling with Angels: Conversations in Modern Theology*. Ed. Mike Higton. Grand Rapids: Eerdmans, 2007.

Yoder, John Howard. *The Politics of Jesus: Vicit Agnus Boster*. Grand Rapids: Eerdmans, 1994.

Žižek, Slavoj. *The Plague of Fantasies*. New York: Verso, 1997.

INDEX

8, 11, 34–37, 40, 43, 50–51, 54,
57, 78, 84, 96, 100, 102, 111–12,
117–19, 122, 125, 130, 137,
152n12; and redemption, 60, 108–
11, 113–19, 126–27, 135, 138;
relationship with creation, 11–12,
41, 43, 45–56, 59–61, 73, 77–78,
84, 94–99, 125–26; and sacrifice,
11, 35, 105, 108, 111, 113–17,
136, 162–63n21; speaking about,
17–18, 41, 51–55, 59–60, 65, 76,
88, 91, 102–3; and violence, 11,
19, 50, 107–9, 118, 123
grace, 95, 100, 109, 124, 126–29,
131, 134, 138, 142; given by God
(through Christ), 59–60, 111,
117–18, 125, 133, 139; receiving,
38, 40, 129

H

Hanby, Michael, 30, 39, 136
Hardt, Michael, 17, 23–32, 34,
146n15, 148n4, 149–150n21,
150n27
Hart, David Bentley, 13, 52, 54–55,
115, 117, 146n15
Hauerwas, Stanley, 161n46
Hick Jr., John, 84, 88
Holy Spirit: gift of, 53; relationship
to the Trinity, 55, 99; work of, 35,
49, 135
human: being, 10, 18, 31–32, 45, 48,
58, 70, 83, 92, 100–101, 133, 139,
159n26; and the natural world, 47,
50, 53, 56, 58; redemption of, 8,
49, 60–61, 94, 113–15, 117–18,
123, 126–28, 135, 144; in relation
to Christ or God, 9, 11, 14, 37,
41–42, 44, 47, 53, 91, 97, 99–100,
105–6, 112, 116, 126, 129–30,
134–35, 140, 142, 150n31
humility (as virtue), 10, 28, 34–35, 37–
39, 103, 127, 130, 139, 161n44;
and Christ, 35, 37, 98, 102

I

imago Dei: human beings as, 47–49,
56, 67, 94–95, 97, 100, 111, 113,
134; natural world as, 48, 56, 100
incarnation, doctrine of. *See* Christ: as
incarnation of God
Irenaeus of Lyons, 2, 5, 8, 18,
110–112
Irigaray, Luce, 66
Islam, 85–90

J

John Paul II, Pope, 100, 102
justice, 19, 28, 32–33, 36–37, 112,
122–24, 131–34, 137, 139,
149n18, 165–66n37; and Christian theology, 8–9, 15, 41; God
and, 106, 109, 138; as virtuous,
30, 34–35

K

Kristeva, Julia, 66

L

language, 17–18, 42, 47, 51, 65–73,
76; the Bible as a literary text, 71;
function of, 18, 65–66, 71, 79, 81
Lindbeck, George, 161n45, 167n1
liturgy, 12, 53, 81, 136

M

Mahmood, Saba, 18, 87, 89–90, 92,
103, 143, 146n15
Marxism, 24, 65, 85, 154n8
McFague, Sallie, 42–46, 51, 54, 58–
60, 142, 152n8, 152n12, 153n27
memory and remembrance, 2, 19,
121–27, 129, 134–40, 163–64n2,
164n3, 165n22; and forgetting,
121, 123–25, 127, 129, 132, 134,
165n28; letting go of, 122, 125;
metanoia, 129; and redemption,
121–23, 126–29; and revenge,
122, 129
Milbank, John, 36, 81, 129, 135,
149n16

CPSIA information can be obtained at www.ICGtesting.com
Printed in the USA
LVOW122017220512

282839LV00006B/1/P

9 780800 698737